TAB

EDITOR: Bill Jamieson
ASSOCIATE EDITORS: Karen Davis, Kathy Reichert
STATISTICIANS/RESEARCH: Greg Innis, Morris Moorawnick
ADVERTISING SALES: Jack Johnson, Jeff Ajluni, Jason O'Connell, Bill Ley
COVER/GRAPHIC DESIGN: Beverly Ostrom
PRODUCTION: North American Graphics, Inc.
PRINTER: The Press Room, Inc.
COVER PHOTO: Mark Hicks
INSIDE PHOTOS: Mark Hicks, Jim Mackey

DETROIT RED WINGS, INC.

Joe Louis Arena — 600 Civic Center Drive — Detroit, MI 48226
Main Phone: (313) 396-7544   P.R. FAX: (313) 567-0296
P.R. Office: (313) 396-7538   Press Box: (313) 396-7957

Owner	Mike Ilitch
Owner/Secretary-Treasurer	Marian Ilitch
President	William Evo
Vice-Presidents	Atanas Ilitch, Christopher Ilitch
Senior Vice-President	Jim Devellano
Drector of Player Personnel/Head Coach	Scotty Bowman
Assistant General Manager/Goaltending Consultant	Ken Holland
Associate Coaches	Barry Smith, Dave Lewis
NHL Scout	Dan Belisle
Director of Player Development/AHL-IHL Scout	Jim Nill
Eastern Canada Scout	Joe McDonnell
Western Canada Scout	Wayne Meier
USA/College Scout	Mark Leach
Western USA Scout	Chris Coury
Director of European Scouting	Hakan Andersson
Czech Republic Scout	Vladimir Havluj
Central Ontario Scout	Paul Crowley
Controller	Paul MacDonald
General Sales Manager	Jack Johnson
Marketing Director	Ted Speers
Public Relations Director	Bill Jamieson
Broadcasting Director	Amy Goan
Broadcasting Manager	Lori Sbroglia
Season Ticket Sales Director	Brad Ebben
Executive Assistant	Nancy Beard
Senior Account Executives	Jeffrey Ajluni, William Ley
Sales Coordinator	Jason O'Connell
Marketing Coordinator	Kevin Vaughn
Public Relations Assistants	Kathy Best, Karen Davis
Accounting Assistant	Cathy Witzke
Administrative Assistant	Kristin Armstrong
Athletic Trainer	John Wharton
Equipment Manager	Paul Boyer
Assistant Equipment Manager	Tim Abbott
Team Physicians	Dr. John Finley, D.O.; Dr. David Collon, M.D.
Team Dentist	Dr. C.J. Regula, D.M.D.
Team Ophthalmologist	Dr. Charles Slater, M.D.

Team Founded	1926
Home Ice/Training Camp Site	Joe Louis Arena
Seating Capacity	19,275
Starting Times	Weekdays 7:35 p.m., Sundays 7:05, Matinees 1:05
Press Box/Radio-TV booths	Jefferson Avenue side of arena, top of seats
Media Lounge	First-floor hallway near Red Wings' dressing room, river side of arena
Rink Dimensions	200 feet by 85 feet; S.A.R. Plastic above boards
Uniforms	Home: Base color white, trimmed in red Road: Base color red, trimmed in white
Radio flagship station	WJR-AM (760)
TV stations	WKBD (Channel 50); PASS Sports; Special Order Sports
Radio announcers	Ken Kal, Paul Woods
TV announcers	Dave Strader, Mickey Redmond

Remember beer?

MIKE ILITCH
Owner

MARIAN ILITCH
Owner/Secretary-Treasurer

Integrity, commitment, enthusiasm and a vast knowledge of hockey, both inside the boards and in the boardrooms. William Evo brings those ingredients and more to his new position as team president.

A former player agent and one-time player in the World Hockey Association, the 41-year-old Detroit native was named to the position by Owner Mike Ilitch last Sept. 5. Evo oversees the Red Wings' organization and works in concert with other team executives and coaches in business and hockey decisions. He also represents the club on the NHL's Board of Governors.

A practicing attorney for 11 years, Evo had been president of the Evo & Mammina law firm in suburban Detroit for the past nine years, concentrating on corporate and contract law and litigation. He also represented several NHL players over the years, along with Hall of Famers such as Alex Delvecchio and Ted Lindsay. When appointed to his position in Detroit's front office, Evo was serving as president and general counsel of the Red Wings' Alumni Association.

Evo was selected once before by the Red Wings — as a player in the third round (45th overall) of the 1974 NHL Entry Draft. However, the right wing opted to sign with the Michigan Stags, the Detroit-based club which had chosen him in that year's WHA draft. He also saw action in the WHA with Cleveland and Edmonton before hanging up the skates in 1979.

The third of 10 children who was born in Detroit and raised in suburban Royal Oak, Evo left home at age 16 to pursue hockey in the junior ranks, playing for three years under future NHL coach Roger Neilson with the Peterborough Petes.

After retiring as a player from the WHA, Evo continued his education, graduating with honors in 1981 from the University of Western Ontario (in London) and receiving a juris doctorate degree in 1984 from the University of Detroit School of Law.

Bill and wife Gail reside in suburban Detroit with son William and daughter Megan.

PROUD SPONSOR

OF THE COOLEST

GAME ON EARTH.

ATANAS ILITCH
Vice-President

CHRISTOPHER ILITCH
Vice-President

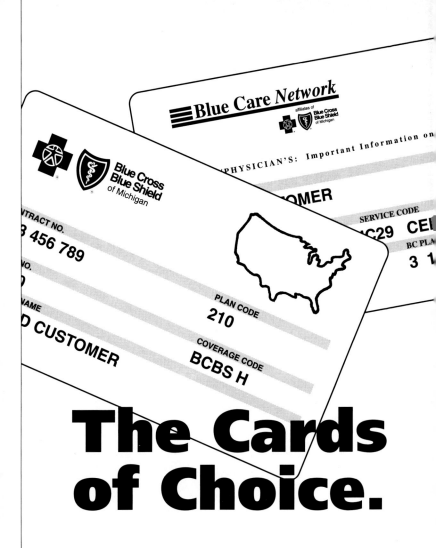

Blue Care Network

affiliates of Blue Cross Blue Shield of Michigan

PHYSICIAN'S: Important Information on

...OMER

Blue Cross Blue Shield of Michigan

...NTRACT NO.
...3 456 789

...NO.
...9

...NAME
...D CUSTOMER

SERVICE CODE

...C29   CE...

BC PLA...

3 1...

PLAN CODE
210

COVERAGE CODE
BCBS H

The Cards
of Choice.

**Blue Cross
Blue Shield
Blue Care Network**
of Michigan

Independent licensees of the Blue Cross and Blue Shield Association

Although he rarely receives public acclaim, Jim Devellano has been a leading architect drawing the blueprint that built the Red Wings from one of the NHL's weakest teams into the powerful Western Conference champions with the league's best regular-season record.

Devellano is in his 14th season with the Red Wings — his sixth as senior vice-president after the first eight as general manager. An excellent judge of talent throughout his 29 years in the NHL, Devellano often departs from administrative duties to scout players on all levels and assist the scouting staff in preparations for the Entry Draft. In addition, he serves as the team's alternate on the NHL's Board of Governors. Jim became a team vice-president Dec. 30, 1985, and assumed his present position July 13, 1990.

Devellano came to Detroit as general manager July 12, 1982, and built a team through the draft, trades and free agency that won two Norris Division regular-season championships (1988 and '89) and twice appeared in the Stanley Cup semifinals ('87 and '88). He also had a hand in developing the Adirondack farm club that won two Calder Cup titles as AHL champions ('86 and '89) under his command.

Devellano, 52, did not play professional hockey but came up through the ranks in various capacities in his native Toronto. He became a scout with the St. Louis Blues in 1967 when the NHL expanded from six to 12 teams. The Blues reached the Stanley Cup final in each of their first three seasons.

Joining the New York Islanders as a scout when that club was founded in 1972, Devellano's scouting skills helped to build a team that won four consecutive Stanley Cup titles (1980-83). In 79-80, he became G.M. of the Islanders' Indianapolis (CHL) farm club and was named Minor League Executive of the Year by The Hockey News in his first year. He returned to New York in '81 as the Islanders' assistant G.M.

"Jimmy D." is single and resides in Detroit.

Scotty Bowman is the winningest coach in NHL history, has seven Stanley Cup rings and already is a member of the Hockey Hall of Fame. But he is not dwelling on past accomplishments or showing any signs of slowing down in a quest to bring the Stanley Cup to Detroit, witnessed by the new three-year contract he signed last July 3.

Bowman is in his 24th season as an NHL coach and third behind the Red Wings' bench. This is his second year as the club's director of player personnel. Last season he orchestrated several key acquisitions and superbly directed a team that won the President's Trophy with the NHL's best regular-season record and reached the Stanley Cup final before losing to the New Jersey Devils.

Bowman has coached teams to six Stanley Cup championships and is bidding to become the first coach to win the Cup with three different teams. He is the only NHL coach to register 1,000 victories overall in the regular season and playoffs. The total was 1,065 entering this season — 913-421-238 in 1,572 regular-season games and 152-92 in 244 playoff contests. He reached the 900 mark in regular-season victories Mar. 25, 1995, at Vancouver after posting his 1,000th overall triumph the season before on Feb. 2, 1994, at Tampa Bay. Scotty has the best regular-season winning percentage (.656) of anyone who has coached at least 600 regular-season games.

Bowman's six Cup titles as a coach are second only to Toe Blake (8). Ten times in 23 seasons, Bowman has been to the Cup final, second behind Dick Irvin (16). Scotty ranks first on the all-time playoff coaching ledger in victories, games, playoff series and series won. He has coached 48 series and won 33. Among those coaching a minimum of 65 postseason games, Bowman's .623 winning percentage is third after Glen Sather (.706) and Blake (.689). In the Stanley Cup finals, Bowman is third in victories with a 24-21 mark in 45 games, trailing Irvin and Blake (32 wins each), and Bowman is third in games in the finals after Irvin (77) and Blake (48).

Bowman, 62, became the 22nd head coach in Detroit history June 15, 1993, signing a two-year deal, and on June 24, 1994, he added the title of director of player personnel.

Before coming to Detroit, Bowman had coached Pittsburgh the previous two seasons, including his most recent Cup title in 1992. Scotty had earned his other Stanley Cup ring in 1991 when he was Pittsburgh's director of player development and recruitment. In 1991-92, Bowman took the reins as the Penguins' coach when the late Bob Johnson became ill. Scotty remained in the dual role through the 92-93 season.

When Detroit won the Central Division last season, it was Bowman's 12th division title. Six times his teams have been first overall in the NHL, and one of his clubs tied for best record. Bowman's teams have amassed 100 or more points 11 times and missed the playoffs only twice.

Bowman broke into the NHL coaching ranks with the St. Louis Blues in the 1967-68 season, when the NHL expanded from six to 12 teams. The Blues advanced to the Cup final in each of their first three seasons and won two division titles.

Moving in 1971 to Montreal — where he earlier had worked and coached in the Canadiens' minor league system — Bowman achieved remarkable success. He won the Stanley Cup five times (1973 and '76 through '79) and rang up six division titles in eight seasons.

In seven of his eight seasons in Montreal, the Canadiens notched more than 100 points and missed the mark once with 99. The three best victory and point totals in NHL history belong to Bowman's Montreal teams (60 wins and 132 points in 76-77, 59 and 129 in 77-78 and 58 and 127 in 75-76). The 76-77 club holds the league record for fewest defeats (8) in a season of 70 or more games.

Bowman went to the Buffalo Sabres in 1979, where he was general manager and shared coaching duties until 1987. He won a division title in his first year behind the Buffalo bench in 79-80.

After leaving the Sabres, Bowman worked for CBC-TV's "Hockey Night in Canada" from 1987 until joining Pittsburgh's front office in June of '90.

Bowman also has been a winner on the international stage, coaching Team Canada to the 1976 Canada Cup title. He also guided Team Canada in the '81 Canada Cup and the NHL All-Stars in a three-game series against the Soviet Union in '79. Scotty was inducted into the Hockey Hall of Fame in 1991.

William Scott Bowman was born Sept. 18, 1933, in Montreal. He and wife Suella have five children, Alicia, David, Stanley, Bob and Nancy, and spend the off-season in suburban Buffalo.

NHL COACHING RECORD

Season	Team	GC	W	L	T	PTS	PCT	FIN	GC	W	L	PCT
				Regular Season						**Playoffs**		
1967-68	St. Louis	58	23	21	14	60	.517	3rd	+18	8	10	.444
1968-69	St. Louis	76	37	25	14	88	.579	1st	+12	8	4	.667
1969-70	St. Louis	76	37	27	12	86	.566	1st	+16	8	8	.500
1970-71	St. Louis	28	13	10	5	31	.554	2nd	6	2	4	.333
1971-72	Montreal	78	46	16	16	108	.692	3rd	6	2	4	.333
1972-73	Montreal	78	52	10	16	120	.769	#1st	*17	12	5	.706
1973-74	Montreal	78	45	24	9	99	.635	2nd	6	2	4	.333
1974-75	Montreal	80	47	14	19	113	.706	@1st	11	6	5	.545
1975-76	Montreal	80	58	11	11	127	.794	#1st	*13	12	1	.923
1976-77	Montreal	80	60	8	12	132	.825	#1st	*14	12	2	.857
1977-78	Montreal	80	59	10	11	129	.806	#1st	*15	12	3	.800
1978-79	Montreal	80	52	17	11	115	.719	1st	*16	12	4	.750
1979-80	Buffalo	80	47	17	16	110	.688	1st	14	9	5	.643
1981-82	Buffalo	35	18	10	7	43	.614	3rd	4	1	3	.250
1982-83	Buffalo	80	38	29	13	89	.556	3rd	10	6	4	.600
1983-84	Buffalo	80	48	25	7	103	.644	2nd	3	0	3	.000
1984-85	Buffalo	80	38	28	14	90	.563	3rd	5	2	3	.400
1985-86	Buffalo	37	18	18	1	37	.500	5th	–	–	–	–
1986-87	Buffalo	12	3	7	2	8	.333	5th	–	–	–	–
1991-92	Pittsburgh	80	39	32	9	87	.544	3rd	*21	16	5	.762
1992-93	Pittsburgh	84	56	21	7	119	.708	#1st	12	7	5	.583
1993-94	DETROIT	84	46	30	8	100	.595	1st	7	3	4	.429
1995	DETROIT	48	33	11	4	70	.729	#1st	+18	12	6	.667
DETROIT TOTALS			**132**	**79**	**41**	**12**	**170**	**.644**		**25**	**15**	**10**	**.667**
NHL TOTALS			**1572**	**913**	**421**	**238**	**2064**	**.656**		**244**	**152**	**92**	**.623**

*-Won Stanley Cup
+-Lost Stanley Cup final
#-First overall in NHL
@-Tied for first overall in NHL

Ken Holland has deftly handled several tasks during 12 years with the Red Wings and is continuing his outstanding work in his second season as assistant general manager while also serving as G.M. of Detroit's Adirondack (AHL) affiliate and goaltending consultant for the entire organization.

In addition to numerous administrative duties, including contract negotiations, Holland has been Detroit's point person at the NHL Entry Draft for the past six years. He's had a hand in selecting several top players, including Keith Primeau, Vyacheslav Kozlov, Darren McCarty, Chris Osgood and Martin Lapointe, along with some top prospects.

Holland, 40, was elevated to his present position June 20, 1994, after five years as amateur scouting director. He had joined the scouting staff in '85 as western Canada scout after finishing his career as a goaltender with Adirondack.

A native of Vernon, BC, Holland played in the junior ranks for Medicine Hat (WHL) in 74-75. He was Toronto's 13th pick (188th overall) in the '75 draft but never saw action with the Maple Leafs. Holland twice signed with NHL teams as a free agent — in '80 with Hartford and '83 with Detroit. He spent most of his pro career with AHL clubs in Binghamton and Springfield, along with Adirondack. He appeared in four NHL games, making his debut with Hartford in 80-81 and playing three contests for Detroit in 83-84.

Ken and wife Cindy have four children, Brad, Julie, Rachel and Greg, and reside in suburban Detroit.

Barry Smith is a keen observer of hockey around the world and always on the lookout for tactics that can make a team improve. His skill as an innovator was manifested last season when he was instrumental in installing the "left wing lock" defensive system he discovered while watching teams in Sweden. The Red Wings had been 16th in the NHL with a 3.24 goals-against average in 1993-94 but soared to second in the league last season with a 2.42 mark.

Smith is in his third season as an assistant coach behind the Detroit bench. Success accompanies Smith wherever he goes, including two Stanley Cup rings as an assistant with the Pittsburgh Penguins and in coaching stints on the college and international levels. Scotty Bowman relies heavily on Smith, who also assisted the legendary head coach at Buffalo and Pittsburgh.

Smith, 44, came to Detroit July 28, 1993, after being an assistant at Pittsburgh for three seasons first under the late Bob Johnson and then two years with Bowman while the Penguins won Stanley Cup titles in 1991 and '92. Smith also spent three years as an assistant at Buffalo.

Barry entered the coaching ranks in 1975 as head coach at Elmira (NY) College while earning a masters degree in education. His clubs won three Eastern Collegiate Athletic Conference titles and twice were NCAA Division III finalists.

Moving to Europe, Smith coached in Sweden from 1981 to '84 and Norway from '84 to '86, serving as an assistant on the Norweigan club in the World Championships. He also scouted European prospects for the Sabres, and in March of '86 he went to Buffalo as Bowman's assistant. Smith worked one year under Bowman and remained in Buffalo until 1989, when he journeyed to Italy for one season to coach the Alleghe club and the Italian National Team. He joined the Penguins in 1990-91 as Johnson's assistant, and also was an aide to Johnson on Team USA in the 1991 Canada Cup.

The Buffalo native received a degree in physical education in 1972 from Ithaca (NY) College, where he starred in hockey and football. He was elected to the school's Hall of Fame in 1992.

Barry and wife Mary have a son, Ryan, and a daughter, Molly, and spend the off-season in suburban Buffalo.

Dave Lewis played nearly 15 seasons as an NHL defenseman and acquired a keen knowledge of the game that has been essential in the Red Wings' rise, especially as one of the league's elite clubs in defensive play and special teams.

Lewis is in his eighth year as a Detroit assistant coach. Impressive is the fact that he has worked under three head coaches in a sport in which assistants usually are tied to the top man. He started with Jacques Demers, continued under Bryan Murray and now assists Scotty Bowman. Lewis' duties also include extensive video work used in pre-scouting opponents.

Lewis, 41, joined the coaching staff immediately after retiring as a player Nov. 6, 1987, amid his 15th NHL season. This is his ninth year in the Detroit organization since signing as a free agent (no compensation) July 28, 1986.

A native of Kindersley, SK, Lewis played junior hockey for Saskatoon (WHL) and was the New York Islanders' second pick (33rd overall) in the 1973 Entry Draft (selected by Jim Devellano, the Islanders' chief scout at the time). Lewis jumped from the junior ranks to the NHL and never played in the minor leagues.

Dave's biggest milestone came when he played in his 1,000th regular-season game Apr. 1, 1987, against Philadelphia at Joe Louis Arena. In all, he played 1,008 regular-season games with the Islanders, Los Angeles, New Jersey and Detroit, recording 36 goals, 187 assists and 953 PIM. He also appeared in 91 playoff games, with one goal, 20 assists and 143 PIM.

Dave and wife Brenda live in suburban Detroit and have a son, Ryan, and daughter, Meagan.

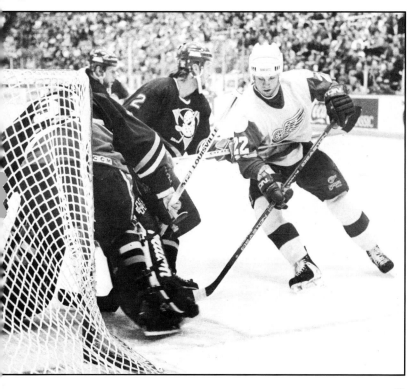

Dan Belisle has a key role whenever the Red Wings' management and coaching staff gather for strategy sessions on player personnel decisions or game plans. Belisle is in his 14th season with the club and 10th as NHL scout, providing valuable information used in making trades and free-agent acquisitions or preparing for opponents.

Belisle, 58, joined the organization in 1982-83 as an assistant coach under Nick Polano. He remained as an assistant to Harry Neale and Brad Park, then assumed his present position in the summer of '86.

Belisle was a successful minor-league coach before becoming head coach at Washington in 78-79, remaining with the Capitals until early in the 79-80 season.

Dan returned to the minors in 80-81 as general manager/coach at Dallas (CHL), guiding that club to the regular-season title and winning the league's Coach of the Year award (one of four times he received such an honor in the minors).

Belisle made his pro coaching debut in 72-73 with Des Moines (IHL) and won the league title in his second season. He moved to Syracuse (NAHL) in 75-76, winning regular-season and playoff championships in his second year, then went to Philadelphia (AHL) in 77-78.

A native of South Porcupine, ON, Belisle spent most of his 15-year playing career as a right wing in the minors, although he played four games for the New York Rangers in the 60-61 season. He retired as a player in '71.

Dan and wife Carol reside in Sarasota, FL, and have three grown children, Debra, Dan Jr. and Dee.

Jim Nill is in his second season in the Red Wings' front office and first in a newly created position as director of player development/AHL-IHL scout. He blends scouting ability and organizational skills to enhance the organization's efficiency.

Nill oversees the development of all Detroit-owned players, with the exception of those at the team's Adirondack (AHL) farm club. He focuses on prospects in the junior leagues and Europe and also scouts the AHL and IHL for potential free agents and trades.

Nill, 37, joined the Red Wings' hierarchy in the summer of 1994 after three seasons with the Ottawa Senators. He started with Ottawa as a scout in October of '91 and two years later became the club's pro scout.

Jim was no stranger to Detroit when he moved into the executive level. He spent his final 2½ years as an NHL player with the Red Wings after being acquired from Winnipeg Jan. 10, 1988, for Mark Kumpel. Nill later went to Adirondack as a player/coach, retiring as a player after the 90-91 season. A right wing in nine NHL seasons, he recorded 58 goals, 87 assists and 854 PIM in 524 regular-season games.

The native of Hanna, AB, played for Medicine Hat (WHL) in the junior ranks, one year at the University of Calgary and was was on the Canadian National and Olympic teams in 79-80. He was St. Louis' fourth pick (89th overall, fifth round) in the '78 Entry Draft and also played for Vancouver and Boston.

Jim and wife Bekki reside in Glens Falls, NY, with daughters Jenna and Kristin and son Trevor.

SCOUTING STAFF

JOE McDONNELL
Eastern Canada

WAYNE MEIER
Western Canada

MARK LEACH
USA/Colleges

CHRIS COURY
Western USA

HAKAN ANDERSSON
Director of
European Scouting

VLADIMIR HAVLUJ
Czech Republic

PAUL CROWLEY
Central Ontario

John Wharton, in his fifth full season with the Red Wings, has used innovative skills to earn the reputation as one of the NHL's top athletic trainers. He came to the club in February of 1991 as strength and conditioning coordinator after five years in the Center for Athletic Medicine at Detroit's Henry Ford Hospital. The Flint native has a bachelor of science degree in sports medicine from Central Michigan University and is a certified strength and conditioning specialist. He was hockey trainer at the '90 Goodwill Games and spent a season with the Detroit Lions. John, wife Jeanne and son Luke reside in suburban Detroit.

Paul Boyer is in his second season as equipment manager. He came to Detroit after one season with the New Jersey Devils. A native of Sault Ste. Marie, ON, Paul earned a bachelor of science degree from nearby Lake Superior State University, then spent five years as the school's hockey trainer before heading for the NHL. He is single and lives in suburban Detroit.

Assistant Equipment Manager Tim Abbott is in his fourth season. The Mt. Clemens native attended L'Anse Creuse High School and Macomb Community College, then spent four years as assistant trainer for Adirondack. Tim, wife Kristen and son Tyler reside in suburban Detroit..

Lending a hand with the busy workload in the dressing room are Johnny Remejes and Wally Crossman.

The Red Wings' medical staff is comprised of Drs. John Finley, D.O.; David Collon, M.D.; C.J. Regula, D.M.D., and Charles Slater, M.D. Dr. Finley has a general practice in Southfield; Dr. Collon is director of orthopedic surgery at the Center for Athletic Medicine at Henry Ford Hospital and also serves the Tigers and Lions; Dr. Regula has a dental practice in Livonia and Dr. Slater an ophthalmology practice in St. Clair.

JOHN WHARTON
Athletic Trainer

PAUL BOYER
Equipment Manager

TIM ABBOTT
Assistant Equipment Manager

JOHNNY REMEJES
Dressing Room Assistant

WALLY CROSSMAN
Dressing Room Assistant

DR. JOHN FINLEY, D.O.
Team Physician

DR. DAVID COLLON, M.D.
Team Physician

DR. C.J. REGULA, D.M.D.
Team Dentist

DR. CHARLES SLATER, M.D.
Team Ophthalmologist

18

It never is easy to follow a legend, but Detroit native Ken Kal is equal to the task in his first season as the Red Wings' play-by-play announcer on flagship station WJR-AM (760) and an extensive radio network. He succeeds Hockey Hall of Famer Bruce Martyn, who retired last June after 31 brilliant seasons behind the mike. Returning for his ninth year is analyst Paul Woods. Kal, 38, had done radio play-by-play of University of Michigan hockey for the past 11 years on Ann Arbor AM stations — seven on WTKA after the first four on WAAM. He also covered the Red Wings as a reporter. Born and raised in the city of Detroit, Kal graduated from Wayne State University in 1979 and immediately joined WAAM, doing sports and working as a disc jockey.

Play-by-play announcer Dave Strader and analyst Mickey Redmond are in their 10th year together on Red Wings television — WKBD (Channel 50), Pro-Am Sports (PASS) and Special Order Sports (pay-per-view). PASS rebroadcasts the majority of its telecasts on the same night games are played.

Woods always has been a fan favorite in Detroit, beginning with a seven-year stint as a player from 1977-78 through 83-84. The native of Hespeler, ON, was drafted by Montreal in '75 but never played for the Canadiens and was obtained by Detroit in the '77 waiver draft. He had 72 goals and 124 assists in 501 regular-season NHL games.

Strader has been on the Detroit scene since the 1985-86 season and gained national acclaim last season for his work on Fox Network telecasts. He came to Detroit after six years as broadcaster and public relations director for the club's Adirondack (AHL) affiliate in his hometown of Glens Falls, NY. A graduate of the University of Massachusetts, he twice was honored by the New York State Broadcasters' Association for play-by-play excellence, and received the Ken McKenzie Award once as the AHL's top P.R. man. Dave also has done games for ESPN.

Redmond is a highly regarded analyst who also works for the Fox Network and previously did games for CBC's Hockey Night in Canada and ESPN. Mickey twice was a 50-goal scorer in five full seasons with Detroit after being acquired from Montreal with Guy Charron and Bill Collins for Frank Mahovlich in January of '71. He scored 52 goals and made the NHL's First All-Star Team in '73, and netted 51 the next season to earn a Second-Team berth. He had 233 goals and 195 assists in 538 regular-season games in nine NHL seasons with Montreal and Detroit.

Toby Cunningham, winner of six local Emmy Awards and four Associated Press honors for production of Red Wings telecasts, is in his 16th season as executive producer for Channel 50 coverage. Jim Holly is in his second year producing PASS games and Special Order Sports telecasts.

Following is the team's radio network (some stations broadcast a limited number of games):

WJR-AM (760), Detroit
WCHT-AM/FM (600/97), Escanaba
WTRX-AM (1330), Flint
WMJZ-AM/FM (900/95.3), Gaylord
WGRY-AM/WQON-FM
  (1230/101.1), Grayling

WCCY-AM (1400), Houghton
WQSN-AM/FM (1470/106.5), Kalamazoo
CKSL-AM (1410), London, ON
WHCH-FM (98.3), Marquette
WPHM-AM (1380), Port Huron
WMAX-AM (1440), Saginaw

KEN KAL

PAUL WOODS

**DAVE STRADER (RIGHT)
AND MICKEY REDMOND**

TOBY CUNNINGHAM

RED WINGS' STAFF

PAUL MacDONALD
Controller

JACK JOHNSON
General Sales Manager

TED SPEERS
Marketing Director

BILL JAMIESON
Public Relations Director

AMY GOAN
Broadcasting Director

LORI SBROGLIA
Broadcasting Manager

BOB KERLIN
Box Office Manager

BRAD EBBEN
Season Ticket Sales Director

NANCY BEARD
Executive Assistant

KATHY BEST
Public Relations Assistant

KAREN DAVIS
Public Relations Assistant

CATHY WITZKE
Accounting Assistant

KRISTIN ARMSTRONG
Administrative Assistant

GAME STAFF

P.A. Announcer	Budd Lynch
Scoreboard Operations Director	Rick Church
Scoreboard Video Coordinator	Sheldon Newman
Video Coordinator	Joe Ducharme
Sound Technician	Steve Kemp
Team Photographer	Mark Hicks
Assistant Team Photographers	Jim Mackey, Tom Albert
Game Staff Coordinator/Statistics & Research	Greg Innis
Statistics & Research Assistant	Morris Moorawnick
Game Staff Assistants	Jerry Brown, Bucky Browning, Dennis Davidson, Marc DesRosiers, Scott Glenn, Lowell Gumbert, Gary Hinds, Kurt Hofner, Lance Hofner, Larry Kosiba, Larry Mach, Gerry McKelvey, Adam Mitchell, Dick Niedermeyer, Jim Omilian, Tom Shaw, Bill Waddell
Media Lounge Receptionist	Barbara Valade
Red Wings' Dressing Room Assistants	Wally Crossman, Johnny Remejes
Visitors' Dressing Room Assistants	Tim Parent, Al Parent

NHL OFF-ICE OFFICIALS

Supervisor & Penalty Timekeeper	Mike Hargraves
Official Scorer	Bill Martin
Game Timekeeper	Ron Idziak
Goal Judges	Jack MacRobert, Chuck Sneddon
Statisticians	Phil Blain, Ron Hayes, Steve Hoesmer, Ken McFadden, Len Paquette
Video Goal Judge	Matt Pavelich
TV Commercial Coordinator	John Vieceli

THE PLAYERS

BERGEVIN Marc

BECAME RED WING: Obtained August 17, 1995, from Tampa Bay
with Ben Hankinson for Shawn Burr, third-round pick in 1996 Entry Draft.

DEFENSE

- 6-1 • 197 lbs.
- Shoots Left
- Born: Montreal, PQ
  August 11, 1965
- Last Amateur Club:
  Chicoutimi Sagueneens (QMJHL)

Career vs. N.H.L.

Team	GP	G	A	PTS
Anaheim	2	0	0	0
Boston	32	3	6	9
Buffalo	27	2	4	6
Calgary	21	2	5	7
Chicago	15	1	3	4
Dallas	42	3	5	8
Detroit	36	1	5	6
Edmonton	23	0	1	1
Florida	9	0	1	1
Hartford	23	1	3	4
Los Angeles	22	1	3	4
Montreal	30	1	2	3
New Jersey	29	1	3	4
NY Islanders	22	1	1	2
NY Rangers	29	1	5	6
Ottawa	10	0	2	2
Philadelphia	32	0	9	9
Pittsburgh	31	2	7	9
Quebec	27	1	4	5
San Jose	8	0	1	1
St. Louis	42	2	7	9
Tampa Bay	0	0	0	0
Toronto	45	1	7	8
Vancouver	21	2	2	4
Washington	25	0	4	4
Winnipeg	23	0	4	4

1995 SEASON — 2-2–4 home, two assists road for Tampa Bay.... One SHG (Jan. 20 season opener vs. Pittsburgh)....Minus-6.... "Plus" or "even" in 24 games....600th NHL game Feb. 24 at Pittsburgh....Missed one game Mar. 12 (elbow), two Apr. 24-26, one Apr. 29 (neck).

CAREER — Initially Chicago's third pick (59th overall) in 1983 draft....Played 60 games for Blackhawks as 19-year-old in 84-85....NHL debut Oct. 21, 1984, vs. Los Angeles.... First NHL goal in second season, Oct. 19, 1985, vs. Detroit (Chris Pusey)....Career-best plus-4 in 86-87....Played parts of five seasons in Chicago, was traded to Islanders in November of 1988....Finished 88-89 season with Islanders, then was dealt to Hartford in late October of '90....Later in 90-91 season, he helped Springfield win Calder Cup as AHL champions....Signed as free agent by Tampa Bay in July of '92 before club's inaugural season....205 regular-season games remain most in Lightning's brief history.... Played for Canada's title-winning team in '94 World Championships.

CAREER — Marc, wife Ruth spent off-season in Tampa Bay area, where he was active in charity events....Enjoys golf.

CAREER

Season	Team	League	GP	G	A	P	PM	GP	G	A	P	PM
			Regular Season					Playoffs				
1982–83	Chicoutimi	QMJHL	64	3	27	30	113	–	–	–	–	–
1983–84	Chicoutimi	QMJHL	70	10	35	45	125	–	–	–	–	–
	Springfield	AHL	7	0	1	1	2	–	–	–	–	–
1984–85	Chicago	NHL	60	0	6	6	54	6	0	3	3	2
	Springfield	AHL	–	–	–	–	–	4	0	0	0	0
1985–86	Chicago	NHL	71	7	7	14	60	3	0	0	0	0
1986–87	Chicago	NHL	66	4	10	14	66	3	1	0	1	2
1987–88	Chicago	NHL	58	1	6	7	85	–	–	–	–	–
	Saginaw	IHL	10	2	7	9	20	–	–	–	–	–
1988–89	Chicago	NHL	11	0	0	0	18	–	–	–	–	–
	NY Islanders	NHL	58	2	13	15	62	–	–	–	–	–
1989–90	NY Islanders	NHL	18	0	4	4	30	–	–	–	–	–
	Springfield	AHL	47	7	16	23	66	17	2	11	13	16
1990–91	Capital Dist.	AHL	7	0	5	5	6	–	–	–	–	–
	Hartford	NHL	4	0	0	0	4	–	–	–	–	–
	Springfield	AHL	58	4	23	27	85	18	0	7	7	26
1991–92	Hartford	NHL	75	7	17	24	64	5	0	0	0	2
1992–93	Tampa Bay	NHL	78	2	12	14	66	–	–	–	–	–
1993–94	Tampa Bay	NHL	83	1	15	16	87	–	–	–	–	–
1994–95	Tampa Bay	NHL	44	2	4	6	51	–	–	–	–	–
NHL Totals			**626**	**26**	**94**	**120**	**647**	**17**	**1**	**3**	**4**	**6**

BROWN Doug

BECAME RED WING: Obtained in NHL Waiver Draft January 18, 1995.

RIGHT WING

- 5-10 • 185 lbs.
- Shoots Right
- Born: Southborough, MA
  June 12, 1964
- Last Amateur Club:
  Boston College (HE)

Career vs. N.H.L.

Team	GP	G	A	PTS
Anaheim	5	2	1	3
Boston	19	7	8	15
Buffalo	16	6	7	13
Calgary	16	1	6	7
Chicago	19	1	3	4
Dallas	19	1	3	4
Detroit	14	2	7	9
Edmonton	20	5	3	8
Florida	4	2	1	3
Hartford	21	12	3	15
Los Angeles	19	0	6	6
Montreal	17	0	2	2
New Jersey	2	0	0	0
NY Islanders	36	5	6	11
NY Rangers	35	11	14	25
Ottawa	6	0	2	2
Philadelphia	37	5	8	13
Pittsburgh	30	8	11	19
Quebec	18	3	6	9
San Jose	10	3	4	7
St. Louis	20	6	3	9
Tampa Bay	3	1	5	6
Toronto	18	2	5	7
Vancouver	18	2	6	8
Washington	33	6	7	13
Winnipeg	17	4	2	6

1995 SEASON — Tied for fourth on team at plus-14....NHL leader in playoffs, also plus-14....Points in 19 of 45 regular-season games...."Plus" or "even" in 34 games....5-7–12 home, 4-5–9 road....Pair of multiple-point games (both twos)....Two goals Feb. 17 vs. Edmonton....Pair of four-game streaks: 1-3–4 Jan. 24-30, 3-2–5 Feb. 12-20....One PPG....1-1–2 on SHGs....2-4–6 on GWGs....2-3–5 on first goals....Assist Jan. 20 in Red Wings debut vs. Chicago....First goal as Red Wing Jan. 30 at Edmonton.

CAREER — Never drafted, he signed with New Jersey as free agent in August of '86....NHL debut Mar. 13, 1987, vs. Islanders....First point assist Mar. 18, 1987, at Winnipeg....First full season in 87-88, being named Devils' top rookie....First goal Oct. 9, 1987, vs. Pittsburgh....Played with Devils in '88 conference final, scoring first playoff OT goal....Led Devils' forwards with plus-18 in 90-91, third overall on team at plus-17 in 91-92....Scored penalty shot Nov. 23, 1991, at Philadelphia vs. Ken Wregget....Signed as free agent by Pittsburgh in September of '93....Career highs in goals (18), assists (37), points (55) in lone season with Penguins (93-94), ranking third on club at plus-19....Career-best four-point game (all assists) Dec. 11, 1993, at Tampa Bay....Team USA in '86, '89, '91 World Championships, '91 Canada Cup....Four seasons at Boston College, making Hockey East First All-Star Team in final two years (84-85, 85-86).

PERSONAL — Doug, wife Maureen have two daughters, Anna and Kaitlin, and son, Patrick....They spend off-season in White Plains, NY....Enjoys golf, tennis....Brother Greg also played in NHL.

CAREER

| Season | Club | League | Regular Schedule | | | | | Playoffs | | | | |
			GP	G	A	P	PM	GP	G	A	P	PM
1982-83	Boston College	ECAC	22	9	8	17	0	–	–	–	–	–
1983-84	Boston College	ECAC	38	11	10	21	6	–	–	–	–	–
1984-85a	Boston College	ECAC	45	37	31	68	10	–	–	–	–	–
1985-86a	Boston College	ECAC	38	16	40	56	16	–	–	–	–	–
1986-87b	New Jersey	NHL	4	0	1	1	0	–	–	–	–	–
	Maine	AHL	73	24	34	58	15	–	–	–	–	–
1987-88	New Jersey	NHL	70	14	11	25	20	19	5	1	6	6
	Utica	AHL	2	0	2	2	2	–	–	–	–	–
1988-89	New Jersey	NHL	63	15	10	25	15	–	–	–	–	–
	Utica	AHL	4	1	4	4	5	–	–	–	–	–
1989-90	New Jersey	NHL	69	14	20	34	16	6	0	1	1	2
1990-91	New Jersey	NHL	58	14	16	30	4	7	2	2	4	2
1991-92	New Jersey	NHL	71	11	17	28	27	–	–	–	–	–
1992-93	New Jersey	NHL	15	0	5	5	2	–	–	–	–	–
	Utica	AHL	25	11	17	28	8	–	–	–	–	–
1993-94c	Pittsburgh	NHL	77	18	37	55	18	6	0	0	0	2
1995d	DETROIT	NHL	45	9	12	21	16	18	4	8	12	2
NHL Totals			**472**	**95**	**129**	**224**	**118**	**56**	**11**	**12**	**23**	**14**

a-Hockey East First All-Star Team.
b-Signed as free agent by New Jersey, August 6, 1986.
c-Signed as free agent by Pittsburgh, Sept. 28, 1993.
d-Acquired by DETROIT in Waiver Draft, January 18, 1995.

CICCARELLI Dino

BECAME RED WING: Obtained June 20, 1992, from Washington for Kevin Miller.

RIGHT WING

- 5-10 • 185 lbs.
- Shoots Right
- Born: Sarnia, ON
  February 8, 1960
- Last Amateur Club:
  London Knights (OHA)

Career vs. N.H.L.

Team	GP	G	A	PTS
Anaheim	7	3	6	9
Boston	34	17	16	33
Buffalo	34	14	12	26
Calgary	42	19	20	39
Chicago	82	46	44	90
Dallas	26	15	15	30
Detroit	64	36	37	73
Edmonton	42	26	17	43
Florida	0	0	0	0
Hartford	35	21	17	38
Los Angeles	42	23	24	47
Montreal	35	10	11	21
New Jersey	47	20	29	49
NY Islanders	46	22	23	45
NY Rangers	48	18	24	42
Ottawa	3	1	2	3
Philadelphia	46	28	17	45
Pittsburgh	47	22	25	47
Quebec	34	22	21	43
San Jose	13	6	5	11
St. Louis	82	52	34	86
Tampa Bay	8	10	6	16
Toronto	81	38	50	88
Vancouver	43	28	23	51
Washington	26	11	11	22
Winnipeg	48	21	39	60

1995 SEASON — Third on club in goals, points, tied for third in assists, was fourth in PPGs (6-11–17)....Points in 28 of 42 games....Goals in 14 outings....11 multiple-point games (one four, two threes, eight twos)....Pair of two-goal games....One four-assist game, four with two....Plus-12...."Plus" or "even" in 34 games....11-game streak (7-10–17) Feb. 20-Mar. 16 (second-best on team in '95, equaled second-highest in career, one shy of 12-game string in '89 for Washington)....Five-game goal streak Feb. 20-Mar. 2....Became 101st NHL player to appear in 1,000 regular-season games Mar. 28 vs. Anaheim....8-16–24 home, 8-11–19 road....3-4–7 on GWGs....1-4–5 on first goals....3-1–4 on ENGs....Missed one game Feb. 10 (facial lacerations), one Apr. 5 (groin)....Led club in goals in playoffs....Paced NHL, tied club record with six playoff PPGs....Three PPGs May 11 in Game 3 at Dallas, tying NHL playoff record for PPGs in one game (one of nine players; only one to do it twice; had been most recent Apr. 29, 1993, in Game 6 at Toronto; this was sixth career playoff hat trick, second as Red Wing).

CAREER — 500th goal Jan. 8, 1994, at Los Angeles....Goal Mar. 9, 1994, at Calgary for 1,000th point....Most recent hat trick in 4-2–6 outing Apr. 5, 1994, at Vancouver (18th NHL hat trick, fourth four-goal game; also notched 500th assist in that game)....Twice has topped 50 goals, 100 points.... 40 or more goals six times, 30 or more 10 times....Fourth in NHL in goals (55), tied for ninth in points (106) with career highs in 81-82 for Minnesota....Fifth in NHL in goals (52), sixth in points (103), second in PPGs (career-high 22) in 86-87....In 92-93, tied Mickey Redmond's club record, was 10th in NHL in PPGs (21)....11-game streak (9-12–21) Mar. 18-Apr. 15, 1993....1-1–2 for first points as Red Wing Oct. 8, 1992, at Los Angeles....Red Wings debut Oct. 6, 1992, at Winnipeg....Career-best 4-3–7 Mar. 18, 1989, for Washington vs. Hartford....12 playoff GWGs (three in OT)....NHL playoff record for goals by rookie (14 in '81 to help Minnesota reach Stanley Cup final)....NHL debut Dec. 13, 1980, vs. Winnipeg....First points 1-2–3 Feb. 7, 1981, at Islanders....Never drafted....Fractured femur in '78 while playing for London (OHA)....Signed with Minnesota as free agent in '79.

PERSONAL — Dino, wife Lynda reside in suburban Detroit with daughters Jenna, Kristen, Ashley....He grew up in nearby Sarnia, ON....Dino is club owner, Sarnia Sting (OHL), Motor City Mustangs (Roller Hockey International) along with brothers Rob, Larry, former teammate Shawn Burr....Enjoys golf....Dedicated to helping hospital burn units.

CAREER

			Regular Schedule					Playoffs				
Season	Club	League	GP	G	A	P	PM	GP	G	A	P	PM
1977-78a	London	OHA	68	72	70	142	49	9	6	10	16	6
1978-79	London	OHL	30	8	11	19	35	7	3	5	8	0
1979-80	London	OHL	62	50	53	103	72	5	2	6	8	15
1980-81	Oklahoma City	CHL	48	32	25	57	45	–	–	–	–	–
	Minnesota	NHL	32	18	12	30	29	19	14	7	21	25
1981-82	Minnesota	NHL	76	55	51	106	138	4	3	1	4	2
1982-83	Minnesota	NHL	77	37	38	75	94	9	4	6	10	11
1983-84	Minnesota	NHL	79	38	33	71	58	16	4	5	9	27
1984-85	Minnesota	NHL	51	15	17	32	41	9	3	3	6	8
1985-86	Minnesota	NHL	75	44	45	89	51	5	0	1	1	6
1986-87	Minnesota	NHL	80	52	51	103	88	–	–	–	–	–
1987-88	Minnesota	NHL	67	41	45	86	79	–	–	–	–	–
1988-89	Minnesota	NHL	65	32	27	59	64	–	–	–	–	–
	Washington	NHL	11	12	12	3	15	6	3	3	6	12
1989-90	Washington	NHL	80	41	38	79	122	8	8	3	11	6
1990-91	Washington	NHL	54	21	18	39	76	11	5	4	9	22
1991-92	Washington	NHL	78	38	38	76	78	7	5	4	9	14
1992-93	DETROIT	NHL	82	41	56	97	81	7	4	2	6	14
1993-94	DETROIT	NHL	66	28	29	57	73	7	5	2	7	14
1995	DETROIT	NHL	42	16	27	43	39	16	9	2	11	22
DETROIT Totals			**190**	**85**	**112**	**197**	**193**	**30**	**18**	**6**	**24**	**52**
NHL Totals			**1015**	**529**	**528**	**1057**	**1113**	**124**	**67**	**43**	**110**	**185**

a-OHA Second All-Star Team (1978).
Signed as a free agent by Minnesota, Sept. 28, 1979.
Traded to Washington by Minnesota with Bob Rouse for Mike Gartner and Larry Murphy, March 7, 1989.
Traded to DETROIT by Washington for Kevin MIller, June 20, 1992.

COFFEY Paul

BECAME RED WING: Obtained January 29, 1993, from Los Angeles with Jim Hiller, Sylvain Couturier for Jimmy Carson, Marc Potvin, Gary Shuchuk.

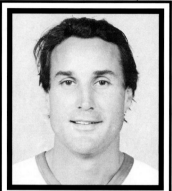

DEFENSE

- 6-0 • 190 lbs.
- Shoots Left
- Born: Weston, ON
  June 1, 1961
- Last Amateur Club:
  Kitchener Rangers (OHA)

Career vs. N.H.L.

Team	GP	G	A	PTS
Anaheim	8	3	8	11
Boston	39	6	29	35
Buffalo	37	3	32	35
Calgary	77	34	66	100
Chicago	50	22	40	62
Dallas	50	19	46	65
Detroit	35	18	34	52
Edmonton	26	6	21	27
Florida	2	0	3	3
Hartford	38	15	44	59
Los Angeles	69	31	62	93
Montreal	39	7	28	35
New Jersey	63	24	44	68
NY Islanders	53	19	47	66
NY Rangers	52	18	59	77
Ottawa	3	1	3	4
Philadelphia	54	16	46	62
Pittsburgh	23	9	18	27
Quebec	37	12	40	52
San Jose	16	2	26	28
St. Louis	44	9	39	48
Tampa Bay	8	1	6	7
Toronto	49	10	41	51
Vancouver	78	27	73	100
Washington	54	21	46	67
Winnipeg	74	25	77	102

1995 SEASON — Won third Norris Trophy as NHL's top defenseman (also won in '85, '86)....NHL First-Team All-Star (other First Team berths in '85, '86, '89, Second Team in '82, '83, '84, '90)....Led NHL defensemen in scoring, tied for sixth overall, ranked second in league in assists, was first in PPG points (4-27–31)....First defenseman in Detroit history to lead team in scoring....Also paced team in assists, plus-minus (plus-18), was fifth in goals....Points in 38 of 45 games....Team-high 13-game streak (6-15–21) Apr. 5-29, tied for third-best in NHL....Goals in 12 outings.... 15 multiple-point games (one four, trio of threes, 11 twos)....Pair of two-goal games....One four-assist game, trio with three, six twos...."Plus" or "even" in 36 games....NHL Player of Month for period Apr. 1-May 3 (7-15–22, plus-8 in 16 outings)....NHL Player of Week Apr. 10-16 (1-5–6, plus-3 in four games).... 5-27–32 home, 9-17–26 road....2-9–11 on GWGs....1-5–6 on first goals....One SHG....Two assists on ENGs....1,300th point with assist Mar. 2 vs. Winnipeg (12th player in NHL history to reach mark).... Missed two games Jan. 30-Feb. 1 (back)....Set club playoff records for points, assists by defenseman, led NHL blue-liners....Moved past Denis Potvin with most playoff points by defenseman, climbed to seventh overall....Tops among defensemen, fourth overall on all-time postseason assist list.

CAREER — NHL all-time leader among defensemen in goals, assists, points....Fourth overall on league ledger in assists, 10th in points....Seven-time scoring leader among defensemen, topping 100 points five times (Bobby Orr, Potvin only other blue-liners to reach 100)....Holds NHL record by goals in one season by defenseman (48 in 85-86)....Second-best assist, point marks by defenseman one season with 90, 138 in 85-86 (Orr 102, 139 in 70-71)....Stanley Cup '84, '85, '87 with Edmonton, '91 in Pittsburgh (with runner-up Oilers '83 final vs. Islanders)....Trying to become seventh player to be on Cup winner with three different teams....League records in '85 for goals, assists, points by defenseman one playoff year....Set Detroit records in 93-94 for points, assists by defenseman....1,000th regular-season game Feb. 4, 1994, vs. Pittsburgh....Started eighth consecutive All-Star Game in '94, made 12th appearance overall....Career-best regular-season outing Mar. 14, 1986, vs. Detroit at Edmonton, tying NHL single-game records for points (8), assists (6) by defenseman....Two assists in Red Wings debut Jan. 30, 1993, at Vancouver, with first goal Feb. 3 that year vs. Chicago....Oilers' first pick (sixth overall) in '80 draft.

PERSONAL — Paul, wife Stephanie have daughter, Savannah, and spend off-season in Muskoka, ON....Enjoys boating.

CAREER

			Regular Schedule					Playoffs				
Season	Club	League	GP	G	A	P	PM	GP	G	A	P	PM
1978-79a	S.S. Marie	OHA	68	17	72	89	103	–	–	–	–	–
1979-80b	S.S. Marie	OHA	23	10	21	31	63	–	–	–	–	–
	Kitchener	OHA	52	19	52	71	130	–	–	–	–	–
1980-81	Edmonton	NHL	74	9	23	32	130	9	4	3	7	22
1981-82c	Edmonton	NHL	80	29	60	89	106	5	1	1	2	6
1982-83c	Edmonton	NHL	80	29	67	96	87	16	7	7	14	14
1983-84c	Edmonton	NHL	80	40	86	126	104	19	8	14	22	21
1984-85de	Edmonton	NHL	80	37	84	121	97	18	12	25	37	44
1985-86de	Edmonton	NHL	79	48	90	138	120	10	1	9	10	30
1986-87	Edmonton	NHL	59	17	50	67	49	17	3	8	11	30
1987-88	Pittsburgh	NHL	46	15	52	67	93	–	–	–	–	–
1988-89e	Pittsburgh	NHL	75	30	83	113	195	11	2	13	15	31
1989-90c	Pittsburgh	NHL	80	29	74	103	95	–	–	–	–	–
1990-91	Pittsburgh	NHL	76	24	69	93	128	12	2	9	11	6
1991-92	Pittsburgh	NHL	54	10	54	64	62	–	–	–	–	–
	Los Angeles	NHL	10	1	4	5	25	6	4	3	7	2
1992-93	Los Angeles	NHL	50	8	49	57	50	–	–	–	–	–
	DETROIT	NHL	30	4	26	30	27	7	2	9	11	2
1993-94	DETROIT	NHL	80	14	63	77	106	7	1	6	7	8
1995de	DETROIT	NHL	45	14	44	58	72	18	6	12	18	10
NHL Totals			1078	358	978	1336	1546	155	53	119	172	226
DETROIT Totals			155	32	143	165	205	32	9	27	36	20

a-OHA 3rd Team All-Star; b-OHA 2nd Team; c-NHL 2nd Team All-Star; d-James Norris Memorial Trophy; e-NHL 1st Team All-Star Team.
Drafted by Edmonton in 1980 Entry Draft (1st choice, 6th overall, 1st Round).
Traded to Pittsburgh by Edmonton with Dave Hunter and Wayne Van Dorp for Craig Simpson, Dave Hannan, Moe Mantha and Chris Joseph, Nov. 24, 1987.
Traded to Los Angeles by Pittsburgh for Brian Benning, Jeff Chychrun and Los Angeles' first round choice (later traded to Phil.) in 1992 Entry Draft, Feb. 19, 1992.
Traded to DETROIT along with Jim Hiller and Sylvain Couturier for Jim Carson, Gary Shuchuk and Mark Potvin, Jan. 29, 1993.

DRAPER Kris

BECAME RED WING: Obtained June 30, 1993, from Winnipeg for future considerations.

CENTER

- 5-11 • 185 lbs.
- Shoots Left
- Born: Toronto, ON
  May 24, 1973
- Last Amateur Club:
  Ottawa 67s (OHL)

Career vs. N.H.L.

Team	GP	G	A	PTS
Anaheim	4	0	1	1
Boston	0	0	0	0
Buffalo	1	1	0	1
Calgary	9	1	2	3
Chicago	6	0	1	1
Dallas	7	0	1	1
Detroit	2	1	0	1
Edmonton	8	1	0	1
Florida	2	0	0	0
Hartford	2	0	0	0
Los Angeles	4	0	0	0
Montreal	2	1	0	1
New Jersey	1	0	0	0
NY Islanders	2	0	0	0
NY Rangers	1	1	0	1
Ottawa	1	0	2	2
Philadelphia	2	0	0	0
Pittsburgh	1	0	0	0
Quebec	1	0	0	0
San Jose	5	0	1	1
St. Louis	7	1	2	3
Tampa Bay	1	0	1	1
Toronto	5	2	0	2
Vancouver	12	0	2	2
Washington	4	0	0	0
Winnipeg	5	1	1	2

1995 SEASON — "Plus" or "even" in 30 of 36 games....Plus-1 overall....Points in six games....Two-game streak (1-3–4) Mar. 22-24, including first two NHL multiple-point games....2-2–4 home, four assists road....One assist on SHG....One assist on ENG....Missed eight games Feb. 7-23 (knee)....Dramatic GWG with 1:45 remaining in third period June 4 vs. Chicago gave Detroit 3-2 victory for 2-0 series lead en route to winning conference championship.

CAREER — Career bests in goals, assists, points, plus-minus (plus-11) in 93-94.... Career-high three-game streak (three goals) Mar. 4-7, 1994....Scored goal in NHL debut Oct. 4, 1990, for Winnipeg vs. Toronto....First goal as Red Wing Feb. 12, 1994, at St. Louis....First NHL assist Jan. 27, 1993, at Chicago....Initially Winnipeg's fourth pick (62nd overall, third round) in '89 draft....Played two seasons for Canadian National Team.

PERSONAL — Single....Spends off-season in West Hill, ON....Enjoys golf....Played baseball, tennis in high school.

CAREER

Season	Club	League	Regular Schedule					Playoffs				
			GP	G	A	P	PM	GP	G	A	P	PM
1988-89	Canadian	National	60	11	15	26	16	–	–	–	–	–
1989-90	Canadian	National	61	12	22	34	44	–	–	–	–	–
1990-91	Winnipeg	NHL	3	1	0	1	5	–	–	–	–	–
	Moncton	AHL	39	19	42	61	35	17	8	11	19	20
1991-92	Winnipeg	NHL	10	2	0	2	2	2	0	0	0	0
	Moncton	AHL	61	11	18	29	113	4	0	1	1	6
1992-93	Moncton	AHL	67	12	23	35	40	5	2	2	4	18
	Winnipeg	NHL	7	0	0	0	0	–	–	–	–	–
1993-94	Adirondack	AHL	46	20	23	43	49	–	–	–	–	–
	DETROIT	NHL	39	5	8	13	31	7	2	2	4	4
1995	DETROIT	NHL	36	2	6	8	22	18	4	1	5	12
NHL Totals			**95**	**10**	**14**	**24**	**62**	**27**	**6**	**3**	**9**	**16**
DETROIT Totals			**75**	**7**	**14**	**21**	**53**	**25**	**6**	**3**	**9**	**16**

Drafted by Winnipeg in 1989 NHL Entry Draft (4th choice, 62nd overall, 3rd round).
Traded to DETROIT from Winnipeg for future considerations, June 30, 1993.

ERREY Bob

BECAME RED WING: Obtained February 28, 1995, from San Jose
for fifth-round pick in 1995 Entry Draft.

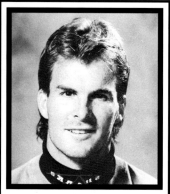

LEFT WING

- 5-11 • 185 lbs.
- Shoots Left
- Born: Montreal, PQ
  September 21, 1964
- Last Amateur Club:
  Peterborough Petes (OHL)

Career vs. N.H.L.

Team	GP	G	A	PTS
Anaheim	8	2	3	5
Boston	27	5	6	11
Buffalo	24	6	8	14
Calgary	31	5	7	12
Chicago	31	8	9	17
Dallas	35	6	6	12
Detroit	22	3	6	9
Edmonton	26	6	5	11
Florida	2	0	0	0
Hartford	23	4	7	11
Los Angeles	30	5	8	13
Montreal	19	4	5	9
New Jersey	51	7	12	19
NY Islanders	53	16	13	29
NY Rangers	52	13	17	30
Ottawa	5	1	1	2
Philadelphia	54	8	16	24
Pittsburgh	2	0	2	2
Quebec	24	8	6	14
San Jose	7	5	2	7
St. Louis	26	8	5	13
Tampa Bay	3	0	0	0
Toronto	27	9	10	19
Vancouver	27	7	4	11
Washington	47	9	13	22
Winnipeg	31	8	3	11

1995 SEASON — Points in 10 of 30 games for Detroit....Tied for fourth on team in overall plus-minus (plus-9)....Season-high five-game streak (2-6–8) Apr. 2-11....Five multiple-point games (two threes, trio of twos)...."Plus" or "even" in 23 games....With Detroit, 2-2–4 home, 4-9–12 road....Three assists on PPGs....1-2–3 on GWGs....Two assists on first goals....1-1–2 on ENGs....Red Wings debut Mar. 2 vs. Winnipeg....1-2–3 Mar. 6 at Vancouver for first points as Red Wing....Was San Jose captain when acquired by Detroit....2-2–4, plus-4 in 13 outings with Sharks.

CAREER — Played on two Stanley Cup winners with Pittsburgh ('91, '92)....Two seasons under Scotty Bowman with Penguins (91-92, 92-93)....Pittsburgh's first pick (15th overall) in '83 draft — same year Peterborough (OHL) teammate Steve Yzerman was Detroit's top choice (fourth overall)....Spent nearly 10 years at Pittsburgh....Career highs in goals (26), assists (32), points (58) in 88-89....Effective penalty killer also has 11 career SHGs....Lone NHL hat trick Oct. 17, 1991, vs. Islanders....Dealt to Buffalo in March of '93 for current Red Wing Mike Ramsey....Signed with Sharks as free agent in summer of '93.

PERSONAL — Bob, wife Tracey have son, Conor, spend off-season in Peterborough, ON....He enjoys golf, water skiing....Third cousin of Detroit great and Hockey Hall of Famer Ted Lindsay.

CAREER

			Regular Schedule					Playoffs				
Season	Club	League	GP	G	A	P	PM	GP	G	A	P	PM
1981-82	Peterborough	AHL	68	29	31	60	39	9	3	1	4	9
1982-83	Peterborough	AHL	67	53	47	100	74	4	1	3	4	7
1983-84	Pittsburgh	NHL	65	9	13	22	29	–	–	–	–	–
1984-85	Pittsburgh	NHL	16	0	2	2	7	–	–	–	–	–
	Baltimore	AHL	59	17	24	41	14	8	3	4	7	11
1985-86	Pittsburgh	NHL	37	11	6	17	8	–	–	–	–	–
	Baltimore	AHL	18	8	7	15	28	–	–	–	–	–
1986-87	Pittsburgh	NHL	72	16	18	34	46	–	–	–	–	–
1987-88	Pittsburgh	NHL	17	3	6	9	18	–	–	–	–	–
1988-89	Pittsburgh	NHL	76	26	32	58	124	11	1	2	3	12
1989-90	Pittsburgh	NHL	78	20	19	39	109	–	–	–	–	–
1990-91	Pittsburgh	NHL	79	20	22	42	115	24	5	3	7	29
1991-92	Pittsburgh	NHL	78	19	16	35	119	14	3	0	3	10
1992-93	Pittsburgh	NHL	54	8	6	14	76	–	–	–	–	–
	Buffalo	NHL	8	1	3	4	4	4	0	1	1	10
1993-94	San Jose	NHL	64	12	18	30	126	14	3	2	5	10
1995	San Jose	NHL	13	2	2	4	27	–	–	–	–	–
	DETROIT	NHL	30	6	11	17	31	18	1	5	6	30
NHL Totals			700	155	176	331	866	85	13	12	25	101

Drafted by Pittsburgh (1st round, 15th Overall) in the 1983 NHL Entry Draft.
Traded to Buffalo by Pittsburgh for Mike Ramsey, March 22, 1993.
Signed as a free agent by San Jose, August 17, 1993.
Traded to DETROIT by San Jose for 5th round pick in 1995 Entry Draft, Feb. 27, 1995.

FEDOROV Sergei

BECAME RED WING: Fourth pick (74th overall) in 1989 Entry Draft.

CENTER

- 6-1 • 200 lbs.
- Shoots Left
- Born: Pskov, Russia
  December 13, 1969
- Last Amateur Club:
  Central Red Army (USSR)

Career vs. N.H.L.

Team	GP	G	A	PTS
Anaheim	8	4	9	13
Boston	9	2	5	7
Buffalo	10	4	8	12
Calgary	16	11	10	21
Chicago	33	13	19	32
Dallas	31	19	22	41
Detroit	–	–	–	–
Edmonton	16	5	10	15
Florida	2	2	0	2
Hartford	10	2	11	13
Los Angeles	18	12	11	23
Montreal	10	5	3	8
New Jersey	8	6	4	10
NY Islanders	10	7	7	14
NY Rangers	9	4	11	15
Ottawa	3	2	1	3
Philadelphia	10	6	11	17
Pittsburgh	10	8	5	13
Quebec	10	1	7	8
San Jose	14	6	11	17
St. Louis	30	11	20	31
Tampa Bay	9	6	10	16
Toronto	32	14	19	33
Vancouver	16	9	12	21
Washington	10	3	4	7
Winnipeg	20	11	19	30

1995 SEASON — Tied for 14th in NHL scoring....Second on club in goals, assists, points, tied for second in PPGs (7-9–16), first in SHGs (3), shared lead in GWGs (5-5–10)....Points in 32 of 42 games....Goals in 17 games....13 multiple-point games (two fours, one three, 10 twos).... Season-high eight-game streak (5-8–13) Mar. 25-Apr. 9....Four goals Feb. 12 vs. Los Angeles (second career hat trick, first four-goal outing; first three in succession for "natural" hat trick)....One four-assist outing (Apr. 19 vs. Winnipeg to equal career best; other Nov. 7, 1991, vs. St. Louis), six with two....Plus-6...."Plus" or "even" in 27 games.... 12-17–29 home, 8-13–21 road....5-5–10 on GWGs....One assist on GTG....2-5–7 on first goals....One assist on ENG....400th NHL point with goal Mar. 25 at Vancouver....Three times blanked in two straight games (not scoreless in as many as three since Mar. 5-7, 1992).... Season debut Jan. 26 after three-game suspension for high-sticking San Jose's Jayson More in Game 7 of '94 playoff series....Missed one game Feb. 7 (flu), one Apr. 11 (hamstring).... NHL playoff leader in points, assists, setting club records....Tied for second in league at plus-13....Points in 14 of 17 playoff outings....Missed one game June 8 (shoulder).

CAREER — Top honors in 93-94: Hart Trophy as MVP (only European winner); Selke Trophy as best defensive forward; Lester B. Pearson Award as top performer in vote by Players' Association; First-Team All-Star; Player of Year by Hockey News, Sporting News, Hockey Digest....Second in NHL in scoring, third in goals, second at plus-48 in 93-94.... Career highs that season in goals, assists, points, plus-minus, GWGs (10), equaled personal best in PPGs (13)....Shares club GWG record initially set by Carson Cooper in 1928-29....One of six Red Wings, second center, to notch 50-goal season; one of five, third center, to get 100 points....Career-high nine-game streak (7-11–18) Nov. 23-Dec. 9, 1993....First NHL hat trick Mar. 1, 1994, vs. Calgary....NHL Co-Player of Month December, 1993, with Buffalo's Dominik Hasek....'92, '94 All-Star games....Runner-up to Guy Carbonneau for 91-92 Selke Trophy despite more first-place votes (22-to-19) in total-points ballot....Second to Ed Belfour for 90-91 Calder Trophy....Four career regular-season OT goals, one in playoffs.... Tied club record for points in one period with 1-3–4 in second vs. Philadelphia Jan. 21, 1992....90-91 All-Rookie Team after pacing freshmen in goals, assists, points....PPG in NHL debut Oct. 4, 1990, at New Jersey....First two assists Oct. 10, 1990, vs. Calgary....'91 Canada Cup....Four years on Central Red Army team....Helped Soviet national team win gold medals in '89, '90 World Championships....Came to Detroit in July, 1990, after leaving Soviet team in Portland, OR (departed before Goodwill Games at Seattle).

PERSONAL — Single....Resides in suburban Detroit....Played tennis in high school.... Likes golf.

CAREER

Season	Club	League	Regular Schedule					Playoffs				
			GP	G	A	P	PM	GP	G	A	P	PM
1986-87	CSKA	Moscow	29	6	6	12	12	–	–	–	–	–
1987-88	CSKA	Moscow	48	7	9	16	20	–	–	–	–	–
1988-89	CSKA	Moscow	44	9	8	17	35	–	–	–	–	–
1989-90	CSKA	Moscow	48	19	10	29	10	–	–	–	–	–
1990-91a	DETROIT	NHL	77	31	48	79	66	7	1	5	6	4
1991-92	DETROIT	NHL	80	32	54	86	72	11	5	5	10	8
1992-93	DETROIT	NHL	73	34	53	87	72	7	3	6	9	23
1993-94bcde	DETROIT	NHL	82	56	64	120	34	7	1	7	8	6
1995	DETROIT	NHL	42	20	30	50	24	17	7	17	24	6
DETROIT and NHL Totals			**354**	**173**	**249**	**422**	**268**	**49**	**17**	**40**	**57**	**47**

a-NHL All-Star Rookie Team.
b-Won Hart Trophy.
c-Won Selke Trophy.
d-Won Lester B. Pearson Award.
e-NHL First All-Star Team.
Drafted by DETROIT in 1989 NHL Entry Draft (4th choice, 74th overall, 4th round).

FETISOV Viacheslav

BECAME RED WING: Obtained April 3, 1995, from New Jersey
for third-round pick in 1995 Entry Draft.

DEFENSE

- 6-1 • 220 lbs.
- Shoots Left
- Born: Moscow, Russia
  April 20, 1958
- Last Amateur Club:
  Central Red Army (USSR)

Career vs. N.H.L.

Team	GP	G	A	PTS
Anaheim	3	0	2	2
Boston	12	2	3	5
Buffalo	16	2	6	8
Calgary	10	0	4	4
Chicago	13	0	5	5
Dallas	12	1	2	3
Detroit	11	0	5	5
Edmonton	12	0	0	0
Florida	3	0	0	0
Hartford	14	0	5	5
Los Angeles	13	0	2	2
Montreal	13	0	7	7
New Jersey	0	0	0	0
NY Islanders	26	0	8	8
NY Rangers	27	3	10	13
Ottawa	4	0	2	2
Philadelphia	30	2	8	10
Pittsburgh	32	2	12	14
Quebec	14	1	7	8
San Jose	10	2	4	6
St. Louis	13	3	7	10
Tampa Bay	5	1	1	2
Toronto	12	0	3	3
Vancouver	11	0	4	4
Washington	28	1	7	8
Winnipeg	11	2	5	7

1995 SEASON — Plus-3 in 14 games for Detroit....Points in nine outings, with assist in debut Apr. 5 at San Jose....Career-high six-game streak (2-8–10) Apr. 13-23...."Plus" or "even" in 10 games.... First goal as Red Wing with PPG Apr. 16 at St. Louis....Three multiple-point games (two threes, one two)....One three-assist outing, one with two....Five assists home, 3-6–9 road....3-2–5 on PPGs....Five assists on GWGs....1-2–3 on first goals....Became free agent after 94-95 season, sat out start in '95, but returned to New Jersey, signing as free agent Feb. 23, getting assist that night vs. Boston....Missed six games with bruised leg, suffered Feb. 25 vs. Washington, returned Mar. 12 at Philadelphia.

CAREER — "Plus" player in all six NHL seasons, with career-best plus-15 in 94-95.... New Jersey's sixth choice (150th overall) in '83 draft, joined club in 89-90, when he had career highs in goals, assists, points....Assist in NHL debut Oct. 5, 1989, at Philadelphia....First goal Oct. 18, 1989, vs. Flyers....Longtime captain of Central Red Army team, which he joined in 74-75, and where he was teammate of Sergei Fedorov, Vladimir Konstantinov....Earned Soviet "Honorned Masters of Sport" award, equivalent of Hockey Hall of Fame....Three times ('84, '86, '90) won Gold Stick Award as Europe's top player....Soviet Player of Year three times ('82, '86, '88)....Nine-time Soviet League All-Star....Pravda Trophy four times as league's top-scoring defenseman.... Played in three Olympics (silver medal in '80, golds in '84, '88)....Performed in 11 World Championships.

PERSONAL — Slava, wife Lada have daughter, Anastasia, spend off-season in West Orange, NJ.

CAREER

| Season | Club | League | Regular Schedule | | | | | Playoffs | | | | |
			GP	G	A	P	PM	GP	G	A	P	PM
1974-75	CSKR	USSR	1	0	0	0	0	–	–	–	–	–
1976-77	CSKR	USSR	35	9	18	27	46	–	–	–	–	–
1978-79	CSKR	USSR	29	10	19	29	40	–	–	–	–	–
1979-80	CSKR	USSR	37	10	14	24	46	–	–	–	–	–
1980-81	CSKR	USSR	48	13	16	29	44	–	–	–	–	–
1981-82ac	CSKR	USSR	46	15	26	41	20	–	–	–	–	–
1982-83ad	CSKR	USSR	43	6	17	23	46	–	–	–	–	–
1983-84a	CSKR	USSR	44	19	30	49	38	–	–	–	–	–
1984-85a	CSKR	USSR	20	13	12	25	6	–	–	–	–	–
1985-86abc	CSKR	USSR	40	15	19	34	12	–	–	–	–	–
1986-87ab	CSKR	USSR	39	13	20	33	18	–	–	–	–	–
1987-88ab	CSKR	USSR	46	18	17	35	26	–	–	–	–	–
1988-89	CSKR	USSR	23	9	8	17	18	–	–	–	–	–
1989-90	New Jersey	NHL	72	8	34	42	52	6	0	2	2	10
1990-91	New Jersey	NHL	67	3	16	19	62	7	0	0	0	17
	Utica	AHL	1	1	1	1	0	–	–	–	–	–
1991-92	New Jersey	NHL	70	3	23	26	108	6	0	3	3	8
1992-93	New Jersey	NHL	76	4	23	27	158	5	0	2	2	4
1993-94	New Jersey	NHL	52	1	14	15	30	14	1	0	1	8
1995e	New Jersey	NHL	4	0	1	1	0	–	–	–	–	–
	DETROIT	NHL	18	3	11	14	2	18	0	8	8	14
NHL Totals			359	22	122	144	412	56	1	15	16	61

a-Soviet National League All-Star Team (1979, 1980, 1982-88).
b-Leningradskaya-Pravda Trophy–Top Scoring Defenseman (1984, 1986-88).
c-Soviet Player of the Year (1982, 1986, 1988).
d-Drafted by New Jersey in 1983 Entry Draft (sixth choice, 150th overall).
e-Signed with New Jersey as a free agent, Feb. 23, 1995.
Traded to DETROIT from New Jersey April 3, 1995 for 3rd round pick in 1995 Entry Draft.

GRIMSON Stu

BECAME RED WING: Obtained from Anaheim Apr. 4, 1995, with Mark Ferner,
sixth-round pick in 1996 Entry Draft for Mike Sillinger, Jason York.

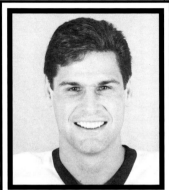

LEFT WING

- 6-5 • 227 lbs.
- Shoots Left
- Born: Kamloops, BC
  May 20, 1965
- Last Amateur Club:
  University of Manitoba (GPAC)

Career vs. N.H.L.

Team	GP	G	A	PTS
Anaheim	1	0	0	0
Boston	6	0	0	0
Buffalo	8	0	0	0
Calgary	15	1	4	5
Chicago	11	0	1	1
Dallas	26	1	1	2
Detroit	27	0	0	0
Edmonton	15	0	0	0
Florida	2	0	0	0
Hartford	7	0	1	1
Los Angeles	14	0	0	0
Montreal	6	0	0	0
New Jersey	8	0	0	0
NY Islanders	7	0	0	0
NY Rangers	7	0	0	0
Ottawa	4	0	0	0
Philadelphia	7	0	0	0
Pittsburgh	7	0	0	0
Quebec	5	0	0	0
San Jose	14	0	1	1
St. Louis	25	1	0	1
Tampa Bay	5	1	1	2
Toronto	24	0	0	0
Vancouver	15	0	0	0
Washington	7	0	1	1
Winnipeg	17	0	0	0

1995 SEASON — Blanked in 11 games with Detroit....Minus-4.... "Plus" or "even" in six games....Overall PIM total (147) topped Red Wings....Lone regular-season point was assist for Anaheim Feb. 9 at Calgary....Minus-7 for Mighty Ducks...."Plus" or "even" in 23 of 31 games for Anaheim....Netted first career playoff goal June 6 at Chicago in Game 3.

CAREER — Twice has been to Stanley Cup final ('95 with Detroit, '92 for Chicago).... Other career playoff point was assist in Game 4 of '92 Cup final vs. Pittsburgh.... Initially selected by Red Wings in 10th round (193rd overall) of '83 draft while in junior ranks at Regina (WHL)....Didn't sign during two-year span, again became eligible for draft, in which he was Calgary's eighth pick (143rd overall, seventh round) in '85.... Played two years at University of Manitoba, where he studied economics....NHL debut Nov. 9, 1988, with Flames at Buffalo....Claimed by Chicago in 1990 waiver draft....First NHL point was assist Mar. 24, 1991, vs. Minnesota....First goal Oct. 24, 1991, vs. Calgary (Mike Vernon in goal)....After three seasons with Blackhawks, was chosen by Anaheim in '93 expansion draft.

PERSONAL — Stu, wife Pam have two daughters, Erin and Hannah, spend off-season in Winnipeg....Enjoys golf, boating....Would like to complete degree in economics when playing days are over.

CAREER

Season	Club	League	Regular Schedule GP	G	A	P	PM	Playoffs GP	G	A	P	PM
1982-83	Regina	WHL	48	0	1	1	105	5	0	0	0	14
1983-84	Regina	WHL	63	8	8	16	131	23	0	1	1	29
1984-85	Regina	WHL	71	24	32	56	248	8	1	2	3	14
1985-86	Univ Manitoba	GPAC	12	7	4	11	113	3	1	1	2	20
1986-87	Univ Manitoba	GPAC	29	8	8	16	67	14	4	2	6	28
1987-88	Salt Lake	IHL	38	9	5	14	268	0	0	0	0	0
1988-89	Salt Lake	IHL	72	9	18	27	397	15	2	3	5	86
	Calgary	NHL	1	0	0	0	5	0	0	0	0	0
1989-90	Salt Lake	IHL	62	8	8	16	319	4	0	0	0	8
	Calgary	NHL	3	0	0	0	17	0	0	0	0	0
1990-91	Chicago	NHL	35	0	1	1	183	5	0	0	0	46
1991-92	Indianapolis	IHL	5	1	1	2	17	0	0	0	0	0
	Chicago	NHL	54	2	2	4	234	14	0	1	1	10
1992-93	Chicago	NHL	78	1	1	2	93	2	0	0	0	4
1993-94	Anaheim	NHL	77	1	5	6	199	0	0	0	0	0
1995	Anaheim	NHL	31	0	1	1	110					
	DETROIT	NHL	11	0	0	0	37	11	1	0	1	26
NHL Totals			**321**	**4**	**11**	**15**	**1088**	**32**	**1**	**1**	**2**	**86**

Drafted by DETROIT in 1983 NHL Entry Draft (10th choice, 193 overall) but did not sign.
Drafted by Calgary in 1985 NHL Entry Draft (8th choice, 143rd overall).
Claimed by Chicago on conditional waivers, Oct. 1, 1990.
Claimed by Anaheim from Chicago in Expansion Draft, June 24, 1993.
Traded to DETROIT with Mark Ferner by Anaheim for Mike Sillinger and Jason York, April 4, 1995.

HANKINSON Ben

BECAME RED WING: Obtained August 17, 1995, from Tampa Bay
with Marc Bergevin for Shawn Burr, third-round pick in 1996 Entry Draft.

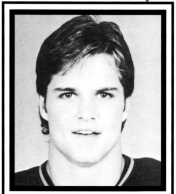

RIGHT WING

- 6-2 • 215 lbs.
- Shoots Right
- Born: Edina, MN
  May 1, 1969
- Last Amateur Club:
  University of Minnesota (WCHA)

Career vs. N.H.L.

Team	GP	G	A	Tp
Anaheim	1	0	0	0
Boston	5	0	0	0
Buffalo	4	0	0	0
Calgary	0	0	0	0
Chicago	0	0	0	0
Dallas	0	0	0	0
Detroit	0	0	0	0
Edmonton	1	0	0	0
Florida	3	0	0	0
Hartford	3	0	1	1
Los Angeles	0	0	0	0
Montreal	2	0	1	1
New Jersey	3	0	0	0
NY Islanders	2	0	0	0
NY Rangers	0	0	0	0
Ottawa	2	1	0	1
Philadelphia	4	0	0	0
Pittsburgh	2	0	0	0
Quebec	5	0	0	0
San Jose	1	0	0	0
St. Louis	0	0	0	0
Tampa Bay	1	2	1	3
Toronto	1	0	0	0
Vancouver	0	0	0	0
Washington	3	0	0	0
Winnipeg	0	0	0	0

1995 SEASON — Began season with New Jersey, going scoreless, minus-6 in eight outings....Traded to Tampa Bay Mar. 14 in four-player deal....Plus-1, two assists in 18 outings with Lightning...."Plus" or "even" in 16 games....First point assist Mar. 27 vs. Montreal....Other assist Apr. 9 at Hartford.

CAREER — Played four years at University of Minnesota (WCHA) after being New Jersey's fifth pick (107th overall, sixth round) in 1987 Entry Draft....WCHA All-Star Team in junior season (89-90)....Team captain in senior year....First pro season with Devils' Utica (AHL) affiliate in 91-92....NHL debut Mar. 20, 1993, vs. Quebec....First NHL points in 2-1–3 performance Mar. 23, 1993, vs. Tampa Bay....Had spent bulk of 92-93 season at Utica, netting team-high 35 goals....Divided 93-94 season between New Jersey and its new Albany (AHL) farm club.

CAREER — Single....Spends off-season in Minnesota....Enjoys working out, playing golf....His father, John, played quarterback for Minnesota Vikings after performing at University of Minnesota.

CAREER

			Regular Season					Playoffs				
Season	Team	League	GP	G	A	P	PM	GP	G	A	P	PM
1987–88	U. Minnesota	WCHA	24	4	7	11	36	–	–	–	–	–
1988–89	U.Minnesota	WCHA	43	7	11	18	115	–	–	–	–	–
1989–90a	U.Minnesota	WCHA	46	25	41	66	34	–	–	–	–	–
1990–91	U.Minnesota	WCHA	43	19	21	40	133	–	–	–	–	–
1991–92	Utica	AHL	77	17	16	33	186	4	3	1	4	2
1992–93	New Jersey	NHL	4	2	1	3	9	–	–	–	–	–
	Utica	AHL	75	35	27	62	145	5	2	2	4	6
1993–94	New Jersey	NHL	13	1	0	1	23	2	1	0	1	4
	Albany	AHL	29	9	14	23	80	5	3	1	4	6
1995	New Jersey	NHL	8	0	0	0	7	–	–	–	–	–
	Tampa Bay	NHL	18	0	2	2	6	–	–	–	–	–
NHL Totals			**43**	**3**	**3**	**6**	**38**	**2**	**1**	**0**	**1**	**4**

a–TO COME

JOHNSON Greg

BECAME RED WING: Obtained from Philadelphia June 20, 1993, for Jim Cummins, fourth-round pick which Detroit acquired from Flyers October 1, 1992, in trade that sent Brent Fedyk to Philadelphia.

LEFT WING/CENTER

- 5-10 • 185 lbs.
- Shoots Left
- Born: Thunder Bay, ON
  March 16, 1971
- Last Amateur Club:
  North Dakota (WCHA)

Career vs. N.H.L.

Team	GP	G	A	PTS
Anaheim	5	0	2	2
Boston	2	0	0	0
Buffalo	2	0	0	0
Calgary	3	0	0	0
Chicago	5	2	0	2
Dallas	7	2	3	5
Detroit	–	–	–	–
Edmonton	6	0	2	2
Florida	0	0	0	0
Hartford	1	0	0	0
Los Angeles	6	0	2	2
Montreal	2	0	2	2
New Jersey	1	0	0	0
NY Islanders	1	0	0	0
NY Rangers	1	0	1	1
Ottawa	1	0	1	1
Philadelphia	1	0	0	0
Pittsburgh	1	2	0	2
Quebec	1	0	0	0
San Jose	5	0	1	1
St. Louis	6	1	1	2
Tampa Bay	2	0	0	9
Toronto	5	1	1	2
Vancouver	4	0	0	0
Washington	0	0	0	0
Winnipeg	6	1	0	1

1995 SEASON — Points in seven of 22 games....Three-game streak (1-2–3) Feb. 17-22, equaling career high....Two-game streak (two goals) Feb. 25-Mar. 2....One multiple-point game (a two)....Plus-1....."Plus" or "even" in 16 games....3-3–6 home, two assists road....Two PPGs....Two assists on PPGs....Two assists on GWGs....Two assists on first goals....One ENG....Missed final nine regular-season games Apr. 16-May 3 (ankle).

CAREER — Goal in NHL debut Oct. 5, 1994, at Dallas....First NHL assist Oct. 13, 1994, vs. St. Louis....Two other three-game streaks in career: 1-3–4 Oct. 23-27, 1-2–3 Dec. 17-21, both 1994....One two-goal game, Nov. 13, 1994, at Pittsburgh....Scored PPG in NHL playoff debut in Game 1 Apr. 18, 1994, vs. San Jose....Played for Team Canada's silver-medal club in '94 Olympics (on loan from Detroit)....Four seasons at North Dakota (WCHA)....Three-time WCHA First-Team All-Star....NCAA West First-Team All-Star in 90-91, Second Team in 91-92, 92-93....Led WCHA in assists in 90-91, 91-92....Third in points, assists in WCHA in 92-93.

PERSONAL — Single....Spends off-season in Thunder Bay, ON....Enjoys golf.

CAREER

Season	Club	League	Regular Schedule					Playoffs				
			GP	G	A	P	PM	GP	G	A	P	PM
1989-90	Univ. of North Dakota	WCHA	44	17	38	55	11	–	–	–	–	–
1990-91*ab*	Univ. of North Dakota	WCHA	38	18	61	79	6	–	–	–	–	–
1991-92*ac*	Univ. of North Dakota	WCHA	39	20	54	74	8	–	–	–	–	–
1992-93	Univ. of North Dakota	WCHA	34	19	45	64	18	–	–	–	–	–
1993-94	DETROIT	NHL	52	6	11	17	22	7	2	2	4	2
	Adirondack	AHL	3	2	4	6	0	4	0	4	4	4
1995	DETROIT	NHL	22	3	5	8	14	1	0	0	0	0
NHL and DETROIT Totals			**74**	**9**	**16**	**25**	**36**	**8**	**2**	**2**	**4**	**2**

Drafted by Philadelphia in 1989 NHL Entry Draft (1st choice, 33rd overall, 2nd round.)
Traded by Philadelphia to DETROIT for Jim Cummins and the Flyers' 4th round pick that DETROIT acquired in the trade that sent Brent Fedyk to the Flyers.

KONSTANTINOV Vladimir

BECAME RED WING: 12th choice (221st overall, 11th round) in 1989 Entry Draft.

DEFENSE

- 6-0 • 190 lbs.
- Shoots Right
- Born: Murmansk, Russia
  March 19, 1967
- Last Amateur Club:
  Central Red Army (USSR)

Career vs. N.H.L.

Team	GP	G	A	PTS
Anaheim	8	2	4	6
Boston	5	1	2	3
Buffalo	7	1	3	4
Calgary	15	0	3	3
Chicago	27	1	8	9
Dallas	26	2	4	6
Detroit	–	–	–	–
Edmonton	13	1	4	5
Florida	2	0	0	0
Hartford	7	0	0	0
Los Angeles	15	1	3	4
Montreal	7	0	0	0
New Jersey	7	1	1	2
NY Islanders	7	1	0	1
NY Rangers	7	1	4	5
Ottawa	4	1	1	2
Philadelphia	7	0	4	4
Pittsburgh	7	0	2	2
Quebec	6	0	1	1
San Jose	15	4	4	8
St. Louis	25	5	9	14
Tampa Bay	9	1	2	3
Toronto	24	2	5	7
Vancouver	14	2	1	3
Washington	8	0	3	3
Winnipeg	16	1	7	8

1995 SEASON — Plus-10...."Plus" or "even" in 39 of 47 games.... Points in 13 games....Four-game streak (2-2–4) Mar. 14-22, equaling career high, capped by assist vs. Winnipeg for 100th NHL point.... Led club defensemen with plus-6 in playoffs....First career playoff goal with GWG 10:35 of second OT in Game 3 June 6 at Chicago.

CAREER — Fourth on club with career-high plus-30 in 93-94....Tied for third on team at plus-22 in 92-93....91-92 NHL All-Rookie Team....Plus-25 as rookie....NHL debut Oct. 3, 1991, at Chicago....First point goal Oct. 17, 1991, vs. St. Louis....First assist Oct. 26, 1991, at Toronto....Seven seasons with Central Red Army....Captain of Red Army, Soviet national teams....Appeared in four World Championships, beginning in '86....Second in scoring among defensemen in Soviet Elite League in 89-90, fifth in 90-91....Also played center earlier in career.

PERSONAL — Vladimir, wife Irina, daughter Anastasia reside in suburban Detroit.... Likes swimming, tennis, golf, traveling.

CAREER

Season	Club	League	Regular Schedule GP	G	A	P	PM	Playoffs GP	G	A	P	PM
1984-85	Central Red Army	Soviet	40	1	4	5	10	–	–	–	–	–
1985-86	Central Red Army	Soviet	26	4	3	7	12	–	–	–	–	–
1986-87	Central Red Army	Soviet	35	2	2	4	19	–	–	–	–	–
1987-88	Central Red Army	Soviet	50	3	6	9	32	–	–	–	–	–
1988-89	Central Red Army	Soviet	37	7	8	15	20	–	–	–	–	–
1989-90	Central Red Army	Soviet	47	14	13	27	44	–	–	–	–	–
1990-91	Central Red Army	Soviet	45	5	12	17	42	–	–	–	–	–
1991-92a	DETROIT	NHL	79	8	26	34	172	11	0	1	1	16
1992-93	DETROIT	NHL	82	5	17	22	137	7	0	1	1	8
1993-94	DETROIT	NHL	80	12	21	33	138	7	0	2	2	4
1995	DETROIT	NHL	47	3	11	14	101	18	1	1	2	22
NHL and DETROIT Totals			**288**	**28**	**75**	**103**	**548**	**43**	**1**	**5**	**6**	**50**

a-Named to Upper Deck All Rookie Team (1991-92).
Drafted by DETROIT in 1989 NHL Entry (12th choice, 221st overall, 11th round).

KOZLOV Vyacheslav

BECAME RED WING: Second choice (45th overall, third round) in 1990 Entry Draft.

LEFT WING
- 5-10 • 180 lbs.
- Shoots Left
- Born: Voskreseksk, Russia May 3, 1972
- Last Amateur Club: Central Red Army (USSR)

Career vs. N.H.L.

Team	GP	G	A	PTS
Anaheim	8	4	4	8
Boston	2	1	0	1
Buffalo	3	0	0	0
Calgary	9	2	3	5
Chicago	13	2	4	6
Dallas	12	4	6	10
Detroit	–	–	–	–
Edmonton	8	2	5	6
Florida	2	0	2	2
Hartford	3	2	3	5
Los Angeles	7	4	5	9
Montreal	2	1	1	2
New Jersey	3	3	1	4
NY Islanders	3	0	1	1
NY Rangers	3	1	1	2
Ottawa	2	1	0	1
Philadelphia	3	1	0	1
Pittsburgh	2	3	0	3
Quebec	2	0	0	0
San Jose	10	6	2	8
St. Louis	12	1	7	8
Tampa Bay	5	0	4	4
Toronto	10	3	5	8
Vancouver	9	4	4	8
Washington	2	0	0	0
Winnipeg	12	6	4	10

1995 SEASON — Sixth on team in goals, seventh in scoring.... Points in 26 of 46 games....Goals in 12 outings....Six multiple-point games (one three, five twos)....One two-goal game....One two-assist game....Season-best seven-game streak (3-6–9) Feb. 3-17....Plus-12.... "Plus" or "even" in 38 outings....8-10–18 home, 5-10–15 road....5-7–12 on PPGs....3-4–7 on GWGs....2-4–6 on first goals....100th NHL point with goal Mar. 14 vs. Los Angeles....Missed one game Apr. 19 (foot)....Shared club lead in goals, was third in NHL in playoffs....Tied for third in scoring....Tied club playoff record with four GWGs, shared NHL lead....Clinched Western Conference title with GWG at 2:25 of second OT in Game 5 June 11 vs. Chicago (first career playoff OTG)....Tied NHL, club records with three assists in one period (Game 1 vs. San Jose May 21).

CAREER — Third on team in goals, tied for fifth in scoring, second in GWGs (6), sixth with plus-27 in 93-94....First NHL hat trick in career-best 3-2–5 outing Jan. 6, 1994, at San Jose....Career-high eight-game streak (8-4–12) Nov. 20-Dec. 3, 1993....One regular-season OTG (Nov. 20, 1993, at New Jersey)....Two assists in NHL debut Mar. 12, 1992, at St. Louis (first on first shift when Sergei Fedorov scored at 1:37 of first period)....First NHL goal Oct. 8, 1992, at Los Angeles....Auto accident in November of '91 limited him to 11 games with Red Army....Rookie of Year in Soviet Elite League in 89-90....Sparkled in '89, '90 World Junior Championships....Helped Soviets win gold medal in '90 Goodwill Games at Seattle....World Championships in '91, '94....'91 Canada Cup.

PERSONAL — Single....Resides in suburban Detroit.

CAREER

			Regular Schedule					Playoffs			
Season	Club	League	GP	G	A	P	PM	GP	G	A	P	PM
1987-88	Khimik	Soviet	2	0	1	1	0	–	–	–	–	–
1988-89	Khimik	Soviet	13	0	1	1	2	–	–	–	–	–
1989-90	Khimik	Soviet	45	14	12	26	38	–	–	–	–	–
1990-91	Khimik	Soviet	45	11	13	24	46	–	–	–	–	–
1991-92	Khimik	Soviet	11	6	5	10	12	–	–	–	–	–
1991-92	DETROIT	NHL	7	0	2	2	2	–	–	–	–	–
1992-93	DETROIT	NHL	17	4	1	5	14	4	0	2	2	2
	Adirondack	AHL	45	23	36	59	54	4	1	1	2	4
1993-94	DETROIT	NHL	77	34	39	73	50	7	2	5	7	12
	Adirondack	AHL	3	0	1	1	0	–	–	–	–	–
1995	DETROIT	NHL	46	13	20	33	45	18	9	7	16	10
NHL and DETROIT Totals			**147**	**51**	**62**	**113**	**111**	**29**	**11**	**14**	**25**	**24**

Drafted by DETROIT in 1990 NHL Entry Draft (2nd choice, 45th overall, 3rd round).

LAPOINTE Martin

BECAME RED WING: First choice (10th overall) in 1991 Entry Draft.

RIGHT WING

- 5-11 • 200 lbs.
- Shoots Right
- Born: Ville Ste-Pierre, PQ
  September 12, 1973
- Last Amateur Club:
  Laval Titan (QMJHL)

Career vs. N.H.L.

Team	GP	G	A	PTS
Anaheim	5	0	1	1
Boston	1	0	0	0
Buffalo	1	0	0	0
Calgary	7	0	1	1
Chicago	12	2	2	4
Dallas	7	1	1	2
Detroit	–	–	–	–
Edmonton	4	1	0	1
Florida	0	0	0	0
Hartford	2	0	0	0
Los Angeles	5	0	0	0
Montreal	3	0	2	2
New Jersey	2	0	1	1
NY Islanders	1	0	0	0
NY Rangers	1	0	0	0
Ottawa	2	1	2	3
Philadelphia	1	0	0	0
Pittsburgh	1	0	0	0
Quebec	2	0	0	0
San Jose	5	2	0	2
St. Louis	9	1	1	2
Tampa Bay	3	0	0	0
Toronto	6	2	0	2
Vancouver	5	1	3	4
Washington	2	0	0	0
Winnipeg	9	1	1	2

1995 SEASON — Points in 10 of 39 games....Career-high three-game streak (2-1–3) Apr. 5-9....Plus-1...."Plus" or "even" in 32 games....Two assists home, 4-4–8 road....1-1–2 on GWGs....1-2–3 on first goals....Played with Adirondack (AHL) during lockout....29-16–45 in 39 games for farm club, with 10 PPGs, five SHGs, five GWGs, plus-12....At time of recall when NHL season began, was second in AHL in goals, led league in in SHGs, was pacing club in plus-minus....Played in AHL All-Star Game, named Player of Game for U.S. club in loss to Canadian team.

CAREER — NHL debut Oct. 5, 1992, at Toronto....First regular-season point with assist Dec. 3, 1992, vs. Calgary....First NHL goal Nov. 21, 1993, at St. Louis....Assist in NHL playoff debut Apr. 26, 1992, vs. Minnesota....Four seasons with Laval (QMJHL)....First All-Star Team in QMJHL in 89-90, Second Team in 90-91....Postseason action with Adirondack's Calder Cup champions in '92.

PERSONAL — Single....Spends off-season in hometown of Ville Ste-Pierre, PQ, near Montreal....Enjoys tennis, squash, weightlifting.

CAREER

Season	Club	League	Regular Schedule					Playoffs				
			GP	G	A	P	PM	GP	G	A	P	PM
1989-90a	Laval	QMJHL	65	42	54	96	77	–	–	–	–	–
1990-91b	Laval	QMJHL	64	44	54	98	66	13	7	14	21	26
1991-92	DETROIT	NHL	4	0	1	1	5	3	0	1	1	4
	Laval	QMJHL	31	25	30	55	81	10	4	10	14	32
1992-93	DETROIT	NHL	3	0	0	0	5	–	–	–	–	–
	Adirondack	AHL	8	1	2	3	9	–	–	–	–	–
	Laval	QMJHL	35	38	51	89	41	5	1	8	9	11
1993-94	DETROIT	NHL	50	8	8	16	55	4	0	0	0	0
	Adirondack	AHL	28	25	21	46	47	4	1	1	2	8
1995	DETROIT	NHL	39	4	6	10	73	2	0	1	1	8
NHL and DETROIT Totals			**96**	**12**	**15**	**27**	**133**	**9**	**0**	**2**	**2**	**18**

a-QMJHL First Team All-Star.
b-QMJHL Second Team All-Star.
Drafted by DETROIT in 1991 NHL Entry Draft (1st choice, 10th overall, 1st round).

LIDSTROM Nicklas

BECAME RED WING: Third choice (53rd overall) in 1989 Entry Draft.

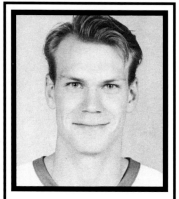

DEFENSE

- 6-2 • 185 lbs.
- Shoots Left
- Born: Vasteras, Sweden
  April 28, 1970
- Last Amateur Club:
  Vasteras (Sweden)

Career vs. N.H.L.

Team	GP	G	A	PTS
Anaheim	8	1	5	6
Boston	6	1	2	3
Buffalo	7	0	3	3
Calgary	15	1	9	10
Chicago	27	5	7	12
Dallas	25	6	8	14
Detroit	–	–	–	–
Edmonton	14	2	7	9
Florida	2	0	1	1
Hartford	7	1	2	3
Los Angeles	15	1	10	11
Montreal	7	0	3	3
New Jersey	7	0	10	10
NY Islanders	7	0	2	2
NY Rangers	7	0	4	4
Ottawa	4	1	1	2
Philadelphia	7	0	0	0
Pittsburgh	7	0	4	4
Quebec	7	3	3	6
San Jose	14	5	11	16
St. Louis	25	4	16	20
Tampa Bay	10	1	7	8
Toronto	25	1	13	14
Vancouver	14	2	8	10
Washington	8	1	4	5
Winnipeg	16	2	5	7

1995 SEASON — Third on team at plus-15, tied for second in PPGs (7-4–11)....Points in 22 of 43 games...."Plus" or "even" in 34 outings....Five-game streak (2-4–6) Mar. 22-30, equaling career best (1-7–8 Nov. 20-27, 1993, 1-5–6 Jan. 31-Feb. 7, 1992)....Four multiple-point games (all twos)....One two-goal game (two PPGs Jan. 24 vs. Vancouver)....Pair of two-assist outings....5-9–14 home, 5-7–12 road....Two assists on GWGs....2-3–5 on first goals....Missed five games Apr. 11-19 (back); never had missed game in NHL career (284 in row; third-longest streak among active players after Trevor Linden, Vincent Damphousse)....Second in playoff scoring among NHL team defensemen after Paul Coffey....With Coffey, tied club postseason record for assists by blue-liner....Tied for third overall in team playoff scoring....GWG at 1:01 of OT June 1 in Game 1 vs. Chicago (first playoff OTG).

CAREER — Third in NHL, second on team with career-high plus-43 in 93-94, when he was second in scoring among club defensemen....Career-best plus-7 outing Jan. 14, 1994, vs. Dallas....Career-high four-assist performance Jan. 6, 1994, at San Jose....One other four-pointer (2-2–4 Nov. 7, 1991, vs. St. Louis)....Runner-up to Pavel Bure for 91-92 Calder Trophy....NHL All-Rookie Team....Third in NHL, third on team at plus-36 in 91-92....Among NHL rookies, was first in plus-minus, first in assists, tied for third in scoring....Ninth in scoring among NHL defensemen, led team blue-liners in 91-92.... Third on team in assists in 91-92, setting club record for assists by rookie defenseman, tying Marcel Dionne's overall team freshman assist mark....Tied Reed Larson's rookie defenseman point mark....In 92-93, was third in scoring among club defensemen.... NHL debut Oct. 3, 1991, at Chicago....First points with two assists Oct. 5, 1991, at Toronto.....First goal was PPG Oct. 17, 1991, vs. St. Louis....Three seasons for Vasteras (Swedish Elite League)....With Sweden in '91 Canada Cup....'91, '94 World Championships, helping Sweden win '91 gold medal....Named one of Sweden's top three players in '90 World Junior Championships.

PERSONAL — Nicklas, Annika, son Kevin Erik spend off-season in Vasteras, Sweden....Enjoys tennis, golf....Played soccer in high school.

CAREER

| Season | Club | League | Regular Schedule | | | | | Playoffs | | | | |
			GP	G	A	P	PM	GP	G	A	P	PM
1988-89	Vasteras	Sweden	19	0	2	2	4	–	–	–	–	–
1989-90	Vasteras	Sweden	39	8	8	16	14	–	–	–	–	–
1990-91	Vasteras	Sweden	20	2	12	14	14	–	–	–	–	–
1991-92a	DETROIT	NHL	80	11	49	60	22	11	1	2	3	0
1992-93	DETROIT	NHL	84	7	34	41	28	7	1	0	1	0
1993-94	DETROIT	NHL	84	10	46	56	26	7	3	2	5	0
1995	DETROIT	NHL	43	10	16	26	6	18	4	12	16	8
NHL and DETROIT Totals			**291**	**38**	**145**	**183**	**82**	**43**	**9**	**16**	**25**	**8**

a-Named to Upper Deck All Rookie Team (1991-92).
Drafted by DETROIT in 1989 NHL Entry (3rd choice, 53rd overall, 3rd round).

McCARTY Darren

BECAME RED WING: Second choice (46th overall) in 1992 Entry Draft.

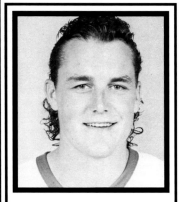

RIGHT WING

- 6-1 • 210 lbs.
- Shoots Right
- Born: Burnaby, BC
  April 1, 1972
- Last Amateur Club:
  Belleville Bulls (OHL)

Career vs. N.H.L.

Team	GP	G	A	PTS
Anaheim	7	3	2	5
Boston	2	0	0	0
Buffalo	2	0	0	0
Calgary	6	0	3	3
Chicago	8	1	0	1
Dallas	9	2	3	5
Detroit	–	–	–	–
Edmonton	6	1	2	3
Florida	2	0	0	0
Hartford	2	0	1	1
Los Angeles	7	0	2	2
Montreal	2	0	1	1
New Jersey	1	0	0	0
NY Islanders	2	0	0	0
NY Rangers	2	0	1	1
Ottawa	2	1	1	2
Philadelphia	2	0	0	0
Pittsburgh	0	0	0	0
Quebec	1	0	0	0
San Jose	7	2	2	4
St. Louis	7	2	1	3
Tampa Bay	2	0	1	1
Toronto	6	0	1	1
Vancouver	5	0	1	1
Washington	0	0	0	0
Winnipeg	8	2	3	5

1995 SEASON — Points in 11 of 31 games....Career-high three-game streak (three assists) Jan. 22-26....3-4–7 home, 2-4–6 road....1-1–2 on PPGs....2-1–3 on GWGs....One assist on first goal....Plus-5...."Plus" or "even" in 27 games....Two multiple-point games (both twos)....Missed eight games Feb. 10-25 (shoulder), two Apr. 1-2 (hand), five Apr. 11-19 (knee).

CAREER — One career OTG (Feb. 12, 1994, at St. Louis)....NHL debut Oct. 5, 1993, at Dallas....First point with assist Oct. 8, 1993, at Los Angeles....First goal Oct. 21, 1993, vs. Winnipeg....Goal in NHL playoff debut Apr. 18, 1994, vs. San Jose....Two seasons at Belleville (OHL), leading league in goals in 91-92 while notching 55-72–127 in 65 outings....Played on line in junior ranks with Brent Gretzky, Wayne's brother.

PERSONAL — Darren, wife Cheryl reside in suburban Detroit....Born in Burnaby, BC, but raised in nearby Leamington, ON....Honored by Royal Canadian Mounted Police for helping juvenile drug prevention programs....Active with Make-a-Wish Foundation....Enjoys golf, softball....Played rugby in high school.

CAREER

Season	Club	League	Regular Schedule					Playoffs				
			GP	G	A	P	PM	GP	G	A	P	PM
1990-91	Belleville	OHL	60	30	37	67	151	6	2	2	4	13
1991-92	Belleville	OHL	65	55	72	127	177	5	1	4	5	13
1992-93	Adirondack	AHL	73	17	19	36	278	11	0	1	1	33
1993-94	DETROIT	NHL	67	9	17	26	181	7	2	2	4	8
1995	DETROIT	NHL	31	5	8	13	88	18	3	2	5	14
NHL and DETROIT Totals			**98**	**14**	**25**	**39**	**269**	**25**	**5**	**4**	**9**	**22**

Drafted by DETROIT in 1992 NHL Entry Draft (2nd choice, 46th overall, 2nd round).

OSGOOD Chris

BECAME RED WING: Third choice (54th overall) in 1991 Entry Draft.

GOALTENDER

- 5-10 • 175 lbs.
- Catches Left
- Born: Peace River, AB
  November 26, 1972
- Last Amateur Club:
  Seattle Thunderbirds (WHL)

Career vs. N.H.L.

Team	GP	MP	GA	SO	GAA	W	L	T
Anaheim	4	220	15	0	4.09	3	0	1
Boston	1	60	1	0	1.00	1	0	0
Buffalo	1	60	3	0	3.00	0	1	0
Calgary	7	423	16	0	2.27	3	3	1
Chicago	3	180	3	0	1.00	3	0	0
Dallas	6	331	13	0	2.36	5	0	0
Detroit	–	–	–	–	–	–	–	–
Edmonton	4	239	12	0	3.01	2	2	0
Florida	2	124	6	0	2.90	2	0	0
Hartford	1	60	0	1	.00	1	0	0
Los Angeles	3	180	10	0	3.33	2	1	0
Montreal	1	30	4	0	8.00	0	1	0
New Jersey	1	27	2	0	4.44	0	0	0
NY Islanders	0	0	0	0	.00	0	0	0
NY Rangers	1	17	0	0	.00	0	0	0
Ottawa	1	59	1	0	1.02	1	0	0
Philadelphia	1	60	3	0	3.00	1	0	0
Pittsburgh	2	120	9	0	4.50	1	1	0
Quebec	3	60	3	0	3.00	1	0	0
San Jose	3	180	3	2	1.00	3	0	0
St. Louis	4	179	10	0	3.35	1	1	2
Tampa Bay	1	60	1	0	1.00	1	0	0
Toronto	4	218	14	0	3.85	1	2	1
Vancouver	3	181	7	0	2.32	3	0	0
Washington	1	5	2	0	24.00	0	0	0
Winnipeg	4	220	8	0	2.18	2	1	0

1995 SEASON — Tied for second in NHL with .917 save percentage (41 goals, 496 shots)....Fourth in league with 2.26 goals-against average....Season-high five-game winning streak Apr. 1-21.... Allowed two goals or less 13 times in 19 outings, all starts....Four-game winning string Feb. 7-22, with 1.00 average during that span....6-0 shutout (16 saves) Feb. 7 vs. San Jose (third regular-season career shutout).

CAREER — Had .622 winning percentage as rookie in 93-94....First two NHL shutouts came in succession in '94: 3-0 Feb. 24 vs. Hartford at Richfield, OH, 2-0 Feb. 26 vs. San Jose (first consecutive shutouts by Detroit goalie since Tim Cheveldae Nov. 13-14, 1992, vs. Pittsburgh, Hartford)....NHL Rookie of Month in February of '94 (7-1-0, 2.30 average, two shutouts in nine outings)....Career-high seven-game winning streak Feb. 11-Mar. 1, 1994....Career-best six-game unbeaten string (4-0-2) Dec. 21-Feb. 2, 1993-94....4-0 shutout in NHL playoff debut Apr. 20, 1994, vs. San Jose (first Detroit rookie shutout since Terry Sawchuk in '51; second Red Wing to post shutout in playoff debut; Norm Smith was other in '36)....First NHL victory 8-3 (23 saves) Oct. 23, 1993, vs. Los Angeles....6-3 defeat Oct. 15, 1993, at Toronto in NHL debut....Three years in junior (WHL) with Medicine Hat, Brandon, Seattle....WHL East Second-Team All-Star with Brandon in 90-91....Seven shutouts as junior....92-93 season at Adirondack (AHL), recording first two pro shutouts.

PERSONAL — Single....Spends off-season in Medicine Hat, AB....Likes golf, tennis.

CAREER

			Regular Schedule								Playoffs						
Season	Club	League	GP	W	L	T	MP	GA	SO	AVG.	GP	W	L	MP	GA	SO	AVG.
1989-90	Medicine Hat	WHL	57	24	28	2	3094	228	0	4.42	3	0	3	173	17	0	5.91
1990-91a	Medicine Hat	WHL	46	23	18	3	2630	173	2	3.95	12	7	5	712	42	0	3.54
1991-92	Medicine Hat	WHL	15	10	3	0	819	44	0	3.22	–	–	–	–	–	–	–
	Brandon	WHL	16	3	10	1	890	60	1	4.04	–	–	–	–	–	–	–
	Seattle	WHL	21	12	7	1	1217	65	1	3.20	15	9	6	904	51	0	3.30
1992-93	Adirondack	AHL	45	19	19	2	2438	159	0	3.91	1	0	1	59	2	0	2.03
1993-94	DETROIT	NHL	41	23	8	5	2206	105	2	2.86	6	3	2	307	12	1	2.35
	Adirondack	AHL	4	3	1	1	240	13	0	3.25	–	–	–	–	–	–	–
1995	DETROIT	NHL	19	14	5	0	1087	41	1	2.26	2	0	0	68	2	0	1.76
NHL and DETROIT Totals			**60**	**37**	**13**	**5**	**3293**	**146**	**3**	**2.66**	**8**	**3**	**2**	**375**	**14**	**1**	**2.24**

a-WHL East Second All-Star Team.
Drafted by DETROIT in 1991 (3rd choice, 54th overall, 3rd round).

1995-1996 DETROIT RED WINGS

PRIMEAU Keith

BECAME RED WING: First Choice (third overall) in 1990 Entry Draft.

LEFT WING

- 6-4 • 210 lbs.
- Shoots Left
- Born: Toronto, ON
  November 24, 1971
- Last Amateur Club:
  Niagara Falls Thunder (OHL)

Career vs. N.H.L.

Team	GP	G	A	PTS
Anaheim	8	4	11	15
Boston	7	2	4	6
Buffalo	6	2	3	5
Calgary	15	4	4	8
Chicago	28	4	8	12
Dallas	25	4	11	15
Detroit	–	–	–	–
Edmonton	15	1	6	7
Florida	2	2	3	5
Hartford	8	2	2	4
Los Angeles	11	4	1	5
Montreal	9	3	3	6
New Jersey	7	2	2	4
NY Islanders	8	4	0	4
NY Rangers	6	2	3	5
Ottawa	4	1	1	2
Philadelphia	6	0	4	4
Pittsburgh	9	0	2	2
Quebec	9	1	3	4
San Jose	13	3	7	10
St. Louis	21	5	4	9
Tampa Bay	9	3	3	6
Toronto	24	5	5	10
Vancouver	13	4	5	9
Washington	8	1	3	4
Winnipeg	18	7	10	17

1995 SEASON — Second on team at plus-17, tied for third in assists, was fourth in points, goals....Points in 25 of 45 games.... Goals in 13 games...."Plus" or "even" in 34 contests....7-13–20 home, 8-14–22 road....1-8–9 on PPGs....3-2–5 on GWGs....4-1–5 on first goals....One assist on SHG....1-3–4 on ENGs....10 multiple-point outings (two fours, trio of threes, five twos)....First two career four-point outings: 1-3–4 Mar. 22 vs. Winnipeg, 2-2–4 Apr. 21 vs. Anaheim....Three four-game streaks, equaling career high: 2-5–7 Mar. 22-28, 4-1–5 Apr. 2-9, 4-5–9 Apr. 16-23....Pair of two-goal games....Pair of three-assist outings, five with two....100th NHL assist Mar. 24 at Calgary....Missed one game Feb. 12 (hand), one Feb. 25 (flu), one Mar. 2 (thumb).

CAREER — In 93-94, was third on team at plus-34, fourth in goals, tied for fifth in scoring, was fifth in assists....Career-high eight-game streak (4-8–12) Feb. 15-Mar. 1, 1994.... First NHL two-goal game Dec. 18, 1992, vs. Boston....NHL debut Oct. 6, 1990, at Washington....First point assist Oct. 10, 1990, vs. Calgary....First goal Dec. 11, 1990, vs. Buffalo....Helped Adirondack (AHL) win '92 Calder Cup....Led OHL in points, goals, was third in assists with Niagara Falls in 89-90....OHL Second-Team All-Star center that season.

PERSONAL — Keith, wife Lisa were married last summer, reside in suburban Detroit....One of founders of Hockey's Helping Hands, which raises funds for charitable works by Sisters of Mercy.....Active with D.A.R.E. (Drug Awareness Resistance Education)....Likes softball, golf, fishing, traveling....Played rugby, volleyball, lacrosse in high school....Brother Wayne No.1 pick by Buffalo in '94 draft.

CAREER

Season	Club	League	Regular Schedule					Playoffs				
			GP	G	A	P	PM	GP	G	A	P	PM
1987-88	Hamilton	OHL	47	6	6	12	69	11	0	2	2	2
1988-89	Niagara Falls	OHL	48	20	35	55	22	17	9	6	15	12
1989-90	Niagara Falls	OHL	65	57	70	127	97	16	16	17	33	49
1990-91	DETROIT	NHL	58	3	12	15	106	5	1	1	2	25
	Adirondack	AHL	6	3	5	8	8	–	–	–	–	–
1991-92	DETROIT	NHL	35	6	10	16	83	11	0	0	0	14
	Adirondack	AHL	42	21	24	45	89	9	1	7	8	27
1992-93	DETROIT	NHL	73	15	17	32	152	7	0	2	2	26
1993-94	DETROIT	NHL	78	31	42	73	173	7	0	2	2	6
1995	DETROIT	NHL	45	15	27	42	99	17	4	5	9	45
DETROIT and NHL Totals			**289**	**70**	**108**	**178**	**613**	**47**	**5**	**10**	**15**	**116**

Drafted by DETROIT in 1990 NHL Entry (1st choice, 3rd overall, 1st round).

1995-1996 DETROIT 15 RED WINGS

RAMSEY Mike

BECAME RED WING: Signed as free agent (no compensation) August 3, 1994.

DEFENSE

- 6-3 • 195 lbs.
- Shoots Left
- Born: Minneapolis, MN
  December 3, 1960
- Last Amateur Club:
  University of Minnesota (WCHA)

Career vs. N.H.L.

Team	GP	G	A	PTS
Anaheim	4	1	0	1
Boston	89	6	21	27
Buffalo	6	0	0	0
Calgary	38	4	7	11
Chicago	37	3	12	15
Dallas	41	4	12	16
Detroit	36	2	15	17
Edmonton	37	0	8	8
Florida	4	0	0	0
Hartford	93	8	24	32
Los Angeles	38	4	17	21
Montreal	89	2	11	13
New Jersey	41	0	10	10
NY Islanders	40	1	7	8
NY Rangers	45	5	7	12
Ottawa	6	0	2	2
Philadelphia	37	3	7	10
Pittsburgh	39	4	20	24
Quebec	89	12	24	36
San Jose	8	0	0	0
St. Louis	40	2	5	7
Tampa Bay	3	1	1	2
Toronto	43	5	15	20
Vancouver	38	3	12	15
Washington	38	3	14	17
Winnipeg	42	4	11	15

1995 SEASON — Plus-11...."Plus" or "even" in 27 of 33 games.... Feb. 20 at Toronto, he became 99th player in NHL history to play 1,000 regular-season games....Two-game streak (two assists) Feb. 12-15, including first point as Red Wing at Los Angeles....1-1-2 home, one assist road....One assist on first goal....Red Wings debut Jan. 20 vs. Chicago....Missed one game Jan. 26 (groin), five Mar. 9-17 (hip).

CAREER — Won gold medal with 1980 U.S. Olympic Team at Lake Placid, NY....All-Star games in '82, '83, '85, played with NHL team in Rendez-vous '87 vs. Russian all-stars....Buffalo's first pick (11th overall) in '79 draft while playing lone season at University of Minnesota (WCHA)....Twice selected Sabres' MVP by teammates (82-83, 86-87)....Three times led Buffalo in plus-minus (plus-19 in 82-83, career-high plus-31 in 84-85, plus-21 in 89-90)....Career highs in assists (31), points (39) in 86-87....Played for Scotty Bowman in Buffalo, Pittsburgh....Canada Cup in '84, '87.

PERSONAL — Mike, wife Jill have daughter, Rachel, spend off-season Chanhassen, MN.

CAREER

Season	Club	League	Regular Schedule					Playoffs				
			GP	G	A	P	PM	GP	G	A	P	PM
1978-79	Univ. of Minnesota	WCHA	26	6	11	17	30	–	–	–	–	–
1979-80	U.S. National Team		56	11	22	33	55	–	–	–	–	–
	U.S. Olympic Team		7	0	2	2	8	–	–	–	–	–
	Buffalo	NHL	13	1	6	7	6	13	1	2	3	12
1980-81	Buffalo	NHL	72	3	14	17	56	8	0	3	3	20
1981-82	Buffalo	NHL	80	7	23	30	56	4	1	1	2	14
1982-83	Buffalo	NHL	77	8	30	38	55	10	4	4	8	15
1983-84	Buffalo	NHL	72	9	22	31	82	3	0	1	1	6
1984-85	Buffalo	NHL	79	8	22	30	102	5	0	1	1	23
1985-86	Buffalo	NHL	76	7	21	28	117	–	–	–	–	–
1986-87	Buffalo	NHL	80	8	31	39	109	–	–	–	–	–
1987-88	Buffalo	NHL	63	5	16	21	77	6	0	3	3	29
1988-89	Buffalo	NHL	56	2	14	16	84	5	1	0	1	11
1989-90	Buffalo	NHL	73	4	21	25	47	6	0	1	1	8
1990-91	Buffalo	NHL	71	6	14	20	46	5	1	0	1	12
1991-92	Buffalo	NHL	66	3	14	17	67	7	0	2	2	8
1992-93	Buffalo	NHL	33	2	8	10	20	–	–	–	–	–
	Pittsburgh	NHL	12	1	2	3	8	12	0	6	6	4
1993-94	Pittsburgh	NHL	65	2	2	4	22	1	0	0	0	0
1995	DETROIT	NHL	33	1	2	3	23	15	0	1	1	4
DETROIT Totals			33	1	2	3	23	15	0	1	1	4
NHL Totals			1021	77	262	339	977	100	8	25	33	166

Drafted by Buffalo in 1979 Entry Draft (1st choice, 11th overall, 1st Round).
Traded to Pittsburgh by Buffalo for Bob Errey, Mar. 22, 1993.
Signed by DETROIT as free agent August 3, 1994.

ROUSE Bob

BECAME RED WING: Signed as free agent (no compensation) August 5, 1994.

DEFENSE

- 6-2 • 210 lbs.
- Shoots Right
- Born: Surrey, BC
  June 18, 1964
- Last Amateur Club:
  Lethbridge Broncos (WHL)

Career vs. N.H.L.

Team	GP	G	A	PTS
Anaheim	8	1	3	4
Boston	26	2	3	5
Buffalo	21	0	4	4
Calgary	31	0	6	6
Chicago	69	3	7	10
Dallas	30	1	9	10
Detroit	56	2	13	15
Edmonton	31	0	5	5
Florida	2	0	1	1
Hartford	22	0	1	1
Los Angeles	30	1	8	9
Montreal	29	2	4	6
New Jersey	30	1	5	6
NY Islanders	32	2	7	9
NY Rangers	30	2	8	10
Ottawa	4	0	0	0
Philadelphia	33	3	3	6
Pittsburgh	33	1	8	9
Quebec	28	0	10	10
San Jose	14	0	2	2
St. Louis	68	8	10	18
Tampa Bay	9	0	2	2
Toronto	45	1	7	8
Vancouver	31	1	3	4
Washington	22	1	5	6
Winnipeg	32	0	9	9

1995 SEASON — Tied for fourth on team at plus-14...."Plus" or "even" in 39 of 48 games....Only Red Wing to appear in every game....Points in five outings....Two multiple-point games (both twos)....1-4–5 home, three assists road....One assist on PPG....1-1–2 on GWGs....One assist on first goal....Red Wings debut Jan. 20 vs. Chicago.... First point with assist Feb. 4 at Los Angeles....Lone goal Mar. 16 vs. Dallas.

CAREER — En route to first appearance in Stanley Cup final, he made fourth trip to conference final (also '90 for Washington, '93, '94 with Toronto)....Career-best plus-15 for Minnesota is 85-86....Minnesota's third pick (80th overall) in '82 draft....Voted Minnesota's top rookie in 84-85....Dealt to Washington late in 88-89 season....Traded to Toronto midway through 90-91 season....Second among Maple Leafs' defensemen with plus-8 in 93-94....Plus-7 in 92-93....Played junior for Billings, Nanaimo, Lethbridge (WHL)....83-84 WHL East Division All-Star.

PERSONAL — Bob, wife Diane reside in suburban Detroit with son Torrey, daughter Calli....He enjoys computers, along with golf, fishing.

CAREER

Season	Club	League	Regular Schedule					Playoffs				
			GP	G	A	P	PM	GP	G	A	P	PM
1980-81	Billings	WHL	70	0	13	13	116	5	0	0	0	2
1981-82	Billings	WHL	71	7	22	29	209	5	0	2	2	10
1982-83	Nanaimo	WHL	29	7	20	27	86	–	–	–	–	–
	Lethbridge	WHL	42	8	30	38	82	20	2	13	15	55
1983-84	Minnesota	NHL	1	0	0	0	0	–	–	–	–	–
	Lethbridge	WHL	71	18	42	60	101	5	0	1	1	28
1984-85	Minnesota	NHL	63	2	9	11	113	–	–	–	–	–
	Springfield	AHL	8	0	3	3	6	–	–	–	–	–
1985-86	Minnesota	NHL	75	1	14	15	151	3	0	0	0	2
1986-87	Minnesota	NHL	72	2	10	12	179	–	–	–	–	–
1987-88	Minnesota	NHL	74	0	12	12	168	–	–	–	–	–
1988-89	Minnesota	NHL	66	4	13	17	124	–	–	–	–	–
	Washington	NHL	13	0	2	2	36	6	2	0	2	4
1989-90	Washington	NHL	70	4	16	20	123	15	2	3	5	47
1990-91	Washington	NHL	47	5	15	20	65	–	–	–	–	–
	Toronto	NHL	13	2	4	6	10	–	–	–	–	–
1991-92	Toronto	NHL	79	3	19	22	97	–	–	–	–	–
1992-93	Toronto	NHL	82	3	11	14	130	21	3	8	11	29
1993-94	Toronto	NHL	63	5	11	16	101	18	0	3	3	29
1995	DETROIT	NHL	48	1	7	8	36	18	0	3	3	8
NHL Totals			**766**	**32**	**143**	**175**	**1333**	**81**	**7**	**17**	**24**	**117**

Drafted by Minnesota in 1982 Entry Draft (3rd choice, 80th overall, 4th Round).
Traded to Washington by Minnesota with Dino Ciccarelli for Mike Gartner and Larry Murphy, March 7, 1989.
Traded to Toronto by Washington with Peter Zezel for Al Iafrate, January 16, 1991.
Signed by DETROIT as a free agent August 5, 1994.

SHEPPARD Ray

BECAME RED WING: Signed as a free agent (no compensation) August 5, 1991.

RIGHT WING

- 6-1 • 195 lbs.
- Shoots Right
- Born: Pembroke, ON May 27, 1966
- Last Amateur Club: Cornwall Royals (OHL)

Career vs. N.H.L.

Team	GP	G	A	PTS
Anaheim	8	7	6	13
Boston	23	9	10	19
Buffalo	10	7	6	13
Calgary	24	11	6	17
Chicago	31	15	16	31
Dallas	33	9	12	21
Detroit	6	1	4	5
Edmonton	22	10	5	15
Florida	2	3	1	4
Hartford	27	11	8	19
Los Angeles	23	8	10	18
Montreal	27	11	9	20
New Jersey	17	6	4	10
NY Islanders	19	3	3	6
NY Rangers	13	9	3	12
Ottawa	4	2	5	7
Philadelphia	16	3	7	10
Pittsburgh	15	6	9	15
Quebec	22	12	8	20
San Jose	14	11	8	19
St. Louis	30	18	9	27
Tampa Bay	9	9	5	14
Toronto	28	16	8	24
Vancouver	23	15	9	24
Washington	17	9	6	15
Winnipeg	24	17	7	24

1995 SEASON — Tied for third in NHL in goals, tied for sixth in PPGs (11-2–13)....Led club in goals, was fifth in scoring, shared lead in GWGs (5-2–7)....Points in 25 of 43 games....Goals in 22 outings....Season-high seven-game streak (10-3-13) Apr. 9-21, with goals in each (tied Washington's Peter Bondra for NHL's best season goal streak)....3-1–4 Jan. 24 vs. Vancouver for sixth regular-season NHL hat trick, fourth as Red Wing, equaled career-high single-game point mark....Six two-goal games....13 multiple-point games (one four, 12 twos)....18-7–25 home, 12-3–15 road....Plus-11...."Plus" or "even" in 32 games....Six first goals....One GTG....One ENG....400th NHL point with assist Mar. 6 at Vancouver....Missed two games Feb. 22-23 (back).

CAREER — Tied for fifth in NHL in goals, tied for 15th in scoring in 93-94....Career highs in goals, assists, points, PPGs (19) that year....Reached 50-goal mark first time Mar. 29, 1994 vs. Hartford (sixth Red Wing, second right wing, to net 50)....Career-best 12-game streak (10-6–16) Feb. 1-23, 1992....Two career regular-season OTGs (recent Jan. 27, 1994, at Chicago)....NHL Player of Week Jan. 17-23, 1994....In 92-93, was fifth on team in goals, points....Second on club in goals, shared lead in PPGs (11) in 91-92....First two goals as Red Wing Oct. 19, 1991, at Quebec....Assist in Red Wings debut Oct. 3, 1991, at Chicago....Buffalo's third pick (60th overall) in '84 draft....87-88 All-Rookie Team, second in voting for Calder Trophy behind Calgary's Joe Nieuwendyk....Led Sabres in goals as rookie....Dealt to Rangers in '90....NHL debut Oct. 8, 1987, vs. Minnesota....First goal Oct. 17, 1987, vs. Quebec....In 85-86 with Cornwall, led OHL in goals, points, won Red Tilson Award (league's top player).

CAREER — Ray, wife Lucie, daughter Lyndsay reside in suburban Detroit....Enjoys golf, riding motorcycle....Played basketball, football in high school....Active in fight against leukemia.

CAREER

| Season | Club | League | Regular Schedule | | | | | Playoffs | | | | |
			GP	G	A	P	PM	GP	G	A	P	PM
1983-84	Cornwall	OHL	68	44	36	80	69	–	–	–	–	–
1984-85	Cornwall	OHL	49	25	33	58	51	9	2	12	14	4
1985-86ab	Cornwall	OHL	63	81	61	142	25	6	7	4	11	0
1986-87	Rochester	AHL	55	18	13	31	11	15	12	3	15	2
1987-88c	Buffalo	NHL	74	38	27	65	14	6	1	1	2	2
1988-89	Buffalo	NHL	67	22	21	43	15	1	0	1	1	0
1989-90	Buffalo	NHL	18	4	2	6	0	–	–	–	–	–
	Rochester	AHL	5	3	5	8	2	17	8	7	15	9
1990-91	NY Rangers	NHL	59	24	34	47	21	–	–	–	–	–
1991-92	DETROIT	NHL	74	36	26	62	27	11	6	2	8	4
1992-93	DETROIT	NHL	70	32	34	66	29	7	2	3	5	0
1993-94	DETROIT	NHL	82	52	41	93	26	7	2	1	3	4
1995	DETROIT	NHL	43	30	10	40	17	17	4	3	7	5
NHL Totals			487	238	184	422	149	49	15	11	26	15
DETROIT Totals			269	150	111	261	99	42	14	9	23	13

a-OHL Player of the Year.
b-OHL First All-Star Team.
c-NHL All Rookie Team.
Drafted by Buffalo in 1984 NHL Entry Draft (3rd choice, 60th overall, 3rd round).
Traded to NY Rangers by Buffalo for cash and future consideration, July 9, 1990.
Signed by DETROIT as free agent August, 1991.

TAYLOR Tim

BECAME RED WING: Signed as free agent July 28, 1993.

LEFT WING

- 6-1 • 185 lbs.
- Shoots Left
- Born: Stratford, ON
  February 6, 1969
- Last Amateur Club:
  London Knights (OHL)

Career vs. N.H.L.

Team	GP	G	A	PTS
Anaheim	2	0	0	0
Boston	0	0	0	0
Buffalo	0	0	0	0
Calgary	1	0	0	0
Chicago	4	0	0	0
Dallas	2	0	2	2
Detroit	–	–	–	–
Edmonton	1	0	0	0
Florida	0	0	0	0
Hartford	0	0	0	0
Los Angeles	1	0	0	0
Montreal	1	1	0	1
New Jersey	0	0	0	0
NY Islanders	0	0	0	0
NY Rangers	0	0	0	0
Ottawa	0	0	0	0
Philadelphia	0	0	0	0
Pittsburgh	0	0	0	0
Quebec	0	0	0	0
San Jose	2	0	0	0
St. Louis	3	0	2	2
Tampa Bay	0	0	0	0
Toronto	3	0	0	0
Vancouver	1	0	0	0
Washington	0	0	0	0
Winnipeg	2	0	0	0

1995 SEASON — Points in three of 22 games....Plus-3...."Plus" or "even" in 20 games....One assist home, three assists road....Two assists on PPGs....One assist on first goal....Two-game streak Mar. 30-Apr. 1, with first two NHL assists, including first Mar. 30 vs. Dallas....One multiple-point game (two assists on PPGs in season finale May 3 at St. Louis).

CAREER — Scored goal in NHL debut Dec. 18, 1993, at Montreal (lone outing for Detroit that season)....Led AHL in scoring in 93-94 with 36-81–117 while playing for Adirondack....AHL First-Team All-Star center in 93-94....Three years in junior ranks with London (OHL), notching 114 points in final season, 88-89, then leading all junior playoff scorers in goals (21), points (46)....Washington's second pick (36th overall) in '89 draft but never played for Capitals.

PERSONAL — Tim, wife Jodilynn have daughter, Brittany, spend off-season in hometown of Stratford, ON....He enjoys woodworking, especially making furniture....Also likes golf.

CAREER

Season	Club	League	Regular Schedule GP	G	A	P	PM	Playoffs GP	G	A	P	PM
1986-87	London	OHL	34	7	9	16	11	–	–	–	–	–
1987-88	London	OHL	64	46	50	96	66	12	9	9	18	28
1988-89	London	OHL	61	34	80	114	93	21	21	25	46	58
1989-90	Baltimore	AHL	79	31	36	67	124	9	2	2	4	4
1990-91	Baltimore	AHL	79	25	42	67	75	5	0	1	1	4
1991-92	Baltimore	AHL	65	9	18	27	131	–	–	–	–	–
1992-93	Batimore	AHL	41	15	16	31	49	–	–	–	–	–
	Hamilton	AHL	36	15	22	37	37	–	–	–	–	–
1993-94	Adirondack	AHL	79	36	81	117	86	12	2	10	12	12
	DETROIT	NHL	1	1	0	1	0	–	–	–	–	–
1995	DETROIT	NHL	22	0	4	4	16	6	0	1	1	12
NHL and DETROIT Totals			**23**	**1**	**4**	**5**	**16**	**6**	**0**	**1**	**1**	**12**

Drafted by Washington in 1988 Entry Draft (2nd choice, 36th overall, 2nd Round).
Signed by DETROIT as a free agent, July 28, 1993.

VERNON Mike

BECAME RED WING: Obtained June 29, 1994, from Calgary for Steve Chiasson.

GOALTENDER

- 5-9 • 165 lbs.
- Catches Left
- Born: Calgary, AB
  February 24, 1963
- Last Amateur Club:
  Calgary Wranglers (WHL)

Career vs. N.H.L.

Team	GP	MP	GA	SO	GAA	W	L	T
Anaheim	8	488	20	1	2.46	5	1	2
Boston	18	1037	59	0	3.41	8	8	2
Buffalo	15	875	50	0	3.43	6	7	2
Calgary	1	60	4	0	4.00	1	0	0
Chicago	19	1076	53	1	2.96	9	9	0
Dallas	23	1319	68	0	3.09	13	7	3
Detroit	21	1220	79	2	3.86	9	10	2
Edmonton	57	3277	172	0	3.15	31	17	6
Florida	1	60	2	0	2.00	1	0	0
Hartford	12	653	28	0	2.57	9	2	1
Los Angeles	39	2046	136	0	3.99	18	16	3
Montreal	19	1151	55	1	2.87	10	7	2
New Jersey	12	679	37	0	3.27	8	4	0
NY Islanders	18	980	55	0	3.37	8	7	2
NY Rangers	16	948	54	1	3.42	9	4	3
Ottawa	3	185	6	0	1.95	2	0	1
Philadelphia	18	1094	49	1	2.69	12	4	2
Pittsburgh	16	915	58	0	3.80	7	7	1
Quebec	18	956	60	0	3.77	10	2	4
St. Louis	25	1480	75	0	3.04	12	10	2
San Jose	16	927	28	2	1.81	14	1	1
Tampa Bay	5	262	17	0	3.89	3	2	0
Toronto	23	1329	66	0	2.98	14	5	3
Vancouver	45	2628	141	1	3.22	28	13	4
Washington	12	709	40	0	3.39	6	3	3
Winnipeg	37	2035	117	0	3.45	15	14	6

1995 SEASON — Tied for fifth among NHL goalies in victories (19)....Club-record 16-game unbeaten streak (13-0-3) Feb. 12-Apr. 13 (shattered team mark held by Terry Sawchuk, who was 8-0-4 in 12 Nov. 27-Dec. 21, 1952)....Career-best 2.52 goals-against average....8-3-3 home, 11-3-1 road....Had .893 save percentage (76 goals, 710 shots)....3-0 shutout (12 saves) Apr. 13 vs. San Jose (first as Red Wing, 10th of career)....Season-high six-game winning streak Mar. 12-30....Four of six defeats by one goal....Allowed two goals or less in 16 outings....Twice dropped two in row (Feb. 4-10, Apr. 27-30)....Second among NHL playoff goalies in victories (12), third in goals-against average (2.31)....Eight-game postseason winning streak May 15-June 6....Fourth playoff shutout with 6-0 triumph (15 saves) May 21 in Game 1 vs. San Jose....Three playoff OT victories (all vs. Chicago in conference final)....Yielded two goals or less in 11 of 18 postseason outings, one goal or less in six contests.

CAREER — Three trips to Stanley Cup final, including '95 with Detroit....Helped Calgary win '89 Cup, beating Montreal in final....16 playoff victories in '89 remains tied for NHL record....Led Calgary to '86 Cup final, bowing to Montreal....Three shutouts for career single-season high in 93-94 for Calgary....Topped 20-victory mark eighth consecutive year in 93-94....Not including lockout-shortened '95 season, he never has won less than 20 games, has topped 30-mark four times....Still Calgary's all-time franchise goalie leader in victories (248)....Paced NHL with 37 victories in 88-89, was second with 31 in 90-91....Second in league in 88-89 with 2.65 goals-against average....NHL Second All-Star Team, runner-up for Vezina Trophy in 88-89....Six All-Star Game appearances ('88, '89, '90, '91, '92, '94; voted starter by fans in '90, '91)....Successive 3-0 shutouts in '92 (Dec. 14 at Detroit, Dec. 15 at Rangers)....Amid that '92 stretch, he had shutout string of 164:40 (nine periods) Dec. 12-19....Started 27 consecutive games Nov. 27-Jan. 26, 1992-93....Has stopped two of six penalty shots in career, most recently against Kevin Miller Dec. 17, 1993, vs. St. Louis....NHL Player of Month in January of '89 (9-0-1, 2.30 average)....9-6 defeat in NHL debut Jan. 3, 1984, at Edmonton....First NHL victory 5-4 OT decision Jan. 9, 1986, vs. Vancouver....First shutout Feb. 21, 1986, at Vancouver....Team Canada silver-medal winner in '91 World Championships....Calgary's second pick (56th overall, third round) in '81 draft....Played junior for Calgary (WHL).

PERSONAL — Mike, wife Jane, both Calgary natives, spend off-season in hometown....Enjoys golf.

CAREER

			Regular Schedule							Playoffs						
Season	Club	League	GP	W	L	T	MP	GA	SO	AVG.	GP	W	L	MP	GA	SO	AVG.
1980-81	Calgary	WHL	59	33	17	1	3154	198	1	3.77	22	–	–	1271	82	1	3.87
1981-82 abc-	Calgary	WHL	42	22	14	2	2329	143	3	3.68	9	–	–	527	30	0	3.42
	Oklahoma City	CHL	–	–	–	–	–	–	–	–	1	0	1	70	4	0	3.43
1982-83	Calgary	NHL	2	0	2	0	100	11	0	6.59	–	–	–	–	–	–	–
	abc-Calgary	WHL	50	19	18	2	2856	155	3	3.26	16	9	7	925	60	0	3.89
1983-84	Calgary	NHL	1	0	1	0	11	4	0	22.22	–	–	–	–	–	–	–
	d-Colorado	CHL	46	30	13	2	2648	148	1	3.35	6	2	4	347	21	0	3.63
1984-85	Monoton	AHL	41	10	20	4	2050	134	0	3.92	–	–	–	–	–	–	–
1985-86	Calgary	NHL	18	9	3	3	921	52	1	3.39	21	12	9	1229	60	0	2.93
	Monoton	AHL	6	3	1	2	374	21	0	3.37	–	–	–	–	–	–	–
	Salt Lake City	IHL	10	–	–	–	600	34	1	3.40	–	–	–	–	–	–	–
1986-87	Calgary	NHL	54	30	21	1	2957	178	1	3.61	5	2	3	263	16	0	3.65
1987-88	Calgary	NHL	64	39	16	7	3565	210	1	3.53	9	4	4	515	34	0	3.96
1988-89 e-	Calgary	NHL	52	37	6	5	2938	130	0	2.65	22	16	5	1381	52	3	2.26
1989-90	Calgary	NHL	47	23	14	9	2795	146	0	3.13	6	2	3	342	19	0	3.33
1990-91	Calgary	NHL	54	31	19	3	3121	172	1	3.31	7	3	4	427	21	0	2.95
1991-92	Calgary	NHL	63	24	30	9	3640	217	0	3.58	–	–	–	–	–	–	–
1992-93	Calgary	NHL	64	29	26	9	3732	203	2	3.26	4	1	1	150	15	0	6.00
1993-94	Calgary	NHL	48	26	17	5	2798	131	3	2.81	7	3	4	466	23	0	2.96
1995	DETROIT	NHL	30	19	6	4	1807	76	1	2.52	18	12	6	1063	41	1	2.31
NHL Totals			**497**	**267**	**161**	**55**	**28385**	**1530**	**10**	**3.23**	**99**	**55**	**39**	**5836**	**281**	**4**	**2.89**

a-WHL First All-Star Team (1982, 1983).
b-WHL Most Valuable Player (1982, 1983).
c-Named WHL's Top Goaltender (1982, 1983).
d-CHL Second All-Star Team.
e-NHL Second All-Star Team.
Drafted by Calgary in the 1981 NHL Entry Draft (2nd Choice, 56th overall, 3rd round).
Traded to DETROIT by Calgary for Steve Chiasson, June 29, 1994.

WALZ Wes

BECAME RED WING: Signed as free agent (no compensation) August 11, 1995.

CENTER

- 5-10 • 185 lbs.
- Shoots Right
- Born: Calgary, AB
  May 15, 1970
- Last Amateur Club:
  Lethbridge Hurricanes (WHL)

Career vs. N.H.L.

Team	GP	G	A	PTS
Anaheim	8	3	4	7
Boston	2	2	0	2
Buffalo	10	1	2	3
Calgary	3	2	2	4
Chicago	9	0	1	1
Dallas	9	0	3	3
Detroit	10	2	2	4
Edmonton	8	0	3	3
Florida	2	0	2	2
Hartford	6	2	1	3
Los Angeles	13	2	6	8
Montreal	6	1	0	1
New Jersey	5	1	0	1
NY Islanders	5	0	0	0
NY Rangers	6	0	3	3
Ottawa	1	2	1	3
Philadelphia	3	0	0	0
Pittsburgh	2	0	0	0
Quebec	8	1	1	2
San Jose	9	0	4	4
St. Louis	8	1	4	5
Tampa Bay	2	0	0	0
Toronto	8	0	3	3
Vancouver	12	1	2	3
Washington	3	2	1	3
Winnipeg	9	4	6	10

1995 SEASON — Points in 15 of 39 games for Calgary....Plus-7.... "Plus" or "even" in 34 outings....4-5–9 home, 2-7–9 road....Four of six goals were PPGs....One GWG....Three multiple-point games: two assists Feb. 26 at Anaheim, 1-1–2 Apr. 17 vs. Los Angeles, two assists Apr. 30 at Vancouver....Trio of two-game streaks: two goals Jan. 24-26, 1-1–2 Feb. 6-9, two assists Mar. 28-31.

CAREER — Personal highs in goals (11), assists (27), points (38), plus-minus (plus-20) in 93-94....Career-best seven-game streak (2-7–9) Jan. 26-Feb. 9, 1994....Initially Boston's third pick (57th overall) in 1989 Entry Draft....NHL debut Feb. 18, 1990, at Vancouver.... First two points in second NHL outing with 1-1–2 Feb. 20, 1990, at Calgary (goal vs. Mike Vernon)....Those were his only NHL games that season....Played in four different cities in 91-92, including Philadelphia after trade to Flyers in January of '92....Signed with Calgary as free agent in August of '93....Starred in junior ranks at Lethbridge (WHL)....League's Rookie of Year in 88-89, then was Player of Year, First-Team East All-Star in 89-90....Twice topped 100-point mark, including 54-86–140 in 89-90....Played for Canada's gold-medal winner in 1990 World Junior Championships.

PERSONAL — Wes, wife Kerry-Anne have son, Kelvin, spend off-season in their native Calgary....Enjoys golf.

CAREER

Season	Team	League	Regular Season					Playoffs				
			GP	G	A	P	PM	GP	G	A	P	PM
1988–89	Lethbridge	WHL	63	29	75	104	32	8	1	5	6	6
1989–90	Boston	NHL	2	1	1	2	0	–	–	–	–	–
	aLethbridge	WHL	56	54	86	140	69	19	13	24	37	33
1990–91	Boston	NHL	56	8	8	16	32	2	0	0	0	0
	Maine	AHL	20	8	12	20	19	2	0	0	0	21
1991–92	Boston	NHL	15	0	3	3	12	–	–	–	–	–
	Maine	AHL	21	13	11	24	38	–	–	–	–	–
	Philadelphia	NHL	2	1	0	1	0	–	–	–	–	–
	Hershey	AHL	41	13	28	41	37	6	1	2	3	0
1992–93	Hershey	AHL	78	35	45	80	106	–	–	–	–	–
1993–94	Calgary	NHL	53	11	27	38	16	6	3	0	3	2
	Saint John	AHL	15	6	6	12	14	–	–	–	–	–
1995	Calgary	NHL	39	6	12	18	11	1	0	0	0	0
NHL Totals			**167**	**27**	**51**	**78**	**67**	**9**	**3**	**0**	**3**	**2**

a–TO COME

YZERMAN Steve

BECAME RED WING: First choice (fourth overall) in 1983 Entry Draft.

CENTER

- 5-11 • 185 lbs.
- Shoots Right
- Born: Cranbrook, BC May 9, 1965
- Last Amateur Club: Peterborough Petes (OHL)

Career vs. N.H.L.

Team	GP	G	A	PTS
Anaheim	7	4	6	10
Boston	28	18	18	36
Buffalo	30	21	33	54
Calgary	38	20	18	38
Chicago	86	40	63	103
Dallas	82	38	72	110
Detroit	–	–	–	–
Edmonton	33	28	25	53
Florida	2	0	6	6
Hartford	27	11	18	29
Los Angeles	36	25	28	53
Montreal	28	16	19	35
New Jersey	29	10	27	37
NY Islanders	26	15	19	34
NY Rangers	27	16	20	36
Ottawa	3	1	1	2
Philadelphia	30	25	25	50
Pittsburgh	29	14	27	41
Quebec	29	18	21	39
San Jose	13	5	13	18
St. Louis	83	37	58	95
Tampa Bay	10	10	13	23
Toronto	83	53	74	127
Vancouver	36	22	24	46
Washington	30	13	26	39
Winnipeg	37	21	25	46

1995 SEASON — Fifth on team in assists, sixth in scoring, seventh in goals....Points in 24 of 47 games....Goals in nine games....Plus-6.... "Plus" or "even" in 30 games....11 multiple-point games (one four, one three, nine twos)....Three two-goal games....One four-assist game, four with two....Season-high six-game streak (4-4–8) Apr. 9-19....6-13–19 both at home, on road....4-15–19 on PPGs....1-4–5 on GWGs....2-3–5 on first goals....2-1–3 on ENGs....Scoreless in six straight games Mar. 14-25, equaling career-high dryspell....Two goals Mar. 6 at Vancouver ended career-high 15-game goal drought....Underwent surgery before season (June 21, 1994, in Los Angeles) to remove herniated disc from neck area.

CAREER — Second on team all-time list in goals, third in assists, points....1,000th point with assist Feb. 24, 1993, at Buffalo)....Hit 1,100 with goal Mar. 4, 1994, vs. Toronto....Has led team in points eight times, goals six, assists eight....Has topped 100-point mark six times (one of 13 in NHL history to do it six times in row)....50 or more goals five times, 60 twice....50-goal mark fewer games (55 in 88-89) than any Red Wing....18 regular-season hat tricks (recent Feb. 14, 1993, at Chicago); needs one to break tie with Gordie Howe for club record....Three "natural" hat tricks (recent Nov. 17, 1990, at Toronto)....122 career PPGs....Club-record 41 SHGs....88-89 Lester B. Pearson Award as top performer in vote by Players' Association (third in Hart Trophy MVP vote tht year)....Club records in goals, assists, points in 88-89 (third in NHL in each)....One of four in NHL history to get 150 or more points, one of six to score minimum of 60 two seasons in row....In 89-90, was second in NHL in goals, third in points....In 92-93, was fourth in league scoring, shared lead in SHGs (7)....Club-record 28-game scoring streak (29-36–65) Nov. 1-Jan. 4, 1988-89....Two six-pointers (2-4 Mar. 15, 1989, at Edmonton, 2-4 Feb. 16, 1990, vs. Philadelphia)....Club-record nine-game goal streak (12 total Nov. 18-Dec. 5, 1988, 14 Jan. 29-Feb. 12, 1992)....3-for-5 on penalty shots....Youngest captain (21) team history in 86-87....Starting center for '93 Campbell Conference All-Stars (2-4–6 in seven All-Star games)....Second to Tom Barrasso for 83-84 Calder Trophy, named top rookie by Sporting News....NHL All-Rookie Team.... Club rookie records in goals, points....1-1–2 in NHL debut Oct. 5, 1983, at Winnipeg.... Missed 26 games in 93-94 (herniated disc), last 16 regular-season games, first 13 playoff contests in '88 (torn posterior cruciate ligament in right knee Mar. 1 vs. Buffalo; same night he first scored 50th goal), final 29 in 85-86 (collarbone), ...'84 Canada Cup....'85, '89, '90 World Championships.

PERSONAL — Steve, wife Lisa reside in suburban Detroit with daughter Isabella....He enjoys golf, squash, racquetball, tennis....Raised in Ottawa suburb of Nepean.

CAREER

Season	Club	League	Regular Schedule					Playoff				
			GP	G	A	P	PM	GP	G	A	P	PM
1981-82	Peterborough	OHL	58	21	43	64	65	6	0	1	1	16
1982-83	Peterborough	OHL	56	42	49	91	33	4	1	4	5	0
1983-84	DETROIT	NHL	80	39	48	87	33	4	3	3	6	0
1984-85	DETROIT	NHL	80	30	59	89	58	3	2	1	3	2
1985-86	DETROIT	NHL	51	14	28	42	16	–	–	–	–	–
1986-87	DETROIT	NHL	80	31	59	90	43	16	5	13	18	8
1987-88	DETROIT	NHL	64	50	52	102	44	3	1	3	4	6
1988-89*a*	DETROIT	NHL	80	65	90	155	61	6	5	5	10	2
1989-90	DETROIT	NHL	79	62	65	127	79	–	–	–	–	–
1990-91	DETROIT	NHL	80	51	57	108	34	7	3	3	6	4
1991-92	DETROIT	NHL	79	45	58	103	64	11	3	5	8	12
1992-93	DETROIT	NHL	84	58	79	137	44	7	4	3	7	4
1993-94	DETROIT	NHL	58	24	58	82	36	3	1	3	4	0
1995	DETROIT	NHL	47	12	26	38	40	15	4	8	12	0
DETROIT and NHL Totals			862	481	679	1160	552	75	31	47	78	38

a-Won the Lester B. Pearson Award.
Drafted by DETROIT in 1983 Entry Draft (1st choice, 4th overall, 1st round).

IN THE WINGS

CURTIS BOWEN

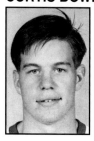

LEFT WING   6-1 — 190 lbs. — SHOOTS LEFT
BORN: KENORA, ONTARIO
MARCH 24, 1974

AMATEUR RECORD

Season	Club	League	Regular Schedule GP	G	A	P	PM	Playoffs GP	G	A	P	PM
1990-91	Ottawa	OHL	42	12	14	26	31	–	–	–	–	–
1991-92	Ottawa	OHL	65	31	45	76	94	11	3	7	10	11
1992-93	Ottawa	OHL	21	9	19	28	51	–	–	–	–	–
1993-94	Ottawa	OHL	52	25	37	62	98	12	5	11	16	14
1994-95	Adirondack	AHL	64	6	11	17	71	4	0	2	2	4

Drafted by DETROIT in 1992 NHL Entry Draft (1st choice, 22nd overall, 1st round).

DAVID CHYZOWSKI

LEFT WING   6-1 — 190 lbs. — SHOOTS LEFT
BORN: EDMONTON, ALBERTA
JULY 11, 1971

Season	Club	League	Regular Schedule GP	G	A	P	PM	Playoffs GP	G	A	P	PM
1987-88	Kamloops	WHL	66	16	17	33	117	18	2	4	6	26
1988-89*a*	Kamloops	WHL	68	56	48	104	139	16	15	13	28	32
1989-90	NY Islanders	NHL	34	8	6	14	45	–	–	–	–	–
	Springfield	AHL	4	0	0	0	7	–	–	–	–	–
	Kamloops	WHL	4	5	2	7	17	17	11	6	17	46
1990-91	NY Islanders	NHL	56	5	9	14	61	–	–	–	–	–
	Capital Dist.	AHL	7	3	6	9	22	–	–	–	–	–
1991-92	NY Islanders	NHL	12	1	1	2	17	–	–	–	–	–
	Capital Dist.	AHL	55	15	18	33	121	6	1	1	2	23
1992-93	Capital Dist.	AHL	66	15	21	36	177	3	2	0	2	0
1993-94	NY Islanders	NHL	3	1	0	1	4	2	0	0	0	0
	Salt Lake	IHL	66	27	13	40	151	–	–	–	–	–
1995	NY Islanders	NHL	13	0	0	0	11	–	–	–	–	–
NHL Totals			**168**	**15**	**16**	**31**	**138**	**2**	**0**	**0**	**0**	**0**

a-WHL West All-Star Team (1989).

SYLVAIN CLOUTIER

CENTER   6-0 — 195 lbs. — SHOOTS LEFT
BORN: MONT-LAURIER, QUEBEC
FEBRUARY 13, 1974

AMATEUR RECORD

Season	Club	League	Regular Schedule GP	G	A	P	PM	Playoffs GP	G	A	P	PM
1991-92	Guelph	OHL	62	35	31	66	74	–	–	–	–	–
1992-93	Guelph	OHL	44	26	29	55	78	5	0	5	5	14
1993-94	Guelph	OHL	66	45	71	116	127	9	7	9	16	32
	Adirondack	AHL	2	0	2	2	2	–	–	–	–	–
1994-95	Adirondack	AHL	71	7	26	33	144	–	–	–	–	–

Drafted by DETROIT in 1992 NHL Entry Draft (3rd choice, 70th overall, 3rd round).

MATHIEU DANDENAULT

RIGHT WING   **6-0 — 180 lbs. — SHOOTS RIGHT**
BORN: SHERBROOKE, QUEBEC
FEBRUARY 3, 1976

AMATEUR RECORD

			Regular Schedule					Playoffs				
Season	Club	League	GP	G	A	P	PM	GP	G	A	P	PM
1994-95	Sherbrooke	QMJHL	67	37	70	107	76	7	1	7	8	10

Drafted by DETROIT in 1994 Entry Draft (2nd choice, 49th overall, 2nd round).

ANDERS ERIKSSON

DEFENSE   **6-3 — 215 lbs. — SHOOTS LEFT**
BORN: BOLLNAS, SWEDEN
JANUARY 9, 1975

			Regular Schedule					Playoffs				
Season	Club	League	GP	G	A	P	PM	GP	G	A	P	PM
1992-93	MoDo	Sweden	20	0	2	2	2	1	0	0	0	0
1993-94	MoDo	Sweden	38	2	8	10	42	–	–	–	–	–
1994-95	MoDo	Sweden	39	3	6	9	54	–	–	–	–	–

Drafted by DETROIT in 1993 NHL Entry Draft (1st choice, 22nd overall, 1st round).

BOB ESSENSA

GOALTENDER   6-0 — 195 lbs. — CATCHES LEFT
BORN: TORONTO, ONTARIO
JANUARY 14, 1965

				Regular Schedule								Playoffs					
Season	Club	League	GP	W	L	T	MP	GA	SO	AVG	GP	W	L	MP	GA	SO	AVG.
1983-84	Mich. State	CCHA	17	11	4	0	946	44	2	2.79	–	–	–	–	–	–	–
1984-85	Mich. State	CCHA	18	15	2	0	1059	29	2	1.64	–	–	–	–	–	–	–
1985-86a	Mich. State	CCHA	23	17	4	1	1333	74	1	3.33	–	–	–	–	–	–	–
1986-87	Mich. State	CCHA	25	19	3	1	1383	64	2	2.78	–	–	–	–	–	–	–
1987-88	Moncton	AHL	27	7	11	1	1287	100	1	4.66	–	–	–	–	–	–	–
1988-89	Winnipeg	NHL	20	6	8	3	1102	68	1	3.70	–	–	–	–	–	–	–
	Fort Wayne	IHL	22	14	7	0	1287	70	0	3.26	–	–	–	–	–	–	–
1989-90	Winnipeg	NHL	36	18	9	5	2035	107	1	3.15	4	2	1	206	12	0	3.50
	Moncton	AHL	6	3	3	0	358	15	0	2.51	–	–	–	–	–	–	–
1990-91	Winnipeg	NHL	55	19	24	6	2916	153	4	3.15	–	–	–	–	–	–	–
	Moncton	AHL	2	1	0	1	125	6	0	2.88	–	–	–	–	–	–	–
1991-92	Winnipeg	NHL	47	21	17	6	2627	126	5	2.88	1	0	0	33	3	0	5.45
1992-93	Winnipeg	NHL	67	33	26	6	3855	227	2	3.53	6	2	4	367	20	0	3.27
1993-94	Winnipeg	NHL	56	19	30	6	3136	201	1	3.85	–	–	–	–	–	–	–
	DETROIT	NHL	13	4	7	2	778	34	1	2.62	2	0	2	109	9	0	4.95
1994-95	San Diego	IHL	16	6	8	1	919	52	0	3.39	1	0	1	59	3	0	3.05
NHL Totals			294	120	121	34	16449	916	15	3.34	13	4	7	715	44	0	3.71
DETROIT Totals			13	4	7	2	778	34	1	2.62	2	0	2	109	9	0	4.95

a-CCHA Second All-Star Team.
Drafted by Winnipeg in 1983 Entry Draft (5th coice, 69th overall, 4th round).
Traded by Winnipeg to DETROIT with Sergie Bautin for Tim Cheveldae and Dallas Drake, Mar. 8, 1994.

JOE FREDERICK

RIGHT WING   6-1 — 190 lbs. — SHOOTS RIGHT
BORN: MADISON, WISCONSIN
AUGUST 6, 1969

PROFESSIONAL RECORD

				Regular Schedule					Playoffs			
Season	Club	League	GP	G	A	P	PM	GP	G	A	P	PM
1990-91	North. Michigan	WCHA	40	9	11	20	77	–	–	–	–	–
1991-92	North. Michigan	WCHA	36	23	8	31	100	–	–	–	–	–
1992-93	North. Michigan	WCHA	29	28	20	48	100	–	–	–	–	–
	Adirondack	AHL	5	0	1	1	2	8	0	0	0	6
	Moncton	AHL	61	11	18	29	113	4	0	1	1	6
1992-93	Moncton	AHL	67	12	23	35	40	5	2	2	4	18
	Winnipeg	NHL	7	0	0	0	0	–	–	–	–	–
1993-94	Adirondack	AHL	46	20	23	43	49	–	–	–	–	–
	DETROIT	NHL	39	5	8	13	31	7	2	2	4	4
NHL Totals			59	8	8	16	40	9	2	2	4	4
DETROIT Totals			39	5	8	13	31	7	2	2	4	4

Drafted by Winnipeg in 1989 NHL Entry Draft (4th choice, 62nd overall, 3rd round).
Traded to DETROIT from Winnipeg for future considerations, June 30, 1993.

YAN GOLUBOVSKY

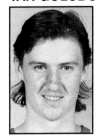

DEFENSE   6-3 — 185 lbs. — SHOOTS LEFT
BORN: NOVOSIBIRSK, RUSSIA
MARCH 9, 1976

			Regular Schedule					Playoffs			
Season	Club	League	GP	G	A	P	PM	GP	G	A	P	PM
1993-94	Moscow Dynamo	CIS	10	0	1	1	–	–	–	–	–	–
1994-95	Adirondack	AHL	57	4	2	6	39	–	–	–	–	–

Drafted by DETROIT in 1993 NHL Entry Draft (1st choice, 23rd overall, 1st round).

KEVIN HODSON

GOALTENDER   6-0 — 182 lbs. — CATCHES LEFT
BORN: WINNIPEG, MANITOBA
MARCH 27, 1972

			AMATEUR RECORD													
			Regular Schedule							Playoffs						
Season	Club	League	GP	W	L	T	MP	GA	SO	AVG.	GP	W	L	MP	GA	SO	AVG.
1990-91	S. Ste. Marie	OHL	30	18	11	0	1638	88	2	3.22	10	9	1	600	28	0	2.87
1991-92	S. Ste. Marie	OHL	50	28	12	4	2722	151	0	3.33	18	12	6	1116	59	1	2.90
1992-93	S. Ste. Marie	OHL	26	18	5	2	1470	76	1	3.10	8	8	0	448	17	0	2.28
1993-94	Adirondack	AHL	37	20	10	4	2083	102	2	2.94	3	0	2	89	10	0	6.74
1994-95	Adirondack	AHL	51	19	22	8	2731	161	1	3.54	4	0	4	237	14	0	3.53

Signed as a free agent by DETROIT May, 1993.

MIKE KNUBLE

RIGHT WING   6-3 — 208 lbs. — SHOOTS RIGHT
BORN: TORONTO, ONTARIO
JULY 4, 1972

			Regular Schedule					Playoffs				
Season	Club	League	GP	G	A	P	PM	GP	G	A	P	PM
1991-92	Univ. of Michigan	CCHA	43	7	8	15	48	–	–	–	–	–
1992-93	Univ. of Michigan	CCHA	39	26	16	42	57	–	–	–	–	–
1993-94	Univ. of Michigan	CCHA	41	32	26	58	71	–	–	–	–	–
1994-95	Univ. of Michigan	CCHA	34	38	22	60	62	–	–	–	–	–
	Adirondack	AHL	3	0	0	0	0	–	–	–	–	–

Drafted by DETROIT in the 1991 NHL Entry Draft (4th choice, 76th overall, 4th round).

NORM MARACLE

GOALTENDER   5-9 — 170 lbs. — CATCHES LEFT
BORN: BELLEVILLE, ONTARIO
OCTOBER 2, 1974

AMATEUR RECORD

			Regular Schedule							Playoffs						
Season	Club	League	GP	W	L	T	MP	GA	SO	AVG.	GP	W	L	MP	GA	SO	AVG.
1991-92	Saskatoon	WHL	29	13	6	3	1529	87	1	3.41	15	9	5	860	37	0	3.38
1992-93a	Saskatoon	WHL	53	27	18	3	1939	160	1	3.27	9	4	5	569	33	0	3.48
1993-94	Saskatoon	WHL	56	41	13	1	3219	148	2	2.76	16	11	5	940	48	1	3.06
1994-95	Adirondack	AHL	39	12	15	2	1997	119	0	3.57	–	–	–	–	–	–	–

a-WHL East Second All-Star Team.
Drafted by DETROIT in 1993 (6th choice, 126th overall, 5th round).

JASON MacDONALD

RIGHT WING   6-0 — 195 lbs. — SHOOTS RIGHT
BORN: CHARLOTTEOWN, PRINCE EDWARD ISLAND
APRIL 1, 1968

AMATEUR RECORD

			Regular Schedule						Playoffs			
Season	Club	League	GP	G	A	P	PM	GP	G	A	P	PM
1990-91	North Bay	OHL	57	12	15	27	126	10	3	3	6	15
1991-92	North Bay	OHL	17	5	8	13	50	–	–	–	–	–
	Owen Sound	OHL	42	17	19	36	129	5	0	3	3	16
1992-93	Owen Sound	OHL	56	46	43	89	197	8	6	5	11	28
1993-94	Owen Sound	OHL	66	55	61	116	177	9	7	11	18	36
	Adirondack	AHL	–	–	–	–	–	1	0	0	0	0
1994-95	Adirondack	AHL	68	14	21	35	238	4	0	0	0	2

Drafted by DETROIT in 1992 NHL Entry Draft (5th choice, 142rd overall, 6th round).

JAMIE PUSHOR

DEFENSE   **6-3 — 192 lbs. — SHOOTS RIGHT**
BORN: LETHBRIDGE, ALBERTA
FEBRUARY 11, 1973

AMATEUR RECORD

			Regular Schedule					Playoffs				
Season	Club	League	GP	G	A	P	PM	GP	G	A	P	PM
1989-90	Lethbridge	WHL	10	0	2	2	0	–	–	–	–	–
1990-91	Lethbridge	WHL	71	1	13	14	193	–	–	–	–	–
1991-92	Lethbridge	WHL	49	2	15	17	232	5	0	0	0	33
1992-93	Lethbridge	WHL	72	6	22	28	200	4	0	1	1	9
1993-94	Adirondack	AHL	73	1	17	18	124	12	0	0	0	22
1994-95	Adirondack	AHL	58	2	11	13	129	4	0	1	1	0

Drafted by DETROIT in 1991 NHL Entry Draft (2nd choice, 32nd overall, 2nd round).

AARON WARD

DEFENSE   **6-2 — 200 lbs. — SHOOTS RIGHT**
BORN: WINDSOR, ONTARIO
JANUARY 17, 1973

			Regular Schedule					Playoffs				
Season	Club	League	GP	G	A	P	PM	GP	G	A	P	PM
1990-91	Univ. of MIchigan	CCHA	46	8	11	19	126	–	–	–	–	–
1991-92	Univ. of Michigan	CCHA	42	7	12	19	64	–	–	–	–	–
1992-93	Univ. of Michigan	CCHA	28	4	8	12	73	–	–	–	–	–
1993-94	Adirondack	AHL	58	4	12	16	87	9	2	6	8	6
	DETROIT	NHL	5	1	0	1	4	–	–	–	–	–
1994-95	Adirondack	AHL	76	11	24	35	87	4	0	1	1	0

Drafted by Winnipeg in 1991 NHL Entry Draft (1st choice, 5th overall, 1st round).
Traded by Winnipeg to DETROIT along with Alan Kerr for Paul Ysebaert, June 11, 1993.

FORWARDS

Player	Position	Hgt	Wgt	Birthplace	Birthdate
BOWEN, Curtis	LW/L	6-1	195	Kenora, Ontario	Mar. 24, 1974
BROWN, Doug	RW/R	5-10	185	Southborough, MA	June 12, 1964
CASSELMAN, Mike	LW/L	5-11	180	Morrisburg, Ontario	Aug. 23, 1968
CICCARELLI, Dino	RW/R	5-10	185	Sarnia, Ontario	Feb. 8, 1960
CLOUTIER, Sylvain	C/L	6-0	195	Mont-Laurier, Quebec	Feb. 13, 1974
DANDENAULT, Mathieu	RW/R	6-0	174	Sherbrooke, Quebec	Feb. 3, 1976
DRAPER, Kris	C/L	5-11	185	Toronto, Ontario	May 24, 1973
ERREY, Bob	LW/L	5-10	185	Montreal, Quebec	Sept. 21, 1964
FEDOROV, Sergei	C/L	6-1	200	Pskov, Russia	Dec. 13, 1969
GRIMSON, Stu	LW/L	6-5	227	Kamloops, B.C.	May 20, 1965
HANKINSON, Ben	RW/R	6-2	210	Edina, MN	May 1, 1969
JOHNSON, Greg	C/R	5-10	185	Thunder Bay, Ontario	Mar. 16, 1971
KNUBLE, Mike	RW/R	6-3	208	Toronto, Ontario	July 4, 1972
KOZLOV, Vyacheslav	C/L	5-10	180	Voskresensk, Russia	May 3, 1972
LAPOINTE, Martin	RW/R	5-11	200	Ville Ste. Pierre, Que.	Sept. 12, 1973
MacDONALD, Jason	RW/R	6-0	195	Charlottetown, PEI	Apr. 1, 1974
McCARTY, Darren	RW/R	6-1	210	Burnaby, B.C.	Apr. 1, 1972
PRIMEAU, Keith	C/L	6-4	210	Toronto, Ontario	Nov. 24, 1971
SHEPPARD, Ray	RW/R	6-1	195	Pembroke, Ontario	May 27, 1966
TAYLOR, Tim	C/L	6-1	185	Stratford, Ontario	Feb 6, 1969
YZERMAN, Steve	C/R	5-11	185	Cranbrook, B.C.	May 9, 1965
WALZ, Wes	C/R	5-10	185	Calgary, Alberta	May 15, 1970

DEFENSEMEN

Player	Position	Hgt	Wgt	Birthplace	Birthdate
BAUTIN, Sergei	Def/L	6-3	210	Rogachev, Russia	Mar. 11, 1967
BERGEVIN, Marc	Def/L	6-1	197	Montreal, Quebec	Aug. 11, 1965
COFFEY, Paul	Def/L	6-1	190	Weston, Ontario	June 1, 1961
ERIKSSON, Anders	Def/L	6-3	218	Bolinas, Sweden	Jan. 9, 1975
FETISOV, Viacheslav	Def/L	6-1	220	Moscow, Russia	April 20, 1958
GOLUBOVSKY, Yan	Def/R	6-3	183	Novosibirsk, Russia	Mar. 9. 1976
KONSTANTINOV, Vlad.	Def/R	5-11	190	Murmansk, Russia	Mar. 19, 1967
LIDSTROM, Nicklas	Def/L	6-2	185	Vasteras, Sweden	Apr. 28, 1970
PUSHOR, Jamie	Def/R	6-3	192	Lethbridge, Alberta	Feb. 11, 1973
RAMSEY, Mike	Def/L	6-3	195	Minneapolis, MN	Dec. 3, 1960
ROUSE, Bob	Def	6-2	210	Surrey, B.C.	June 18, 1964
WARD, Aaron	Def/R	6-2	200	Windsor, Onatario	Jan. 1, 1973

FORWARDS 1994-95 Club/League	Regular Season					Playoffs				
	GP	G	A	TP	PM	GP	G	A	TP	PM
Adirondack (AHL)	64	6	11	17	71	4	0	2	2	4
Detroit (NHL)	45	9	12	21	16	18	4	8	12	2
Adirondack (AHL)	77	17	38	55	34	12	2	4	6	10
Detroit (NHL)	42	16	27	43	39	16	9	2	11	22
Adirondack (AHL)	71	7	26	33	144	–	–	–	–	–
Sherbrooke (QMJHL)	67	37	70	107	76	7	1	7	8	10
Detroit (NHL)	39	5	8	13	31	7	2	2	4	4
San Jose (NHL)	13	2	2	4	27	–	–	–	–	–
Detroit (NHL)	30	6	11	17	31	18	1	5	6	30
Detroit (NHL)	42	20	30	50	24	17	7	17	24	6
Anaheim (NHL)	31	0	1	1	110	–	–	–	–	–
Detroit (NHL)	11	0	0	0	37	11	1	0	1	26
New Jersey (NHL)	8	0	0	0	7	–	–	–	–	–
Tampa Bay (NHL)	18	0	2	2	6	–	–	–	–	–
Detroit (NHL)	22	3	5	8	14	1	0	0	0	0
Michigan (CCHA)	34	38	22	60	62					
Adirondack (AHL)						3	0	0	0	0
Detroit (NHL)	46	13	20	33	45	18	9	7	16	10
Detroit (NHL)	39	4	6	10	73	2	0	1	1	8
Adirondack (AHL)	68	14	21	35	238	4	0	0	0	2
Detroit (NHL)	31	5	8	13	88	18	3	2	5	14
Detroit (NHL)	45	15	27	42	99	17	4	5	9	45
Detroit (NHL)	43	30	10	40	17	17	4	3	7	5
Detroit (NHL)	22	0	4	4	16	6	0	1	1	12
Detroit (NHL)	47	12	26	38	40	15	4	8	12	0
Calgary (NHL)	39	6	12	18	11	1	0	0	0	0

DEFENSEMEN 1994-95 Club/League	Regular Season					Playoffs				
	GP	G	A	TP	PM	GP	G	A	TP	PM
Winnipeg (NHL)	59	0	7	7	78	–	–	–	–	–
Detroit (NHL)	1	0	0	0	0	–	–	–	–	–
Adirondack (AHL)	9	1	5	6	6	–	–	–	–	–
Tampa Bay (NHL)	44	2	4	6	51	–	–	–	–	–
Detroit (NHL)	45	14	44	58	72	18	6	12	18	10
MoDo (Sweden)	39	3	6	9	54	–	–	–	–	–
New Jersey (NHL)	4	0	1	1	0					
Detroit (NHL)	18	3	12	15	2	18	0	8	8	14
Adirondack (AHL)	57	4	2	6	39	–	–	–	–	–
Detroit (NHL)	47	3	11	14	101	18	1	1	2	22
Detroit (NHL)	43	10	16	26	6	18	4	12	16	8
Adirondack (AHL)	58	2	11	13	129	4	0	1	1	0
Detroit (NHL)	33	1	2	3	23	15	0	1	1	4
Detroit (NHL)	48	1	7	8	36	18	0	3	3	8
Adirondack (AHL)	76	11	24	35	87	4	0	1	1	0

GOALTENDERS Player	Catch	Hgt	Wgt	Birthplace	Birthdate
ESSENSA, Bob	L	6-0	185	Toronto, Ontario	Jan. 14, 1965
HODSON, Kevin	L	6-0	182	Winnipeg, Manitoba	Mar. 27, 1972
MARACLE, Norm	L	5-9	175	Belleville, Ontario	Oct. 2, 1974
OSGOOD, Chris	L	5-10	160	Peace River, Alberta	Nov. 26, 1972
VERNON, Mike	L	5-9	170	Calgary, Alberta	Feb. 24, 1963

GOALTENDERS

1994-95 Club/League	GP	Mins	GA	SO	Avg.	(W-L-T)
San Diego(IHL)	16	919	52	0	3.39	6-8-1
Playoffs (NHL)	1	59	3	0	3.05	0-1
Adirondack (AHL)	51	2731	161	1	3.54	19-22-8
Playoffs (AHL)	4	237	14	0	3.53	0-2
Adirondack(AHL)	39	1997	119	0	3.57	12-15-2
Playoffs (WHL)						11-5
Detroit (NHL)	19	1087	41	1	2.26	14-5-0
Playoffs (NHL)	2	68	2	0	1.76	0-0
Detroit (NHL)	30	1807	76	1	2.52	19-6-4
Playoffs (NHL)	18	1063	41	1	2.31	12-6

WESTERN CONFERENCE

CENTRAL DIVISION

	GP	W	L	T	GF	GA	PTS	PCTG
DETROIT	**48**	**33**	**11**	**4**	**180**	**117**	**70**	**.72**
ST. LOUIS	48	28	15	5	178	135	61	.63
CHICAGO	48	24	19	5	156	115	53	.55
TORONTO	48	21	19	8	135	146	50	.52
DALLAS	48	17	23	8	136	135	42	.43
WINNIPEG	48	16	25	7	157	177	39	.40

PACIFIC DIVISION

	GP	W	L	T	GF	GA	PTS	PCTG
CALGARY	48	24	17	7	163	135	55	.57
VANCOUVER	48	18	18	12	153	148	48	.50
SAN JOSE	48	19	25	4	129	161	42	.43
LOS ANGELES	48	16	23	9	142	174	41	.42
EDMONTON	48	17	27	4	136	183	38	.39
ANAHEIM	48	16	27	5	125	164	37	.38

EASTERN CONFERENCE

NORTHEAST DIVISION

	GP	W	L	T	GF	GA	PTS	PCTG
QUEBEC	48	30	13	5	185	134	65	.67
PITTSBURGH	48	29	16	3	181	158	61	.63
BOSTON	48	27	18	3	150	127	57	.59
BUFFALO	48	22	19	7	130	119	51	.53
HARTFORD	48	19	24	5	127	141	43	.44
MONTREAL	48	18	23	7	125	148	43	.44
OTTAWA	48	9	34	5	117	174	23	.24

ATLANTIC DIVISION

	GP	W	L	T	GF	GA	PTS	PCTG
PHILADELPHIA	48	28	16	4	150	132	60	.625
NEW JERSEY	48	22	18	8	136	121	52	.54
WASHINGTON	48	22	18	8	136	120	52	.54
NY RANGERS	48	22	23	3	139	134	47	.49
FLORIDA	48	20	22	6	115	127	46	.47
TAMPA BAY	48	17	28	3	120	144	37	.38
NY ISLANDERS	48	15	28	5	126	158	35	.36

1995 NHL SEASON SCORING LEADERS

		GP	G	A	PTS	+/-	PIM	PP	SH	GW	GT	S	PCT
Jaromir Jagr	Pittsburgh	48	32	38	70	23	37	8	3	7	0	192	16.7
Eric Lindros	Philadelphia	46	29	41	70	27	60	7	0	4	1	144	20.1
Alexei Zhamnov	Winnipeg	48	30	35	65	5	20	9	0	4	0	155	19.4
Joe Sakic	Quebec	47	19	43	62	7	30	3	2	5	0	157	12.1
Ron Francis	Pittsburgh	44	11	48	59	30	18	3	0	1	0	94	11.7
Theoren Fleury	Calgary	47	29	29	58	6	112	9	2	5	0	173	16.8
PAUL COFFEY	**DETROIT**	**45**	**14**	**44**	**58**	**18**	**72**	**4**	**1**	**2**	**0**	**181**	**7.7**
Mikael Renberg	Philadelphia	47	26	31	57	20	20	8	0	4	0	143	18.2
John LeClair	Mtl/Phi	46	26	28	54	20	30	6	0	7	0	131	19.8
Mark Messier	NY Rangers	46	14	39	53	8	40	3	3	2	0	126	11.1
Adam Oates	Boston	48	12	41	53	11-	8	4	1	2	0	109	11.0
Bernie Nicholls	Chicago	48	22	29	51	4	32	11	2	5	0	114	19.3
Keith Tkachuk	Winnipeg	48	22	29	51	4-	152	7	2	2	1	129	17.1
Brett Hull	St. Louis	48	29	21	50	13	10	9	3	6	0	200	14.5
Joe Nieuwendyk	Calgary	46	21	29	50	11	33	3	0	4	0	122	17.2
SERGEI FEDOROV	**DETROIT**	**42**	**20**	**30**	**50**	**6**	**24**	**7**	**3**	**5**	**0**	**147**	**13.6**
Peter Forsburg	Quebec	47	15	35	50	17	16	3	0	3	0	86	17.4
Owen Nolan	Quebec	46	30	19	49	21	46	13	2	8	0	137	21.9
Teemu Selanne	Winnipeg	45	22	26	48	1	2	8	2	1	1	167	13.2
Mark Recchi	Phi/Mtl	49	16	32	48	9-	28	9	0	3	0	121	13.2
Wayne Gretzky	Los Angeles	48	11	37	48	20-	6	3	0	1	0	142	7.7
Pierre Turgeon	NYI/Mtl	49	24	23	47	0	14	5	2	4	0	160	15.0
Mats Sundin	Toronto	47	23	24	47	5-	14	9	0	4	1	173	13.3
Alexander Mogilny	Buffalo	44	19	28	47	0	36	12	0	2	1	148	12.8

*-Rookie

1995 NHL SEASON GOALTENDING LEADERS
(Minimum 13 games played)

	GP	MINS	GA	SO	AVG	W-L-T
Dominik Hasek, Buffalo	41	2416	85	5	2.11	19-14-7
Rick Tabaracci, Wsh/Cgy	13	596	21	0	2.11	3-3-3
Jim Carey, Washington	28	1604	57	4	2.13	18-6-3
CHRIS OSGOOD, DETROIT	**19**	**1087**	**41**	**1**	**2.26**	**14-5-0**
Ed Belfour, Chicago	42	2450	93	5	2.28	22-15-3

*-Rookie

Paul Coffey led all NHL defensemen in scoring and paced Red Wings in points while tying for sixth overall in NHL.

1995 STANLEY CUP PLAYOFF RESULTS
(All Best-of-Seven Series)

CONFERENCE QUARTERFINALS

EASTERN CONFERENCE

SERIES 'A'

SAT.	MAY 6	NY RANGERS	4	AT	QUEBEC	5
MON.	MAY 8	NY RANGERS	8	AT	QUEBEC	3
WED.	MAY 10	QUEBEC	3	AT	NY RANGERS	4
FRI.	MAY 12	QUEBEC	2	AT	NY RANGERS	3*
SUN.	MAY 14	NY RANGERS	2	AT	QUEBEC	4
TUE.	MAY 16	QUEBEC	2	AT	NY RANGERS	4

*STEVE LARMER SCORED AT 8:09 OF OVERTIME
(NY RANGERS WON SERIES 4-2)

SERIES 'B'

SUN.	MAY 7	BUFFALO	3	AT	PHILADELPHIA	4*
MON.	MAY 8	BUFFALO	1	AT	PHILADELPHIA	3
WED.	MAY 10	PHILADELPHIA	1	AT	BUFFALO	3
FRI.	MAY 12	PHILADELPHIA	4	AT	BUFFALO	2
SUN.	MAY 14	BUFFALO	4	AT	PHILADELPHIA	6

*KARL DYKHUIS SCORED AT 10:06 OF OVERTIME
(PHILADELPHIA WON SERIES 4-1)

SERIES 'C'

SAT.	MAY 6	WASHINGTON	5	AT	PITTSBURGH	4
MON.	MAY 8	WASHINGTON	3	AT	PITTSBURGH	5
WED.	MAY 10	PITTSBURGH	2	AT	WASHINGTON	6
FRI.	MAY 12	PITTSBURGH	2	AT	WASHINGTON	6
SUN.	MAY 14	WASHINGTON	5	AT	PITTSBURGH	6*
TUE.	MAY 16	PITTSBURGH	7	AT	WASHINGTON	1
THU.	MAY 18	WASHINGTON	0	AT	PITTSBURGH	3

*LUC ROBITAILLE SCORED AT 4:30 OF OVERTIME
(PITTSBURGH WON SERIES 4-3)

SERIES 'D'

SUN.	MAY 7	NEW JERSEY	5	AT	BOSTON	0
MON.	MAY 8	NEW JERSEY	3	AT	BOSTON	0
WED.	MAY 10	BOSTON	3	AT	NEW JERSEY	2
FRI.	MAY 12	BOSTON	0	AT	NEW JERSEY	1*
SUN.	MAY 14	NEW JERSEY	3	AT	BOSTON	2

*RANDY McKAY SCORED AT 8:51 OF OVERTIME
(NEW JERSEY WON SERIES 4-1)

WESTERN CONFERENCE

SERIES 'E'

SUN.	MAY 7	DALLAS	3	AT	DETROIT	4
TUE.	MAY 9	DALLAS	1	AT	DETROIT	4
THU.	MAY 11	DETROIT	5	AT	DALLAS	1
SUN.	MAY 14	DETROIT	1	AT	DALLAS	4
MON.	MAY 15	DALLAS	1	AT	DETROIT	3

(DETROIT WON SERIES 4-1)

SERIES 'F'

SUN.	MAY 7	SAN JOSE	5	AT	CALGARY	4
TUE.	MAY 9	SAN JOSE	5	AT	CALGARY	4*
THU.	MAY 11	CALGARY	9	AT	SAN JOSE	2
SAT.	MAY 13	CALGARY	6	AT	SAN JOSE	4
MON.	MAY 15	SAN JOSE	0	AT	CALGARY	5
WED.	MAY 17	CALGARY	3	AT	SAN JOSE	5
FRI.	MAY 19	SAN JOSE	5	AT	CALGARY	4**

*ULF DAHLEN SCORED AT 12:21 OF OVERTIME
**RAY WHITNEY SCORED AT 21:54 OF OVERTIME
(SAN JOSE WON SERIES 4-3)

SUN.	MAY 7	VANCOUVER	1	AT	ST. LOUIS	2
TUE.	MAY 9	VANCOUVER	5	AT	ST. LOUIS	3
THU.	MAY 11	ST. LOUIS	1	AT	VANCOUVER	6
SAT.	MAY 13	ST. LOUIS	5	AT	VANCOUVER	2
MON.	MAY 15	VANCOUVER	6	AT	ST. LOUIS	5*
WED.	MAY 17	ST. LOUIS	8	AT	VANCOUVER	2
FRI.	MAY 19	VANCOUVER	5	AT	ST. LOUIS	3

*CLIFF RONNING SCORED AT 1:48 OF OVERTIME
(VANCOUVER WON SERIES 4-3)

SERIES 'H'

SUN.	MAY 7	TORONTO	5	AT	CHICAGO	3
TUE.	MAY 9	TORONTO	3	AT	CHICAGO	0
THU.	MAY 11	CHICAGO	3	AT	TORONTO	2
SAT.	MAY 13	CHICAGO	3	AT	TORONTO	1
MON.	MAY 15	TORONTO	2	AT	CHICAGO	4
WED.	MAY 17	CHICAGO	4	AT	TORONTO	5*
FRI.	MAY 19	TORONTO	2	AT	CHICAGO	5

*RANDY WOOD SCORED AT 10:00 OF OVERTIME
(CHICAGO WON SERIES 4-3)

CONFERENCE SEMIFINALS

EASTERN CONFERENCE

SERIES 'I'

SUN.	MAY 21	NY RANGERS	4	AT	PHILADELPHIA	5*
MON.	MAY 22	NY RANGERS	3	AT	PHILADELPHIA	4**
WED.	MAY 24	PHILADELPHIA	5	AT	NY RANGERS	2
FRI.	MAY 26	PHILADELPHIA	4	AT	NY RANGERS	1

*ERIC DESJARDINS SCORED AT 7:03 OF OVERTIME
**KEVIN HALLER SCORED AT 25 SECONDS OF OVERTIME
(PHILADELPHIA WON SERIES 4-0)

SERIES 'J'

SAT.	MAY 20	NEW JERSEY	2	AT	PITTSBURGH	3
MON.	MAY 22	NEW JERSEY	4	AT	PITTSBURGH	2
WED.	MAY 24	PITTSBURGH	1	AT	NEW JERSEY	5
FRI.	MAY 26	PITTSBURGH	1	AT	NEW JERSEY	2*
SUN.	MAY 28	NEW JERSEY	4	AT	PITTSBURGH	1

*NEAL BROTEN SCORED AT 18:36 OF OVERTIME
(NEW JERSEY WON SERIES 4-1)

WESTERN CONFERENCE

SERIES 'K'

SUN.	MAY 21	SAN JOSE	0	AT	DETROIT	6
TUE.	MAY 23	SAN JOSE	2	AT	DETROIT	6
THU.	MAY 25	DETROIT	6	AT	SAN JOSE	2
SAT.	MAY 27	DETROIT	6	AT	SAN JOSE	2

(DETROIT WON SERIES 4-0)

SERIES 'L'

SUN.	MAY 21	VANCOUVER	1	AT	CHICAGO	2*
TUE.	MAY 23	VANCOUVER	0	AT	CHICAGO	2
THU.	MAY 25	CHICAGO	3	AT	VANCOUVER	2**
SAT.	MAY 27	CHICAGO	4	AT	VANCOUVER	3***

*JOE MURPHY SCORED AT 9:04 OF OVERTIME
**CHRIS CHELIOS SCORED AT 6:22 OF OVERTIME
***CHRIS CHELIOS SCORED AT 5:35 OF OVERTIME
(CHICAGO WON SERIES 4-0)

EASTERN CONFERENCE

SERIES 'M'

SAT.	JUNE 3	NEW JERSEY	4	AT	PHILADELPHIA	1
MON.	JUNE 5	NEW JERSEY	5	AT	PHILADELPHIA	2
WED.	JUNE 7	PHILADELPHIA	3	AT	NEW JERSEY	2*
SAT.	JUNE 10	PHILADELPHIA	4	AT	NEW JERSEY	2
SUN.	JUNE 11	NEW JERSEY	3	AT	PHILADELPHIA	2
TUE.	JUNE 13	PHILADELPHIA	2	AT	NEW JERSEY	4

*ERIC LINDROS SCORED AT 4:19 OF OVERTIME
(NEW JERSEY WON SERIES 4-2)

WESTERN CONFERENCE

SERIES 'N'

THU.	JUNE 1	CHICAGO	1	AT	DETROIT	2*
SUN.	JUNE 4	CHICAGO	2	AT	DETROIT	3
TUE.	JUNE 6	DETROIT	4	AT	CHICAGO	3**
THU.	JUNE 8	DETROIT	2	AT	CHICAGO	5
SUN.	JUNE 11	CHICAGO	1	AT	DETROIT	2***

*NICKLAS LIDSTROM SCORED AT 1:01 OF OVERTIME
**VLADIMIR KONSTANTINOV SCORED AT 29:25 OF OVERTIME
***VYACHESLAV KOZLOV SCORED AT 22:25 OF OVERTIME
(DETROIT WON SERIES 4-1)

SERIES 'O'

SAT.	JUNE 17	NEW JERSEY	2	AT	DETROIT	1
TUE.	JUNE 20	NEW JERSEY	4	AT	DETROIT	2
THU.	JUNE 22	DETROIT	2	AT	NEW JERSEY	5
SAT.	JUNE 24	DETROIT	2	AT	NEW JERSEY	5

(NEW JERSEY WON SERIES 4-0)

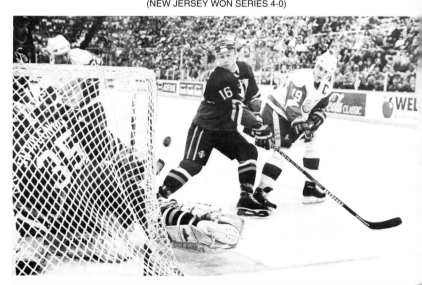

1995 NHL PLAYOFF SCORING LEADERS

		GP	G	A	PTS	+/-	PM	PP	SH	GW	OT	S	PCT
SERGEI FEDOROV	DETROIT	17	7	17	24	13	6	3	0	0	0	53	13.2
Stephane Richer	New Jersey	19	6	15	21	9	2	3	1	2	0	55	10.9
Neal Broten	New Jersey	20	7	12	19	13	6	1	0	4	1	47	14.9
Ron Francis	Pittsburgh	12	6	13	19	3	4	2	0	0	0	30	20.0
Denis Savard	Chicago	16	7	11	18	12	10	3	0	0	0	39	17.9
PAUL COFFEY	DETROIT	18	6	12	18	4	10	2	1	0	0	74	8.1
John MacLean	New Jersey	20	5	13	18	8	14	2	0	0	0	57	8.7
Claude Lemieux	New Jersey	20	13	3	16	12	20	0	0	3	0	65	20.0
V. KOZLOV	DETROIT	18	9	7	16	12	10	1	0	4	1	45	0.0
NICKLAS LIDSTROM	DETROIT	18	4	12	16	4	8	3	0	2	1	37	10.8
Jaromir Jagr	Pittsburgh	12	10	5	15	3	6	2	1	1	0	55	18.2
Rod Brind'Amour	Philadelphia	15	6	9	15	5	8	2	1	1	0	28	21.4
Eric Lindros	Philadelphia	12	4	11	15	7	18	0	0	1	1	28	14.3
Larry Murphy	Pittsburgh	12	2	13	15	3	0	1	0	0	0	35	5.7
Theoren Fleury	Calgary	7	7	7	14	8	2	2	1	0	0	40	17.5
Brian Leetch	NY Rangers	10	6	8	14	1-	8	3	0	1	0	46	13.0
Pavel Bure	Vancouver	11	7	6	13	1-	10	2	2	0	0	39	17.9
Mikael Renberg	Philadelphia	15	6	7	13	5	6	2	0	0	0	45	13.3
Mark Messier	NY Rangers	10	3	10	13	11-	8	2	0	1	0	26	11.5

1995 NHL PLAYOFF GOALTENDING LEADERS
(Minimum 7 games played)

		GP	MINS	GA	SO	AVG	W-L
Martin Brodeur	New Jersey	20	1222	34	3	1.67	16-4
Ed Belfour	Chicago	16	1014	37	1	2.19	9-7
Mike Vernon	DETROIT	18	1063	41	1	2.31	12-6
Ron Hextall	Philadelphia	15	897	42	0	2.81	10-5
Felix Potvin	Toronto	7	424	20	1	2.83	3-4

1995 NHL ALL-STARS

FIRST TEAM	POS	SECOND TEAM
DOMINIK HASEK, Buffalo	G	ED BELFOUR, Chicago
PAUL COFFEY, DETROIT	D	RAY BOURQUE, Boston
CHRIS CHELIOS, Chicago	D	LARRY MURPHY, Pittsburgh
ERIC LINDROS, Philadelphia	C	ALEXEI ZHAMNOV, Winnipeg
JAROMIR JAGR, Pittsburgh	RW	THEOREN FLEURY, Calgary
JOHN LeCLAIR, Philadelphia	LW	KEITH TKACHUK, Winnipeg

NORRIS
(Defenseman)
PAUL COFFEY
Detroit

HART
(MVP)
LESTER B. PEARSON
(NHLPA Top Player)
ERIC LINDROS
Philadelphia

ROSS
(Top Scorer)
JAROMIR JAGR
Pittsburgh

SELKE
(Defensive Forward)
LADY BYNG
(Sportsmanship)
RON FRANCIS
Pittsburgh

VEZINA
(Goalie)
DOMINIK HASEK
Buffalo

JENNINGS
(Team GAA)
ED BELFOUR
Chicago

CALDER
(Rookie)
PETER FORSBERG
Quebec

ADAMS
(Coach)
MARC CRAWFORD
Quebec

CONN SMYTHE
(Playoff MVP)
CLAUDE LEMIEUX
New Jersey

CLANCY
(Humanitarian Efforts)
JOE NIEUWENDYK
Calgary

MASTERTON
(Perseverance)
PAT LaFONTAINE
Quebec

1995 DETROIT RED WINGS' STATISTICS
(48 Games, Jan. 20 – May 3)

	GP	G	A	PTS	+/-	PIM	PP	SH	GW	GT	S	PCT
Paul Coffey	45	14	44	58	18	72	4	1	2	0	181	7.
Sergei Fedorov	42	20	30	50	6	24	7	3	5	0	147	13.
Dino Ciccarelli	42	16	27	43	12	39	6	0	3	0	106	15.
Keith Primeau	45	15	27	42	17	99	1	0	3	0	96	15.
Ray Sheppard	43	30	10	40	11	17	11	0	5	1	125	24.
Steve Yzerman	47	12	26	38	6	40	4	0	1	0	134	9.
Vyacheslav Kozlov	46	13	20	33	12	45	5	0	3	0	97	13.
Nicklas Lidstrom	43	10	16	26	15	6	7	0	0	0	90	11.
Doug Brown	45	9	12	21	14	16	1	1	2	0	69	13.
Bob Errey SJ	13	2	2	4	4	27	0	0	0	0	19	10.
DET	30	6	11	17	9	31	0	0	1	0	53	11.
TOT	43	8	13	21	13	58	0	0	1	0	72	11.
Viacheslav Fetisov NJ	4	0	1	1	2-	0	0	0	0	0	1	.
DET	14	3	11	14	3	2	3	0	0	0	36	8.
TOT	18	3	12	15	1	2	3	0	0	0	37	8.
Shawn Burr	42	6	8	14	13	60	0	0	3	0	65	9.
Vlad. Konstantinov	47	3	11	14	10	101	0	0	0	0	57	5.
Darren McCarty	31	5	8	13	5	88	1	0	2	0	27	18.
Martin Lapointe	39	4	6	10	1	73	0	0	1	0	46	8.
Greg Johnson	22	3	5	8	1	14	2	0	0	0	32	9.
Kris Draper	36	2	6	8	1	22	0	0	0	0	44	4.
+Mike Sillinger	13	2	6	8	3	2	0	0	0	0	11	18.
Bob Rouse	48	1	7	8	14	36	0	0	1	0	51	2.
Mark Howe	18	1	5	6	3-	10	0	0	1	0	14	7.
Mike Krushelnyski	20	2	3	5	3	6	0	0	0	0	20	10.
★Tim Taylor	22	0	4	4	3	16	0	0	0	0	21	.
Terry Carkner	20	1	2	3	7	21	0	0	0	0	9	11.
Mike Ramsey	33	1	2	3	11	23	0	0	0	0	29	3.
★+Jason York	10	1	2	3	0	2	0	0	0	0	6	16.
Mark Ferner ANA	14	0	1	1	4-	6	0	0	0	0	15	.
DET	3	0	0	0	0	0	0	0	0	0	1	.
TOT	17	0	1	1	4-	6	0	0	0	0	16	.
Stu Grimson ANA	31	0	1	1	7-	110	0	0	0	0	14	.
DET	11	0	0	0	4-	37	0	0	0	0	4	.
TOT	42	0	1	1	11-	147	0	0	0	0	18	.
★Aaron Ward	1	0	1	1	1	2	0	0	0	0	0	.
#Bob Halkidis	4	0	0	0	2	6	0	0	0	0	0	.
Andrew McKim	2	0	0	0	0	2	0	0	0	0	0	.
Chris Osgood	19	0	0	0	0	2	0	0	0	0	0	.
Mike Vernon	30	0	0	0	0	8	0	0	0	0	0	.
BENCH	–	–	–	–	–	10	–	–	–	–	–	.
TOTALS	**48**	**180**	**310**	**490**		**932**	**52**	**5**	**33**	**1**	**1571**	**11.**

GOALTENDERS	GP	MIN	GAA	W	L	T	EN	SO	GA	SA	SPCT
Chris Osgood	19	1087	2.26	14	5	0	0	1	41	496	.91
Mike Vernon	30	1807	2.52	19	6	4	0	1	76	710	.89
TOTALS	**48**	**@2900**	**2.42**	**33**	**11**	**4**	**0**	**2**	**117**	**1206**	**.90**

@-Includes minutes goalie out of net
★-Rookie
+-Traded
#-Claimed on waivers

1995 DETROIT RED WINGS' PLAYOFF STATISTICS
(18 Games, May 7 – June 24)

	GP	G	A	PTS	+/-	PIM	PP	SH	GW	OT	S	PCT.
Sergei Fedorov	17	7	17	24	13	6	3	0	0	0	53	13.2
Paul Coffey	18	6	12	18	4	10	2	1	0	0	74	8.1
Vyacheslav Kozlov	18	9	7	16	12	10	1	0	4	1	45	20.0
Nicklas Lidstrom	18	4	12	16	4	8	3	0	2	1	37	10.8
Doug Brown	18	4	8	12	14	2	0	1	1	0	27	14.8
Steve Yzerman	15	4	8	12	2-	0	2	0	1	0	37	10.8
Dino Ciccarelli	16	9	2	11	4-	22	6	0	2	0	49	18.4
Keith Primeau	17	4	5	9	2-	45	2	0	0	0	34	11.8
Viacheslav Fetisov	18	0	8	8	1	14	0	0	0	0	31	.0
Ray Sheppard	17	4	3	7	6-	5	2	0	0	0	41	9.8
Bob Errey	18	1	5	6	0	30	1	0	0	0	18	5.6
Kris Draper	18	4	1	5	2-	12	0	1	1	0	22	18.2
Darren McCarty	18	3	2	5	3	14	0	0	0	0	31	9.7
Bob Rouse	18	0	3	3	2	8	0	0	0	0	16	.0
Vlad. Konstantinov	18	1	1	2	6	22	0	0	1	1	25	4.0
Shawn Burr	16	0	2	2	2-	6	0	0	0	0	20	.0
Stu Grimson	11	1	0	1	0	26	0	0	0	0	3	33.3
Martin Lapointe	2	0	1	1	1	8	0	0	0	0	0	.0
Mike Ramsey	15	0	1	1	2	4	0	0	0	0	7	.0
Tim Taylor	6	0	1	1	4-	12	0	0	0	0	11	.0
Mark Howe	3	0	0	0	2	0	0	0	0	0	1	.0
Greg Johnson	1	0	0	0	1	0	0	0	0	0	0	.0
Mike Krushelnyski	8	0	0	0	1	0	0	0	0	0	1	.0
Chris Osgood	2	0	0	0	0	0	0	0	0	0	0	.0
Mike Vernon	18	0	0	0	0	0	0	0	0	0	0	.0
TOTALS	**18**	**61**	**99**	**160**		**264**	**22**	**3**	**12**	**3**	**583**	**10.5**

GOALTENDERS	GP	MIN	GAA	W	L	EN	SO	GA	SA	SPCT.
Chris Osgood	2	68	1.76	0	0	0	0	2	25	.920
Mike Vernon	18	1063	2.31	12	6	1	1	41	370	.889
TOTALS	**18**	**+1133**	**2.33**	**12**	**6**	**1**	**1**	**+44**	**+396**	**.889**

Rookie
-Includes minutes goalie out of net, empty net goals, shots

Game	Date	Opposition	W-L-T	Score	Record
1	1-20-95	Chicago	W	4-1	1-0-
2	1-22-95	Calgary	L	1-4	1-1-
3	1-24-95	Vancouver	W	6-3	2-1-
4	1-26-95	Calgary	W	5-1	3-1-
5	1-29-95	Edmonton	W	5-2	4-1-
6	1-31-95	@ Edmonton	W	4-2	5-1-
7	2- 1-95	@ Calgary	L	1-2	5-2-
8	2- 3-95	@ Anaheim	W	5-2	6-2-
9	2- 4-95	@ Los Angeles	L	3-4	6-3-
10	2- 7-95	San Jose	W	6-0	7-3-
11	2-10-95	Toronto	L	1-2	7-4-
12	2-12-95	Los Angeles	T (OT)	4-4	7-4-
13	2-15-95	@ Winnipeg	W	5-1	8-4-
14	2-17-95	Edmonton	W	4-2	9-4-
15	2-20-95	@ Toronto	W	4-2	10-4-
16	2-22-95	Toronto	W	4-1	11-4-
17	2-23-95	@ Chicago	W	4-2	12-4-
18	2-25-95	St. Louis	L	2-3	12-5-
19	3- 2-95	Winnipeg	W	6-1	13-5-
20	3- 5-95	@ Edmonton	L	2-4	13-6-
21	3- 6-95	@ Vancouver	W	5-3	14-6-
22	3- 9-95	@ Anaheim	T (OT)	4-4	14-6-
23	3-12-95	@ St. Louis	W	2-1	15-6-
24	3-14-95	Los Angeles	W	5-2	16-6-
25	3-16-95	Dallas	W	5-4	17-6-
26	3-17-95	Vancouver	W	3-1	18-6-
27	3-22-95	Winnipeg	W	6-3	19-6-
28	3-24-95	@ Calgary	L	2-3	19-7-
29	3-25-95	@ Vancouver	W	2-1	20-7-
30	3-28-95	Anaheim	W	6-4	21-7-
31	3-30-95	Dallas	W	3-2	22-7-
32	4- 1-95	@ Dallas	W	3-2	23-7-
33	4- 2-95	St. Louis	T (OT)	3-3	23-7-
34	4- 5-95	@ San Jose	W	5-3	24-7-
35	4- 7-95	@ Toronto	W	4-2	25-7-
36★	4- 9-95	@ Chicago	W	4-1	26-7-
37	4-11-95	@ Dallas	W	4-1	27-7-
38	4-13-95	San Jose	W	3-0	28-7-
39	4-14-95	@ Chicago	W	3-1	29-7-
40	4-16-95	@ St. Louis	L	5-6	29-8-
41	4-19-95	Winnipeg	T (OT)	5-5	29-8-
42	4-21-95	Anaheim	W	6-5	30-8-
43	4-23-95	@ San Jose	W	5-1	31-8-
44	4-25-95	@ Los Angeles	L	1-5	31-9-
45+	4-27-95	@ Winnipeg	L	3-4	31-10-
46#	4-29-95	Dallas	W	4-2	32-10-
47	4-30-95	Chicago	L	0-4	32-11-
48	5- 3-95	@ St. Louis	W	3-2	33-11-

★-Clinched playoff berth 4-10 when San Jose lost @ Calgary
+-Clinched Western Conference, Central Division when St. Louis lost @ Edmonton
#-Clinched President's Trophy

a-Vernon replaced Osgood 8:38 of 1st period.

ts	GF	GA	Goalie	Deciding Goal
2	4	1	VERNON	COFFEY
2	5	5	Vernon	Nieuwendyk
4	11	8	VERNON	BURR
6	16	9	OSGOOD	FEDOROV
8	21	11	OSGOOD	CICCARELLI
0	25	13	VERNON	SHEPPARD
0	26	15	Osgood	Titov
2	31	17	VERNON	McCARTY
2	34	21	Vernon	Tocchett
4	40	21	OSGOOD	BROWN
4	41	23	Vernon	Yake
5	45	27	VERNON	Quinn
7	50	28	OSGOOD	BURR
9	54	30	OSGOOD	BROWN
1	58	32	VERNON	LAPOINTE
3	62	33	OSGOOD	BURR
5	66	35	VERNON	FEDOROV
5	68	38	*a*-Osgood/ Vernon	Carbonneau
7	74	39	VERNON	FEDOROV
7	76	43	Osgood	Buchberger
9	81	45	VERNON	ERREY
0	85	49	VERNON	Kariya
2	87	50	VERNON	SHEPPARD
4	92	52	OSGOOD	PRIMEAU
6	97	56	VERNON	ROUSE
8	100	57	OSGOOD	BROWN
0	106	60	VERNON	KOZLOV
0	108	63	Osgood	McCarthy
2	110	64	VERNON	PRIMEAU
4	116	68	VERNON	SHEPPARD
6	119	70	VERNON	FEDOROV
8	122	72	OSGOOD	CICCARELLI
9	125	75	VERNON	Elik
1	130	78	OSGOOD	FEDOROV
3	134	80	VERNON	KOZLOV
5	138	81	VERNON	PRIMEAU
7	142	82	OSGOOD	COFFEY
9	145	82	VERNON	SHEPPARD
1	148	83	OSGOOD	YZERMAN
1	153	89	Vernon	Zombo
2	158	94	VERNON	SHEPPARD
4	164	99	OSGOOD	McCARTY
6	169	100	VERNON	CICCARELLI
6	170	105	Osgood	Todd
6	173	109	Vernon	Tkachuk
8	177	111	OSGOOD	SHEPPARD
8	177	115	Vernon	Murphy
0	180	117	VERNON	HOWE

1995 GAME-BY-GAME HOME RESULTS

GAME	DAY	DATE	OPPONENT	SCORE	RESULT	W-L-T	ATTENDANCE
1	Fri.	Jan. 20	Chicago	4-1	W	1-0-0	19,875
2	Sun.	Jan. 22	Calgary	1-4	L	1-1-0	19,683
3	Tue.	Jan. 24	Vancouver	6-3	W	2-1-0	19,099
4	Thu.	Jan. 26	Calgary	5-1	W	3-1-0	19,264
5	Sat.	Jan. 28	Edmonton	5-2	W	4-1-0	19,680
6	Tue.	Feb. 7	San Jose	6-0	W	5-1-0	19,431
7	Fri.	Feb. 10	Toronto	1-2	L	5-2-0	19,875
8	Sun.	Feb. 12	Los Angeles	4-4 OT	T	5-2-1	19,875
9	Fri.	Feb. 17	Edmonton	4-2	W	6-2-1	19,875
10	Wed.	Feb. 22	Toronto	4-1	W	7-2-1	19,875
11	Sat.	Feb. 25	St. Louis	2-3	L	7-3-1	19,875
12	Thu.	Mar. 2	Winnipeg	6-1	W	8-3-1	19,875
13	Tue.	Mar. 14	Los Angeles	5-2	W	9-3-1	19,875
14	Thu.	Mar. 16	Dallas	5-4	W	10-3-1	19,875
15	Fri.	Mar. 17	Vancouver	3-1	W	11-3-1	19,875
16	Wed.	Mar. 22	Winnipeg	6-3	W	12-3-1	19,807
17	Tue.	Mar. 28	Anaheim	6-4	W	13-3-1	19,875
18	Thu.	Mar. 30	Dallas	3-2	W	14-3-1	19,875
19	Sun.	Apr. 2	St. Louis	3-3 OT	T	14-3-2	19,875
20	Thu.	Apr. 13	San Jose	3-0	W	15-3-2	19,875
21	Wed.	Apr. 19	Winnipeg	5-5 OT	T	15-3-3	19,875
22	Fri.	Apr. 21	Anaheim	6-5	W	16-3-3	19,875
23	Sat.	Apr. 29	Dallas	4-2	W	17-3-3	19,875
24	Sun.	Apr. 30	Chicago	0-4	L	17-4-3	19,875

Home Attendance: 474,714
Average: 19,780

1995 GAME-BY-GAME ROAD RESULTS

GAME	DAY	DATE	OPPONENT	SCORE	RESULT	W-L-T	ATTENDANCE
1	Mon.	Jan. 30	Edmonton	4-2	W	1-0-0	12,120
2	Wed.	Feb. 1	Calgary	1-2	L	1-1-0	18,212
3	Fri.	Feb. 3	Anaheim	5-2	W	2-1-0	17,174
4	Sat.	Feb. 4	Los Angeles	3-4	L	2-2-0	16,005
5	Wed.	Feb. 15	Winnipeg	5-1	W	3-2-0	12,299
6	Mon.	Feb. 20	Toronto	4-2	W	4-2-0	15,746
7	Thu.	Feb. 23	Chicago	4-2	W	5-2-0	22,073
8	Sun.	Mar. 5	Edmonton	2-4	L	5-3-0	12,780
9	Mon.	Mar. 6	Vancouver	5-2	W	6-3-0	14,115
10	Thu.	Mar. 9	Anaheim	4-4 OT	T	6-3-1	17,174
11	Sun.	Mar. 12	St. Louis	2-1	W	7-3-1	20,297
12	Fri.	Mar. 24	Calgary	2-3	L	7-4-1	20,230
13	Sat.	Mar. 25	Vancouver	2-1	W	8-4-1	16,083
14	Sat.	Apr. 1	Dallas	3-2	W	9-4-1	16,924
15	Wed.	Apr. 5	San Jose	5-3	W	10-4-1	17,190
16	Fri.	Apr. 7	Toronto	4-2	W	11-4-1	15,746
17	Sun.	Apr. 9	Chicago	4-1	W	12-4-1	22,227
18	Tue.	Apr. 11	Dallas	4-1	W	13-4-1	16,924
19	Fri.	Apr. 14	Chicago	3-1	W	14-4-1	22,279
20	Sun.	Apr. 16	St. Louis	5-6	L	14-5-1	20,162
21	Sun.	Apr. 23	San Jose	5-1	W	15-5-1	17,190
22	Tue.	Apr. 25	Los Angeles	1-5	L	15-6-1	16,005
23	Thu.	Apr. 27	Winnipeg	3-4	L	15-7-1	14,081
24	Wed.	May 3	St. Louis	3-2	W	16-7-1	20,228

Road Attendance: 412,634
Average: 17,193

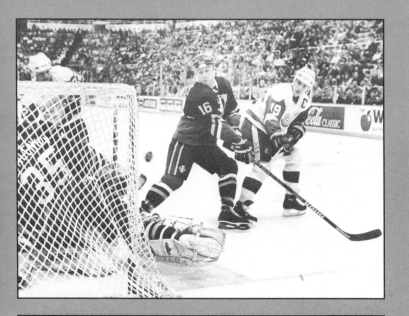

HIGH SCHTICKING YEAR-ROUND

Uncommon Comedy

We offer sharp-edged comedy which
can be preceded by a
wonderful dinner at Risata.

We're open year-round in the heart of
Detroit's exciting Theatre District.

TIX
(313) 965-2222

SHOWS: Wednesday thru Sunday

NEXT TO THE FOX THEATRE

TEAM	W	L	T	P	GF	GA	PPG	SHG	PM
Anaheim	0	3	1	1	15	21	5	0	72
DETROIT	3	0	1	7	21	15	4	0	92

at Anaheim (1-0-1)	**at DETROIT (2-0-0)**
Feb. 2 – DETROIT 5, Anaheim 2	March 28 – DETROIT 6, Anaheim 4
March 9 – DETROIT 4, Anaheim 4	April 21 – DETROIT 6, Anaheim 5
Totals – DETROIT 9, Anaheim 6	Totals – DETROIT 12, Anaheim 9

ANAHEIM MIGHTY DUCKS

PLAYER	GP	G	A	P	PM	+/-
Kariya	4	4	1	5	0	1-
Carback	4	3	1	4	4	2-
Krygier	4	2	2	4	4	2-
Van Allen	4	0	4	4	4	2-
Dollas	4	1	2	3	0	8-
York	1	0	3	3	0	–
Sacco	4	2	0	2	0	2-
Lebeau	4	0	2	2	0	–
Sillinger	1	1	0	1	0	1-
Karpa	2	1	0	1	24	1-
Douris	4	1	0	1	2	1-
Lambert	1	0	1	1	0	1
Holan	2	0	1	1	2	2
Kurvers	2	0	1	1	0	2-
Dirk	3	0	1	1	10	1-
Corkum	4	0	1	1	0	–
Ladouceur	4	0	1	1	2	1
Ferner	1	0	0	0	0	–
Semenov	1	0	0	0	0	2-
Sweeney	1	0	0	0	0	1-
Williams	1	0	0	0	0	1-
Grimson	2	0	0	0	4	1-
Rucchin	2	0	0	0	0	1-
Valk	2	0	0	0	0	–
Ewen	3	0	0	0	14	2-
Karpov	3	0	0	0	2	4-
Tverdovsky	4	0	0	0	0	4-
Totals	**4**	**15**	**21**	**36**	**72**	**–**

DETROIT RED WINGS

PLAYER	GP	G	A	P	PM	+/-
Primeau	4	2	7	9	14	7
Sheppard	4	5	1	6	0	1
Fedorov	4	1	4	5	2	2
Ciccarelli	4	0	5	5	4	5
Coffey	4	2	2	4	6	2
Yzerman	4	2	2	4	2	1
Lidstrom	4	1	3	4	0	4
Kozlov	4	2	1	3	2	1-
Errey	3	1	2	3	6	3
Konstantinov	4	1	2	3	26	1-
Brown	3	2	0	2	0	–
McCarty	3	2	0	2	11	1
Johnson	2	0	2	2	0	1
Rouse	4	0	2	2	4	6
Carkner	1	0	1	1	0	2
Fetisov	1	0	1	1	0	1
Krushelnyski	1	0	1	1	0	–
Sillinger	1	0	1	1	0	1-
Lapointe	2	0	1	1	0	1
Draper	4	0	1	1	4	2-
Ferner	1	0	0	0	0	–
Grimson	1	0	0	0	4	1-
Halkidis	1	0	0	0	0	–
Howe	1	0	0	0	0	1
York	1	0	0	0	0	1-
Burr	2	0	0	0	2	1
Ramsey	2	0	0	0	5	1
Taylor	2	0	0	0	0	2
Totals	**4**	**21**	**39**	**60**	**92**	**–**

GOALIE:	GP	MP	GA	ENG	SO	AVG
Herbert (0-2-1)	4	174	15	0	0	5.17
Shtalenkov (0-1-0)	2	69	6	0	0	5.22
Totals (0-3-1)	**4**	**243**	**21**	**0**	**0**	**5.19**

GOALIE:	GP	MP	GA	ENG	SO	AVG
Vernon (2-0-1)	3	185	10	0	0	3.24
Osgood (1-0-0)	1	60	5	0	0	5.00
Totals (3-0-1)	**4**	**245**	**15**	**0**	**0**	**3.67**

TEAM	W	L	T	P	GF	GA	PPG	SHG	PM
Calgary	3	1	0	6	10	9	2	1	89
DETROIT	1	3	0	2	9	10	1	1	118

at Calgary (0-2-0)
Feb. 1 – Calgary 2, DETROIT 1
March 24 – Calgary 3, DETROIT 2
Totals – Calgary 5, DETROIT 3

at DETROIT (1-1-0)
Jan. 22 – Calgary 4, DETROIT 1
Jan. 26 – DETROIT 5, Calgary 1
Totals – DETROIT 6, Calgary 5

CALGARY FLAMES

PLAYER	GP	G	A	P	PM	+/-
Titov	4	2	2	4	0	3
Housley	4	2	1	3	2	3
Nieuwendyk	4	1	2	3	4	–
Fleury	4	0	3	3	8	3-
Walz	3	2	0	2	0	1
Roberts	3	1	1	2	4	–
McCarthy	1	1	0	1	0	2
Kruse	4	1	0	1	11	–
Kennedy	2	0	1	1	4	–
Kisio	2	0	1	1	0	3
Dahl	3	0	1	1	2	–
Keczmer	3	0	1	1	0	1
Musil	3	0	1	1	4	1-
Chiasson	4	0	1	1	2	2-
Otto	4	0	1	1	19	1-
Patrick	4	0	1	1	0	1-
Allison	1	0	0	0	0	–
Greig	1	0	0	0	2	–
Nylander	1	0	0	0	0	1
Yawney	2	0	0	0	5	1
Stern	3	0	0	0	18	2-
Reichel	4	0	0	0	2	3-
Sullivan	4	0	0	0	2	2-
Zalapski	4	0	0	0	0	1-
Totals	**4**	**10**	**17**	**21**	**89**	**–**

DETROIT RED WINGS

PLAYER	GP	G	A	P	PM	+/-
Coffey	3	2	1	3	4	3
Draper	4	1	2	3	4	4
Lidstrom	4	0	3	3	0	2
Fedorov	3	2	0	2	0	3-
Krushelnyski	2	1	1	2	2	3
Yzerman	4	1	1	2	4	–
McCarty	4	0	2	2	15	3
Burr	4	1	0	1	22	2
Sheppard	4	1	0	1	5	1-
Halkidis	1	0	1	1	2	2
Brown	4	0	1	1	0	1-
Ciccarelli	4	0	1	1	4	1-
Konstantinov	4	0	1	1	12	1
Kozlov	4	0	1	1	19	2-
Primeau	4	0	1	1	8	–
Errey	1	0	0	0	0	1-
Sillinger	1	0	0	0	0	–
Taylor	1	0	0	0	2	–
Howe	2	0	0	0	2	2-
Carkner	3	0	0	0	2	1-
Ramsey	3	0	0	0	4	2-
Lapointe	4	0	0	0	2	3-
Rouse	4	0	0	0	5	3-
Totals	**4**	**9**	**16**	**25**	**118**	**–**

GOALIE:	GP	MP	GA	ENG	SO	AVG
Kidd (3-1-0)	4	230	9	0	0	2.35
Muzzatti (0-0-0)	1	10	0	0	0	.00
Totals (3-1-0)	**4**	**240**	**9**	**0**	**0**	**2.25**

GOALIE:	GP	MP	GA	ENG	SO	AVG
Vernon (0-1-0)	1	60	4	0	0	4.00
Osgood (1-2-0)	3	178	6	0	0	2.02
Totals (1-3-0)	**4**	**238**	**10**	**0**	**0**	**2.52**

Last DETROIT win at Calgary — Mar. 3, 1994 (5-1)

DETROIT VS. CHICAGO 1995 SEASON

TEAM	W	L	T	P	GF	GA	PPG	SHG	PM
Chicago	1	4	0	2	9	15	2	1	132
DETROIT	4	1	0	8	15	9	5	0	87

at Chicago (3-0-0)	at DETROIT (1-1-0)
Feb. 23 – DETROIT 4, Chicago 2	Jan. 20 – DETROIT 4, Chicago 1
April 9 – DETROIT 4, Chicago 1	April 30 – Chicago 4, DETROIT 0
April 14 – DETROIT 3, Chicago 1	
Totals – DETROIT 11, Chicago 4	Totals – Chicago 5, DETROIT 4

CHICAGO BLACKHAWKS

PLAYER	GP	G	A	P	PM	+/-
Amonte	5	1	2	3	6	2-
Shantz	5	1	2	3	2	2
Nicholls	5	0	3	3	0	–
Murphy	5	2	0	2	12	1-
Savard	3	1	1	2	4	1-
Suter	5	1	1	2	6	3-
Weinrich	5	0	2	2	2	1-
Daze	1	1	0	1	0	1
Graham	4	1	0	1	14	2-
Poulin	5	1	0	1	19	2-
B. Sutter	5	0	1	1	0	2-
Dubinsky	1	0	0	0	0	–
Horacek	1	0	0	0	0	–
R. Sutter	1	0	0	0	0	–
Ysebaert	1	0	0	0	0	1-
Roenick	2	0	0	0	0	3-
Russell	2	0	0	0	0	1
Ruuttu	2	0	0	0	0	1
Smyth	2	0	0	0	2	–
Carney	3	0	0	0	2	2-
Craven	3	0	0	0	0	1-
Diduck	3	0	0	0	4	1
Grieve	3	0	0	0	0	1-
Cummins	4	0	0	0	20	1
Krivokrasov	4	0	0	0	4	1-
Chelios	5	0	0	0	9	3-
Smith	5	0	0	0	26	1
Totals	**5**	**9**	**12**	**21**	**132**	**–**

DETROIT RED WINGS

PLAYER	GP	G	A	P	PM	+/-
Yzerman	5	4	1	5	5	1
Ciccarelli	3	3	2	5	6	4
Coffey	5	2	3	5	0	–
Sheppard	3	2	2	4	0	2
Fedorov	4	1	2	3	4	1-
Primeau	5	1	2	3	13	–
Kozlov	4	1	1	2	2	1
Fetisov	2	0	2	2	0	1
Errey	3	0	2	2	0	2
Lapointe	5	0	2	2	20	–
Lidstrom	4	1	0	1	0	–
Sillinger	1	0	1	1	0	1
Howe	3	0	1	1	2	1-
Brown	4	0	1	1	4	1
Burr	5	0	1	1	4	2
York	1	0	0	0	0	–
Draper	2	0	0	0	0	–
Grimson	2	0	0	0	11	1-
Carkner	3	0	0	0	4	1
Johnson	3	0	0	0	0	1
Krushelnyski	3	0	0	0	2	–
McCarty	3	0	0	0	2	3-
Ramsey	3	0	0	0	0	2
Taylor	4	0	0	0	2	1-
Konstantinov	5	0	0	0	0	–
Rouse	5	0	0	0	4	3
Totals	**5**	**15**	**23**	**38**	**87**	**–**

GOALIE:	GP	MP	GA	ENG	SO	AVG
Belfour (1-4-0)	5	299	13	2	1	2.61
Totals (1-4-0)	**5**	**299**	**13**	**2**	**1**	**2.61**

GOALIE:	GP	MP	GA	ENG	SO	AVG
Vernon (3-1-0)	4	240	8	0	0	2.00
Osgood (1-0-0)	1	60	1	0	0	1.00
Totals (4-1-0)	**5**	**300**	**9**	**0**	**0**	**1.80**

Last Chicago win at Chicago — Oct. 23, 1993 (4-2)

TEAM	W	L	T	P	GF	GA	PPG	SHG	PM
Dallas	0	5	0	0	11	19	2	0	122
DETROIT	5	0	0	10	19	11	7	0	100

at Dallas (2-0-0)
April 1 – DETROIT 3, Dallas 2
April 11 – DETROIT 4, Dallas 1

Totals – DETROIT 7, Dallas 3

at DETROIT (3-0-0)
March 16 – DETROIT 5, Dallas 4
March 30 – DETROIT 3, Dallas 2
April 29 – DETROIT 4, Dallas 2
Totals – DETROIT 12, Dallas 8

DALLAS STARS

PLAYER	GP	G	A	P	PM	+/-
Millen	5	1	3	4	4	–
D. Hatcher	5	2	1	3	8	–
Ledyard	4	1	2	3	2	–
Zezel	5	1	2	3	0	-2
Donnelly	5	1	1	2	15	–
Adams	2	1	0	1	0	-1
Courtnall	2	1	0	1	0	1
Modano	2	1	0	1	0	–
Evason	5	1	0	1	2	-3
Gagner	5	1	0	1	11	1
Marshall	1	0	1	1	0	1
Zmolek	4	0	1	1	4	-1
Cavallini	5	0	1	1	0	2
K. Hatcher	5	0	1	1	13	-4
Kennedy	5	0	1	1	0	-2
Ludwig	5	0	1	1	2	-1
Langenbrunner	1	0	0	0	2	–
Lawrence	1	0	0	0	0	–
May	1	0	0	0	0	1
Matvichuk	2	0	0	0	0	-2
Moog	2	0	0	0	10	–
Gilchrist	3	0	0	0	0	1
Churla	4	0	0	0	39	-3
Harvey	4	0	0	0	4	-1
Klatt	4	0	0	0	0	-2
Broten	5	0	0	0	6	-1
Totals	**5**	**11**	**15**	**26**	**122**	**–**

DETROIT RED WINGS

PLAYER	GP	G	A	P	PM	+/-
Ciccarelli	5	3	4	7	2	1
Coffey	5	2	5	7	4	-1
Fedorov	4	1	6	7	2	–
Sheppard	5	3	2	5	0	3
Yzerman	5	0	5	5	0	-1
Lidstrom	4	2	0	2	0	-2
Burr	5	2	0	2	6	2
Carkner	3	1	1	2	7	2
Errey	5	1	1	2	2	-1
Rouse	5	1	1	2	9	5
Taylor	2	0	2	2	0	1
Primeau	5	0	2	2	11	1
Lapointe	3	1	0	1	10	1
McCarty	3	1	0	1	12	1
Konstantinov	5	1	0	1	17	1
York	1	0	1	1	2	-1
Kozlov	5	0	1	1	6	1
Grimson	1	0	0	0	2	1
Howe	1	0	0	0	2	–
Johnson	1	0	0	0	0	1
Fetisov	2	0	0	0	0	–
Krushelnyski	2	0	0	0	0	–
Osgood	3	0	0	0	2	–
Ramsey	3	0	0	0	2	1
Brown	5	0	0	0	0	1
Draper	5	0	0	0	0	-2
Totals	**5**	**19**	**31**	**50**	**100**	**–**

GOALIE:	GP	MP	GA	ENG	SO	AVG
Moog (0-2-0)	2	85	5	0	0	3.53
Wakaluk (0-2-0)	3	153	10	1	0	3.92
Fernandez (0-1-0)	1	59	3	0	0	3.05
Totals (0-5-0)	**5**	**297**	**18**	**1**	**0**	**3.64**

GOALIE:	GP	MP	GA	ENG	SO	AVG
Vernon (2-0-0)	2	120	6	0	0	3.00
Osgood (3-0-0)	3	180	5	0	0	1.67
Totals (5-0-0)	**5**	**300**	**11**	**0**	**0**	**2.22**

Last Dallas win at DETROIT — Oct. 25, 1993 (5-3)
Last Dallas win at Dallas — Apr. 14, 1994 (4-3)

DETROIT VS. EDMONTON 1995 SEASON

TEAM	W	L	T	P	GF	GA	PPG	SHG	PM
Edmonton	1	3	0	2	10	15	1	2	85
DETROIT	3	1	0	6	15	10	5	1	69

at Edmonton (1-1-0)
Jan. 30 – DETROIT 4, Edmonton 2
March 5 – Edmonton 4, DETROIT 2
Totals – DETROIT 6, Edmonton 6

at DETROIT (2-0-0)
Jan. 28 – DETROIT 5, Edmonton 2
Feb. 17 – DETROIT 4, Edmonton 2
Totals – DETROIT 9, Edmonton 4

EDMONTON OILERS

PLAYER	GP	G	A	P	PM	+/-
Corson	4	2	2	4	4	2
Arnott	4	0	4	4	2	4
Oliver	4	2	1	3	2	3
Kennedy	4	1	1	2	9	1
Marchant	4	1	1	2	4	–
Fraser	1	1	0	1	0	1
Buchberger	4	1	0	1	8	2
Maltby	4	1	0	1	8	1-
Oksiuta	4	1	0	1	2	7-
Mironov	2	0	1	1	4	1
Mark	3	0	1	1	2	–
Marchment	4	0	1	1	17	3-
Richardson	4	0	1	1	2	4
Stapleton	4	0	1	1	4	5-
Weight	4	0	1	1	6	1-
DeBrusk	1	0	0	0	0	–
McAmmond	1	0	0	0	0	1-
Nilsson	1	0	0	0	0	1-
Smyth	1	0	0	0	0	–
Esau	2	0	0	0	2	1-
Olausson	2	0	0	0	2	–
Kravchuk	3	0	0	0	0	3-
Pearson	3	0	0	0	7	1-
Thornton	4	0	0	0	0	2-
Totals	**4**	**10**	**15**	**25**	**85**	**–**

DETROIT RED WINGS

PLAYER	GP	G	A	P	PM	+/-
Fedorov	4	2	3	5	0	–
Brown	4	3	1	4	2	4
Sheppard	4	3	1	4	4	1-
Yzerman	4	2	2	4	0	1-
Kozlov	4	1	3	4	2	–
Primeau	4	0	4	4	9	2-
Lidstrom	4	1	2	3	2	3-
Ciccarelli	3	1	1	2	2	2-
Sillinger	2	0	2	2	0	1
Coffey	3	0	2	2	2	1-
Johnson	3	0	2	2	8	1
York	1	1	0	1	0	1
Krushelnyski	3	1	0	1	2	1
McCarty	3	0	1	1	5	1
Konstantinov	4	0	1	1	4	1
Errey	1	0	0	0	5	1-
Halkidis	1	0	0	0	2	–
Taylor	1	0	0	0	0	1
Vernon	1	0	0	0	2	–
Burr	2	0	0	0	0	1-
Carkner	2	0	0	0	2	3
Howe	2	0	0	0	4	–
Draper	3	0	0	0	4	1
Lapointe	3	0	0	0	4	1-
Ramsey	3	0	0	0	0	–
Rouse	4	0	0	0	4	2
Totals	**4**	**15**	**25**	**40**	**69**	**–**

GOALIE:	GP	MP	GA	ENG	SO	AVG
Brathwaite (0-1-0)	2	90	4	1	0	2.67
Ranford (1-2-0)	3	148	10	0	0	4.05
Totals (1-3-0)	**4**	**238**	**14**	**1**	**0**	**3.53**

GOALIE:	GP	MP	GA	ENG	SO	AVG
Osgood (2-1-0)	3	180	8	0	0	2.67
Vernon (1-0-0)	1	60	2	0	0	2.00
Totals (3-1-0)	**4**	**240**	**10**	**0**	**0**	**2.50**

Last Edmonton win at DETROIT — Nov. 9, 1993 (4-2)

TEAM	W	L	T	P	GF	GA	PPG	SHG	PM
Los Angeles	2	1	1	3	15	13	3	1	64
DETROIT	1	2	1	3	13	15	5	2	59

at Los Angeles (0-2-0)
Feb. 4 – Los Angeles 4, DETROIT 3
April 25 – Los Angeles 5, DETROIT 1
Totals – Los Angeles 9, DETROIT 4

at DETROIT (1-0-1)
Feb. 12 – DETROIT 4, Los Angeles 4
March 14 – DETROIT 5, Los Angeles 2
Totals – DETROIT 9, Los Angeles 6

LOS ANGELES KINGS

PLAYER	GP	G	A	P	PM	+/-
Tocchet	3	4	3	7	16	1
Kurri	3	1	4	5	0	1
Todd	3	2	1	3	0	2
Zhitnik	2	1	2	3	4	–
Quinn	4	1	2	3	0	4
Gretzky	4	0	3	3	0	3-
McSorley	4	0	3	3	4	–
Lang	4	2	0	2	0	–
Burridge	3	1	1	2	0	1
Petit	3	1	1	2	0	3
Sydor	4	1	1	2	4	2
Shuchuk	2	0	2	2	0	3
Crowder	2	1	0	1	10	2
Cowie	2	0	1	1	2	2
Granato	2	0	1	1	2	2
Huddy	2	0	1	1	2	1
Snell	3	0	1	1	2	2
Conacher	4	0	1	1	0	1-
Blake	1	0	0	0	0	1-
R. Brown	1	0	0	0	0	–
Donnelly	1	0	0	0	0	1-
K. Brown	2	0	0	0	0	1-
Perreault	2	0	0	0	6	–
O'Donnell	3	0	0	0	2	1-
Druce	4	0	0	0	4	–
Lacroix	4	0	0	0	4	–
Totals	**4**	**15**	**28**	**43**	**64**	**–**

DETROIT RED WINGS

PLAYER	GP	G	A	P	PM	+/-
Fedorov	4	6	0	6	0	3
Kozlov	4	2	4	6	0	1
Ciccarelli	3	1	3	4	4	1-
Coffey	4	1	3	4	0	–
Primeau	3	2	1	3	0	5-
Brown	4	0	3	3	0	4
Konstantinov	4	0	2	2	6	2-
Lidstrom	4	0	2	2	0	2-
Yzerman	4	0	2	2	19	1
Sheppard	4	1	0	1	4	4-
Ramsey	2	0	1	1	0	2-
Rouse	4	0	1	1	0	1-
Carkner	1	0	0	0	0	1
Fetisov	1	0	0	0	0	2-
Howe	1	0	0	0	0	–
McKim	1	0	0	0	0	–
Taylor	1	0	0	0	2	–
Errey	2	0	0	0	2	1-
Johnson	2	0	0	0	0	3-
Krushelnyski	2	0	0	0	0	–
Sillinger	2	0	0	0	2	1-
York	2	0	0	0	0	–
Draper	3	0	0	0	0	–
Lapointe	3	0	0	0	2	1-
McCarty	3	0	0	0	6	2-
Burr	4	0	0	0	12	4-
Totals	**4**	**13**	**22**	**35**	**59**	**–**

GOALIE:	GP	MP	GA	ENG	SO	AVG
Hrudey (2-1-1)	4	245	13	0	0	3.18
Totals (2-1-1)	**4**	**245**	**13**	**0**	**0**	**3.18**

GOALIE:	GP	MP	GA	ENG	SO	AVG
Vernon (0-1-1)	2	124	8	0	0	3.87
Osgood (1-1-0)	2	120	7	0	0	3.50
Totals (1-2-1)	**4**	**144**	**15**	**0**	**0**	**3.69**

Last DETROIT win at Los Angeles — Jan. 8, 1994 (6-3)
Last Los Angeles win at DETROIT — Mar. 20, 1993 (9-3)

DETROIT VS. ST. LOUIS

1995 SEASON

TEAM	W	L	T	P	GF	GA	PPG	SHG	PM
St. Louis	2	2	1	4	15	15	5	2	107
DETROIT	2	2	1	4	15	15	8	0	115

at St. Louis (2-1-0)
March 12 – DETROIT 2, St. Louis 1
April 16 – St. Louis 6, DETROIT 5
May 3 – DETROIT 3, St. Louis 2
Totals – DETROIT 10, St. Louis 9

at DETROIT (0-1-1)
Feb. 25 – St. Louis 3, DETROIT 2
April 2 – DETROIT 3, St. Louis 3

Totals – St. Louis 6, DETROIT 5

ST. LOUIS BLUES

PLAYER	GP	G	A	P	PM	+/-
Hull	5	6	1	7	0	1
Carbonneau	4	1	2	3	0	2
Duchesne	4	1	2	3	8	4
MacInnis	4	1	2	3	4	2-
Laperriere	5	1	2	3	10	1
Shanahan	5	0	3	3	9	3-
Elik	2	1	1	2	0	1
Anderson	5	1	1	2	0	2-
Gilbert	5	1	1	2	0	2
McRae	3	0	2	2	17	2
Norton	4	0	2	2	14	1
Houlder	3	1	0	1	0	2
Zombo	3	1	0	1	2	–
Dufresne	3	0	1	1	6	1
Tardif	3	0	1	1	4	–
Baron	4	0	1	1	2	3-
Tikkanen	4	0	1	1	6	2
Chasse	5	0	1	1	8	1
Batters	1	0	0	0	2	–
Hollinger	1	0	0	0	2	–
Johnson	1	0	0	0	0	–
Roberts	2	0	0	0	2	1
Twist	2	0	0	0	4	–
Lidster	3	0	0	0	0	2
Karamnov	4	0	0	0	0	1
Creighton	5	0	0	0	7	3-
Totals	**5**	**15**	**24**	**39**	**107**	**–**

DETROIT RED WINGS

PLAYER	GP	G	A	P	PM	+/-
Fetisov	2	2	3	5	2	1
Coffey	4	1	4	5	14	1-
Primeau	4	2	2	4	17	–
Sheppard	4	3	0	3	2	1
Howe	3	1	2	3	0	–
Errey	4	1	2	3	12	1
McCarty	2	1	1	2	2	–
Ciccarelli	5	1	1	2	0	2-
Taylor	3	0	2	2	4	–
Yzerman	4	0	2	2	0	3-
Kozlov	5	0	2	2	6	1
Johnson	2	1	0	1	0	1
Fedorov	4	1	0	1	4	4-
Brown	5	1	0	1	0	2-
York	1	0	1	1	0	–
Burr	5	0	1	1	4	1-
Draper	5	0	1	1	2	–
Lapointe	5	0	1	1	27	2
Rouse	5	0	1	1	6	2-
Ferner	1	0	0	0	0	–
Krushelnyski	1	0	0	0	0	–
Sillinger	1	0	0	0	0	–
Carkner	2	0	0	0	2	1-
Grimson	2	0	0	0	2	1-
Ramsey	3	0	0	0	2	1-
Konstantinov	4	0	0	0	7	1-
Lidstrom	4	0	0	0	0	2-
Totals	**5**	**15**	**26**	**41**	**115**	**–**

GOALIE:	GP	MP	GA	ENG	SO	AVG
Joseph (1-2-0)	4	199	8	0	0	2.41
Casey (1-0-1)	2	105	7	0	0	4.00
Totals (2-2-1)	**5**	**304**	**15**	**0**	**0**	**2.96**

GOALIE:	GP	MP	GA	ENG	SO	AVG
Vernon (2-1-1)	5	295	12	0	0	2.44
Osgood (0-1-0)	1	9	3	0	0	20.00
Totals (2-2-1)	**5**	**304**	**15**	**0**	**0**	**2.96**

Last DETROIT win at DETROIT — Dec. 9, 1993 (3-2)

DETROIT VS. SAN JOSE 1995 SEASON

TEAM	W	L	T	P	GF	GA	PPG	SHG	PM
San Jose	0	4	0	0	4	19	2	0	79
DETROIT	4	0	0	8	19	4	5	0	58

at San Jose (2-0-0)
April 5 – DETROIT 5, San Jose 3
April 23 – DETROIT 5, San Jose 1
Totals – DETROIT 10, San Jose 4

at DETROIT (2-0-0)
Feb. 7 – DETROIT 6, San Jose 0
April 13 – DETROIT 3, San Jose 0
Totals – DETROIT 9, San Jose 0

SAN JOSE SHARKS

PLAYER	GP	G	A	P	PM	+/-
Dahlen	4	1	1	2	0	3-
Friesen	4	1	1	2	0	4-
Pederson	4	0	2	2	2	6-
Nazarov	3	1	0	1	2	–
Baker	4	1	0	1	2	4-
Larionov	4	0	1	1	0	5-
More	4	0	1	1	0	1-
Odgers	4	0	1	1	12	3-
Ozolinsh	4	0	1	1	2	6-
Byakin	1	0	0	0	0	2-
Donovan	1	0	0	0	0	1-
Norton	1	0	0	0	2	1-
Sykora	1	0	0	0	0	–
Duchesne	2	0	0	0	0	2-
Janney	3	0	0	0	2	2-
Kyte	3	0	0	0	7	3-
Miller	3	0	0	0	2	4-
Rathje	3	0	0	0	6	3-
Tancill	3	0	0	0	0	–
Cronin	4	0	0	0	23	1-
Falloon	4	0	0	0	15	1-
Makarov	4	0	0	0	0	5-
Whitney	4	0	0	0	2	4-
Totals	**4**	**4**	**8**	**12**	**79**	**–**

DETROIT RED WINGS

PLAYER	GP	G	A	P	PM	+/-
Yzerman	4	1	6	7	2	3
Coffey	4	0	6	6	0	4
Fetisov	3	1	4	5	0	4
Sheppard	4	3	1	4	0	3
Brown	4	1	3	4	4	6
Ciccarelli	3	3	0	3	6	2
Errey	3	2	1	3	2	3
Fedorov	3	1	2	3	0	–
Primeau	4	1	2	3	0	5
Burr	3	0	3	3	4	4
Sillinger	1	2	0	2	0	2
Kozlov	4	2	0	2	0	3
Lidstrom	3	1	1	2	0	5
Lapointe	2	1	0	1	2	1
Draper	2	0	1	1	4	1
McCarty	3	0	1	1	10	1
Rouse	4	0	1	1	2	5
Carkner	1	0	0	0	0	–
Ferner	1	0	0	0	0	–
Howe	1	0	0	0	0	1
Grimson	2	0	0	0	16	–
Johnson	2	0	0	0	0	1
Krushelnyski	2	0	0	0	0	1
Taylor	2	0	0	0	4	–
Ramsey	3	0	0	0	2	3
Konstantinov	4	0	0	0	0	2
Totals	**4**	**19**	**32**	**51**	**58**	**–**

GOALIE:	GP	MP	GA	ENG	SO	AVG
Flaherty (0-2-0)	3	149	8	1	0	3.22
Irbe (0-2-0)	2	91	10	0	0	6.59
Totals (0-4-0)	**4**	**240**	**18**	**1**	**0**	**4.50**

GOALIE:	GP	MP	GA	ENG	SO	AVG
Osgood (2-0-0)	2	120	3	0	1	1.50
Vernon (2-0-0)	2	120	1	0	1	.50
Totals (4-0-0)	**4**	**240**	**4**	**0**	**2**	**1.00**

Last San Jose win at San Jose — Nov. 23, 1993 (6-4)

TEAM	W	L	T	P	GF	GA	PPG	SHG	PM
Toronto	1	3	0	2	7	13	9	0	32
DETROIT	3	1	0	6	13	7	2	0	62

at Toronto (2-0-0)	at DETROIT (1-1-0)
Feb. 20 – DETROIT 4, Toronto 2	Feb. 10 – Toronto 2, DETROIT 1
April 7 – DETROIT 4, Toronto 2	Feb. 22 – DETROIT 4, Toronto 1
Totals – DETROIT 8, Toronto 4	Totals – DETROIT 5, Toronto 2

TORONTO MAPLE LEAFS

PLAYER	GP	G	A	P	PM	+/-
Sundin	4	1	2	3	0	–
Andreychuk	4	2	0	2	4	1-
Gill	4	1	1	2	2	2-
Wood	4	1	1	2	0	2
Borschevsky	3	0	2	2	0	2
Butcher	4	0	2	2	2	–
Yake	1	1	0	1	0	1
Eastwood	3	1	0	1	2	1-
Ward	3	0	1	1	2	–
Ellett	4	0	1	1	4	5-
Ridley	4	0	1	1	0	1-
Berg	1	0	0	0	2	2-
Dipietro	1	0	0	0	0	1-
Domi	1	0	0	0	0	–
Hendrickson	1	0	0	0	0	–
Hogue	1	0	0	0	0	2-
Manderville	1	0	0	0	0	1-
Martin	1	0	0	0	0	1
Berehowsky	2	0	0	0	0	1-
Mironov	2	0	0	0	0	2
Warriner	2	0	0	0	0	1-
Gartner	3	0	0	0	0	3-
Gilmour	3	0	0	0	4	1-
Rychel	3	0	0	0	6	–
Craig	4	0	0	0	2	4-
Jonsson	4	0	0	0	0	2-
Macoun	4	0	0	0	2	1-
Totals	**4**	**7**	**11**	**18**	**32**	**–**

DETROIT RED WINGS

PLAYER	GP	G	A	P	PM	+/-
Coffey	4	1	4	5	28	3
Ciccarelli	3	3	1	4	2	3
Kozlov	4	2	1	3	2	3
Primeau	4	2	1	3	2	4
Burr	3	1	2	3	2	2
Fedorov	4	0	3	3	4	–
Lapointe	4	2	0	2	0	1
Johnson	3	1	1	2	4	–
Howe	2	0	2	2	0	2-
Sillinger	3	0	2	2	0	1
Konstantinov	4	0	2	2	4	2
Lidstrom	4	0	2	2	0	5
Sheppard	2	1	0	1	0	–
Errey	1	0	1	1	0	1
Brown	4	0	1	1	2	4-
Draper	1	0	0	0	0	–
Fetisov	1	0	0	0	0	1-
Grimson	1	0	0	0	0	1-
Krushelnyski	1	0	0	0	0	–
McCarty	1	0	0	0	2	–
McKim	1	0	0	0	2	–
York	2	0	0	0	0	1
Taylor	3	0	0	0	0	–
Ramsey	4	0	0	0	6	3
Rouse	4	0	0	0	0	3-
Yzerman	4	0	0	0	2	2
Totals	**4**	**13**	**23**	**36**	**62**	**–**

GOALIE:	GP	MP	GA	ENG	SO	AVG
Rhodes (1-1-0)	2	119	4	1	0	2.02
Potvin (0-2-0)	2	118	7	1	0	3.56
Totals (1-3-0)	**4**	**237**	**11**	**2**	**0**	**2.78**

GOALIE:	GP	MP	GA	ENG	SO	AVG
Vernon (2-1-0)	3	179	6	0	0	2.01
Osgood (1-0-0)	1	60	1	0	0	1.00
Totals (3-1-0)	**4**	**239**	**7**	**0**	**0**	**1.76**

Last Toronto win at Toronto — Feb. 15, 1994 (5-4 OT)

DETROIT VS. VANCOUVER

1995 SEASON

TEAM	W	L	T	P	GF	GA	PPG	SHG	PM
Vancouver	0	4	0	0	7	16	3	0	85
DETROIT	4	0	0	8	16	7	4	1	83

at Vancouver (2-0-0)
March 6 – DETROIT 5, Vancouver 2
March 25 – DETROIT 2, Vancouver 1
Totals – DETROIT 7, Vancouver 3

at DETROIT (2-0-0)
Jan. 24 – DETROIT 6, Vancouver 3
March 17 – DETROIT 3, Vancouver 1
Totals – DETROIT 9, Vancouver 4

VANCOUVER CANUCKS

PLAYER	GP	G	A	P	PM	+/-
Adams	4	1	2	3	2	–
Peca	3	2	0	2	0	1-
Bure	4	1	1	2	15	4-
Courtnall	4	1	1	2	9	3-
Brown	2	0	2	2	0	–
Gelinas	4	0	2	2	10	2
Lafayette	2	1	0	1	0	1
Momesso	4	1	0	1	14	5-
Diduck	2	0	1	1	2	1-
McIntyre	3	0	1	1	2	1
Linden	4	0	1	1	0	3-
Ronning	4	0	1	1	0	5-
Antoski	1	0	0	0	2	–
Leeman	1	0	0	0	0	2-
Whitmore	1	0	0	0	5	–
Namestnikov	2	0	0	0	0	–
Odjick	2	0	0	0	4	2-
Ruuttu	2	0	0	0	0	–
Slegr	2	0	0	0	2	1-
Babych	3	0	0	0	2	8-
Beranek	3	0	0	0	0	3-
Cullimore	3	0	0	0	2	1-
Hunter	3	0	0	0	2	1
Lumme	3	0	0	0	2	–
Murzyn	3	0	0	0	8	3
Hedican	4	0	0	0	2	8-
Totals	**4**	**7**	**12**	**19**	**85**	**–**

DETROIT RED WINGS

PLAYER	GP	G	A	P	PM	+/-
Sheppard	4	3	3	6	0	4
Coffey	4	1	5	6	4	5
Fedorov	3	2	3	5	6	5
Yzerman	4	2	3	5	6	2
Lidstrom	4	2	2	4	2	4
Kozlov	4	1	3	4	4	4
Errey	3	1	2	3	0	3
Brown	4	1	2	3	4	4
Primeau	4	1	1	2	17	2
Burr	4	1	0	1	0	–
Konstantinov	4	1	0	1	11	3
Ward	1	0	1	1	2	1
Lapointe	3	0	1	1	4	1
McCarty	3	0	1	1	6	–
Ciccarelli	4	0	1	1	5	2-
Carkner	1	0	0	0	2	–
Halkidis	1	0	0	0	2	–
Howe	1	0	0	0	0	–
Krushelnyski	1	0	0	0	0	–
Taylor	1	0	0	0	0	–
York	1	0	0	0	0	–
Johnson	2	0	0	0	2	1-
Ramsey	3	0	0	0	2	2
Vernon	3	0	0	0	4	–
Draper	4	0	0	0	0	1-
Rouse	4	0	0	0	0	1
Totals	**4**	**16**	**28**	**44**	**83**	**–**

GOALIE:	GP	MP	GA	ENG	SO	AVG
McLean (0-3-0)	3	177	12	1	0	4.07
Whitmore (0-1-0)	1	59	3	0	0	3.05
Totals (0-4-0)	**4**	**239**	**15**	**1**	**0**	**3.77**

GOALIE:	GP	MP	GA	ENG	SO	AVG
Vernon (3-0-0)	3	180	6	0	0	2.00
Osgood (1-0-0)	1	60	1	0	0	1.00
Totals (4-0-0)	**4**	**240**	**7**	**0**	**0**	**1.75**

Last Vancouver win at DETROIT — Feb. 8, 1994 (6-3)
Last Vancouver win at Vancouver — Dec. 17, 1991 (2-1)

TEAM	W	L	T	P	GF	GA	PPG	SHG	PM
Winnipeg	1	3	1	3	14	25	3	0	90
DETROIT	3	1	1	7	25	14	6	0	79

at Winnipeg (1-1-0)	at DETROIT (2-0-1)
Feb. 15 – DETROIT 5, Winnipeg 1	March 2 – DETROIT 6, Winnipeg 1
April 27 – Winnipeg 4, DETROIT 3	March 22 – DETROIT 6, Winnipeg 3
	April 19 – DETROIT 5, Winnipeg 5
Totals – DETROIT 8, Winnipeg 5	Totals – DETROIT 17, Winnipeg 9

WINNIPEG JETS

PLAYER	GP	G	A	P	PM	+/-
Selanne	4	2	3	5	0	1
Tkachuk	5	2	2	4	12	–
Zhamnov	5	2	2	4	0	3-
Numminen	4	1	3	4	0	–
Korolev	5	1	3	4	0	–
Quintal	5	1	2	3	7	4-
Emerson	5	0	3	3	4	1-
Shannon	5	2	0	2	0	1
Olczyk	2	0	2	2	0	–
Drake	4	1	0	1	4	4-
King	5	1	0	1	11	3-
Manson	5	1	0	1	18	6-
Brown	1	0	1	1	0	1-
Ulanov	1	0	1	1	0	2-
Eastwood	2	0	1	1	0	–
Martin	2	0	1	1	0	1
Gilhen	5	0	1	1	6	4-
Romaniuk	1	0	0	0	0	2-
Shannon	1	0	0	0	2	3-
Cheveldae	2	0	0	0	2	–
Mikulchik	2	0	0	0	2	2
Murray	2	0	0	0	0	–
Domi	3	0	0	0	0	4-
Eagles	3	0	0	0	0	2-
Grosek	3	0	0	0	0	–
Steen	3	0	0	0	0	1-
Thompson	3	0	0	0	0	4-
Wilkinson	4	0	0	0	22	2-
Totals	**5**	**14**	**25**	**39**	**90**	**–**

DETROIT RED WINGS

PLAYER	GP	G	A	P	PM	+/-
Coffey	5	2	9	11	10	4
Fedorov	5	3	7	10	2	4
Ciccarelli	5	1	8	9	4	5
Primeau	4	4	4	8	8	5
Sheppard	5	5	0	5	2	3
Kozlov	4	2	3	5	2	1
Lidstrom	4	2	1	3	2	4
McCarty	3	1	2	3	17	3
Konstantinov	5	0	3	3	12	4
Draper	3	1	1	2	2	–
Ramsey	4	1	1	2	0	4
Burr	5	1	1	2	4	6
Yzerman	5	0	2	2	0	1
Johnson	2	1	0	1	0	1-
Brown	4	1	0	1	0	1
Fetisov	2	0	1	1	0	1-
Krushelnyski	2	0	1	1	0	2-
Lapointe	5	0	1	1	2	1-
Rouse	5	0	1	1	2	1
Howe	1	0	0	0	0	–
Sillinger	1	0	0	0	0	–
Grimson	2	0	0	0	2	1-
Taylor	2	0	0	0	2	–
Carkner	3	0	0	0	2	–
Errey	4	0	0	0	2	–
Vernon	4	0	0	0	2	–
Totals		**5**	**25**	**46**	**71**	**79**	–

GOALIE:	GP	MP	GA	ENG	SO	AVG
Khabibulin	3	180	13	1	0	4.33
(1-2-0)						
Cheveldae	2	125	11	0	0	5.28
(0-1-1)						
Totals (1-3-1)	**5**	**305**	**24**	**1**	**0**	**4.72**

GOALIE:	GP	MP	GA	ENG	SO	AVG
Osgood (1-0-0)	1	60	1	0	0	1.00
Vernon (2-1-1)	4	244	13	0	0	3.20
Totals (3-1-1)	**5**	**304**	**14**	**0**	**0**	**2.76**

Last Winnipeg win at DETROIT — Nov. 19, 1992 (5-3)

TEAM	W	L	GF	GA	PPG	SHG	PM
Dallas	1	4	10	17	3	1	95
DETROIT	4	1	17	10	9	0	88

GAME	DATE	VENUE	RESULT	SCORE	GOALIE	WINNING GOAL
1	May 7	Detroit	W	4-3	VERNON	Kozlov
2	May 9	Detroit	W	4-1	VERNON	Lidstrom
3	May 11	Dallas	W	5-1	VERNON	Kozlov
4	May 14	Dallas	L	1-4	Vernon	K. Hatcher
5	May 15	Detroit	W	3-1	VERNON	Ciccarelli

DALLAS STARS

PLAYER	GP	G	A	P	PM	+/-
K. Hatcher	5	2	1	3	2	4-
Broten	5	1	2	3	2	2-
Evason	5	1	2	3	12	1
Adams	5	2	0	2	0	1
Gagner	5	1	1	2	4	–
Cavallini	5	0	2	2	6	2
Matvichuk	5	0	2	2	4	3-
Zezel	3	1	0	1	0	–
Klatt	5	1	0	1	0	–
Millen	5	1	0	1	2	1-
Ludwig	4	0	1	1	2	5
Donnelly	5	0	1	1	6	–
Gilchrist	5	0	1	1	2	1-
Boyer	2	0	0	0	0	–
Lalor	3	0	0	0	2	2
Ledyard	3	0	0	0	2	2-
Churla	5	0	0	0	20	1-
Harvwey	5	0	0	0	8	1-
Kennedy	5	0	0	0	9	1-
Moog	5	0	0	0	2	–
Zmolek	5	0	0	0	10	2-
Totals	**5**	**10**	**13**	**23**	**95**	**–**

DETROIT RED WINGS

PLAYER	GP	G	A	P	PM	+/-
Lidstrom	5	3	3	6	4	–
Coffey	5	1	5	6	10	1
Kozlov	5	3	2	5	0	3
Yzerman	5	1	4	5	0	1
Fedorov	5	0	5	5	4	4
Ciccarelli	3	4	0	4	6	1-
Primeau	5	2	1	3	8	3-
McCarty	5	1	1	2	4	1
Errey	5	0	2	2	4	1
Draper	5	1	0	1	4	–
Sheppard	5	1	0	1	5	4-
Brown	5	0	1	1	0	4
Fetisov	5	0	1	1	8	1-
Konstantinov	5	0	1	1	6	2
Ramsey	5	0	1	1	0	2
Rouse	5	0	1	1	6	1-
Krushelnyski	2	0	0	0	0	1-
Burr	5	0	0	0	4	2-
Grimson	5	0	0	0	15	–
Totals	**5**	**17**	**28**	**45**	**88**	**–**

GOALIE:	GP	MP	GA	ENG	SO	AVG
Moog (1-4)	5	277	16	0	0	3.47
Wakaluk	1	20	1	0	0	3.00
Totals (1-4)	**5**	**297**	**17**	**0**	**0**	**3.43**

GOALIE:	GP	MP	GA	ENG	SO	AVG
Vernon (4-1)	5	300	10	0	0	2.00
Totals (4-1)	**5**	**300**	**10**	**0**	**0**	**2.00**

TEAM	W	L	GF	GA	PPG	SHG	PM
San Jose	0	4	6	24	3	0	49
DETROIT	4	0	24	6	6	2	45

GAME	DATE	VENUE	RESULT	SCORE	GOALIE	WINNING GOAL
1	May 21	Detroit	W	6-0	VERNON	Ciccarelli
2	May 23	Detroit	W	6-2	VERNON	Yzerman
3	May 25	San Jose	W	6-2	VERNON	Kozlov
4	May 27	San Jose	W	6-2	VERNON	Brown

SAN JOSE SHARKS

PLAYER	GP	G	A	P	PM	+/-
Larionov	4	0	3	3	0	3-
Rathje	4	2	0	2	0	8-
Whitney	4	2	0	2	2	5-
Dahlen	4	1	1	2	0	7-
More	4	0	2	2	0	6-
Ozolinsh	4	0	2	2	2	6-
Makarov	4	1	0	1	0	2-
Friesen	4	0	1	1	0	6-
Kyte	4	0	1	1	2	4-
Cronin	2	0	0	0	0	–
Miller	2	0	0	0	2	1-
Baker	4	0	0	0	2	5-
Donovan	4	0	0	0	6	2-
Falloon	4	0	0	0	0	4-
Janney	4	0	0	0	0	4-
Kroupa	4	0	0	0	4	2-
Odgers	4	0	0	0	19	1-
Pederson	4	0	0	0	2	4-
Tancill	4	0	0	0	8	6-
Totals	**4**	**6**	**10**	**16**	**49**	**–**

DETROIT RED WINGS

PLAYER	GP	G	A	P	PM	+/-
Fedorov	4	4	7	11	2	8
Kozlov	4	4	5	9	6	9
Brown	4	3	3	6	0	7
Coffey	4	3	3	6	0	5
Yzerman	4	1	4	5	0	4
Ciccarelli	4	3	1	4	6	1
Sheppard	4	2	1	3	0	3
Errey	4	1	2	3	2	4
Lidstrom	4	0	3	3	4	6
McCarty	4	2	0	2	0	4
Draper	4	1	1	2	0	2
Fetisov	4	0	2	2	4	7
Primeau	4	0	2	2	4	2
Burr	4	0	1	1	2	1-
Rouse	4	0	1	1	0	5
Grimson	2	0	0	0	9	–
Krushelnyski	2	0	0	0	0	1
Konstantinov	4	0	0	0	2	4
Ramsey	4	0	0	0	4	3
Totals	**4**	**24**	**36**	**60**	**45**	**–**

GOALIE:	GP	MP	GA	ENG	SO	AVG
Flaherty (0-3)	3	180	18	0	0	6.00
Irbe (0-1)	1	60	6	0	0	6.00
Totals (0-4)	**4**	**240**	**24**	**0**	**0**	**6.00**

GOALIE:	GP	MP	GA	ENG	SO	AVG
Vernon (4-0)	4	240	6	0	1	1.50
Totals (4-0)	**4**	**240**	**6**	**0**	**1**	**1.50**

TEAM	W	L	GF	GA	PPG	SHG	PM
Chicago	1	4	12	13	5	0	62
DETROIT	4	1	13	12	3	0	83

GAME	DATE	VENUE	RESULT	SCORE	GOALIE	WINNING GOAL
1	June 1	Detroit	W	2-1	VERNON	Lidstrom
2	June 4	Detroit	W	3-2	VERNON	Draper
3	June 6	Chicago	W	4-3	VERNON	Konstantinov
4	June 8	Chicago	L	2-5	Vernon (L)/ Osgood	Graham
5	June 11	Detroit	W	2-1	VERNON	Kozlov

CHICAGO BLACKHAWKS

PLAYER	GP	G	A	P	PM	+/-
Savard	5	4	2	6	4	2
Murphy	5	3	1	4	6	–
Chelios	5	1	3	4	2	1
Craven	5	0	3	3	0	1-
Graham	5	1	1	2	4	1
Suter	2	0	2	2	2	2-
Amonte	5	1	0	1	4	1
Nicholls	5	1	0	1	6	2-
Shantz	5	1	0	1	2	2-
Carney	3	0	1	1	0	–
Poulin	5	0	1	1	2	2-
Roenick	5	0	1	1	10	1-
Weinrich	5	0	1	1	0	1
Krivokrasov	2	0	0	0	2	1-
Cummins	3	0	0	0	0	–
Belfour	5	0	0	0	2	–
Daze	5	0	0	0	2	2-
Diduck	5	0	0	0	2	5-
Russell	5	0	0	0	2	1
Smith	5	0	0	0	10	2-
Sutter	5	0	0	0	0	1-
Totals	**5**	**12**	**16**	**28**	**62**	**–**

DETROIT RED WINGS

PLAYER	GP	G	A	P	PM	+/-
Lidstrom	5	1	4	5	0	4
Primeau	5	2	2	4	25	2
Coffey	5	1	3	4	0	1
Fedorov	4	0	3	3	0	–
Draper	5	2	0	2	4	1-
Brown	5	1	1	2	0	2
Sheppard	5	1	1	2	0	2-
Fetisov	5	0	2	2	2	–
Grimson	2	1	0	1	0	1
Yzerman	2	1	0	1	0	–
Ciccarelli	5	1	0	1	4	1
Konstantinov	5	1	0	1	6	1
Kozlov	5	1	0	1	4	1
Taylor	4	0	1	1	10	3-
Burr	5	0	1	1	0	2
Errey	5	0	1	1	20	2
McCarty	5	0	1	1	6	1
Rouse	5	0	1	1	2	–
Howe	1	0	0	0	0	2
Johnson	1	0	0	0	0	1
Krushelnyski	2	0	0	0	0	–
Ramsey	4	0	0	0	0	1-
Totals	**5**	**13**	**21**	**34**	**83**	**–**

GOALIE:	GP	MP	GA	ENG	SO	AVG
Belfour (1-4)	5	352	13	0	0	2.22
Totals (1-4)	**5**	**352**	**13**	**0**	**0**	**2.22**

GOALIE:	GP	MP	GA	ENG	SO	AVG
Vernon (4-1)	5	317	11	0	0	2.08
Osgood	1	36	1	0	0	1.67
Totals (4-1)	**5**	**353**	**12**	**0**	**0**	**2.04**

DETROIT VS. NEW JERSEY 1995 PLAYOFFS

TEAM	W	L	GF	GA	PPG	SHG	PM
New Jersey	4	0	16	7	3	0	56
DETROIT	0	4	7	16	4	1	48

GAME	DATE	VENUE	RESULT	SCORE	GOALIE	WINNING GOAL
1	June 17	Detroit	L	1-2	Vernon	Lemieux
2	June 20	Detroit	L	2-4	Vernon	Dowd
3	June 22	New Jersey	L	2-5	Vernon (L)/ Osgood	Broten
4	June 24	New Jersey	L	2-5	Vernon	Broten

NEW JERSEY DEVILS

PLAYER	GP	G	A	P	PM	+/-
Broten	4	3	3	6	4	5
Maclean	4	1	4	5	0	5
Richer	4	2	2	4	2	1
Niedermayer	4	1	3	4	0	5
Guerin	4	0	4	4	12	4
Chambers	4	2	1	3	0	3
Driver	4	1	2	3	0	4
Lemieux	4	2	0	2	4	2
Dowd	1	1	1	2	2	2
Brylin	3	1	1	2	4	2
Holik	4	1	1	2	8	–
Chorske	3	0	2	2	0	1
Albelin	4	0	2	2	2	1
Stevens	4	0	2	2	4	5
McKay	4	1	0	1	0	–
Rolston	2	0	1	1	0	2
Carpenter	4	0	1	1	2	1
Zelepulkin	3	0	0	0	4	3
Brodeur	4	0	0	0	2	–
Daneyko	4	0	0	0	6	2
Peluso	4	0	0	0	0	–
Totals	**4**	**16**	**30**	**46**	**56**	**–**

DETROIT RED WINGS

PLAYER	GP	G	A	P	PM	+/-
Fedorov	4	3	2	5	0	1
Brown	4	0	3	3	2	1
Fetisov	4	0	3	3	0	5-
Ciccarelli	4	1	1	2	6	5-
Coffey	4	1	1	2	0	3-
Lidstrom	4	0	2	2	0	6-
Kozlov	4	1	0	1	0	1-
Yzerman	4	1	0	1	0	7-
Lapointe	2	0	1	1	8	1
Sheppard	3	0	1	1	0	3-
Burr	2	0	0	0	0	1-
Grimson	2	0	0	0	2	1-
Howe	2	0	0	0	0	–
Krushelnyski	2	0	0	0	0	1
Ramsey	2	0	0	0	0	2-
Taylor	2	0	0	0	2	1-
Primeau	3	0	0	0	8	3-
Draper	4	0	0	0	4	3-
Errey	4	0	0	0	4	7-
Konstantinov	4	0	0	0	8	1-
McCarty	4	0	0	0	4	3-
Rouse	4	0	0	0	0	2-
Totals	**4**	**7**	**14**	**21**	**48**	**–**

GOALIE:	GP	MP	GA	ENG	SO	AVG
Brodeur (4-0)	5	240	7	0	0	1.75
Totals (4-0)	**5**	**240**	**7**	**0**	**0**	**1.75**

GOALIE:	GP	MP	GA	ENG	SO	AVG
Vernon (0-4)	5	206	14	1	0	4.08
Osgood	1	32	1	0	0	1.88
Totals (0-4)	**5**	**238**	**15**	**1**	**0**	**3.78**

1995 RECORD BY MONTHS

	OVERALL				
MONTH	GP	W	L	T	P
January	6	5	1	0	10
February	12	7	4	1	15
March	13	10	2	1	21
April	16	10	4	2	22
May	1	1	0	0	2

	HOME					ROAD				
MONTH	GP	W	L	T	P	GP	W	L	T	P
January	5	4	1	0	8	1	1	0	0	2
February	6	3	2	1	7	6	4	2	0	8
March	7	7	0	0	14	6	3	2	1	7
April	6	3	1	2	8	10	7	3	0	14
May	0	0	0	0	0	1	1	0	0	2

1995 RECORD BY DAYS

	OVERALL				
DAY	GP	W	L	T	P
Sunday	9	3	4	2	8
Monday	3	3	0	0	6
Tuesday	6	5	1	0	10
Wednesday	7	5	1	1	11
Thursday	8	6	1	1	13
Friday	9	7	2	0	14
Saturday	6	4	2	0	8

	HOME					ROAD				
DAY	GP	W	L	T	P	GP	W	L	T	P
Sunday	4	0	2	2	2	5	3	2	0	6
Monday	0	0	0	0	0	3	3	0	0	6
Tuesday	4	4	0	0	8	2	1	1	0	2
Wednesday	3	2	0	1	5	4	3	1	0	6
Thursday	5	5	0	0	10	3	1	1	1	3
Friday	5	4	1	0	8	4	3	1	0	6
Saturday	3	2	1	0	4	3	2	1	0	4

1995 RECORD ON SUCCESSIVE DAYS

1st Game:	6-2-0, 12 points	
2nd Game:	5-2-1, 11 points	

1995 RECORD VS. DIVISIONS

Central:	17-5-2, 36 points;	H: 7-3-2,	R: 10-2-0
Pacific:	16-6-2, 34 points;	H: 10-1-1,	R: 6-5-1

1995 SHOTS BY PERIODS

	1st	2nd	3rd	OT	Total	Avg.	Pctg.
Detroit	554	533	469	15	1571	32.7	11.5
Opponents	362	427	410	7	1206	25.1	9.7

1995 GOALS BY PERIODS

	1st	2nd	3rd	OT	Total	Avg.
Detroit	63	61	56	0	180	3.8
Opponents	42	38	37	0	117	2.4

1995 FIRST GOAL

Scoring First:	22-3-2, 46 points
Opposition Scoring First:	11-8-2, 24 points

1995 HOLDING LEAD

Leading After One Period:	20-1-2, 42 points
Trailing After One Period:	3-6-2, 8 points
Tied After One Period:	10-4-0, 20 points
Leading After Two Periods:	26-0-2, 54 points
Trailing After Two Periods:	2-10-1, 5 points
Tied After Two Periods:	5-1-1, 11 points

1995 CLOSE DECISIONS

One-Goal Games:	7-7, 14 points
Two-Goal Games:	10-1, 20 points

1995 GOAL MARGINS

Scoring 0 Goals:	1 defeat, 0 points
Scoring 1 Goal:	0-4-0, 0 points
Scoring 2 Goals:	2-3-0, 4 points
Scoring 3 Goals:	6-2-1, 13 points
Scoring 4 Goals:	10-0-2, 22 points
Scoring 5 Goals:	9-1-1, 19 points
Scoring 6 Goals:	6-0-0, 12 points
Allowing 0 Goals:	2 shutouts, 4 points
Allowing 1 Goal:	12-0-0, 24 points
Allowing 2 Goals:	13-2-0, 26 points
Allowing 3 Goals:	3-2-1, 7 points
Allowing 4 Goals:	2-5-2, 6 points
Allowing 5 Goals:	1-1-1, 3 points
Allowing 6 Goals:	0-1-0, 0 points

——1995 POWER-PLAY GOALS & PENALTY KILLING——

Red Wings had 52 in 215 attempts,
Power-play percentage, 24.2,
2nd in NHL

Opponents had 28 in 206 attempts,
Penalty killing percentage 86.4,
2nd in NHL

vs. ANAHIEM MIGHTY DUCKS

RED WINGS (4-12) – Coffey,
Kozlov, Sheppard, Yzerman

MIGHTY DUCKS (5-18) – Kariya (2), Dollas,
J. Sacco, Sillinger

vs. CALGARY FLAMES

RED WINGS (1-21) – Fedorov

FLAMES (2-21) – Roberts, Walz

vs. CHICAGO BLACKHAWKS

RED WINGS (5-26) – Yzerman (2),
Ciccarelli, Coffey, Lidstrom

BLACKHAWKS (2-20) – Graham, Poulin

vs. DALLAS STARS

RED WINGS (7-21) – Ciccarelli (2),
Lidstrom (2), Sheppard (2), Fedorov

STARS (2-21) – D. Hatcher, Ledyard

vs. EDMONTON OILERS

RED WINGS (5-20) – Brown, Fedorov,
Kozlov, Lidstrom, Sheppard

OILERS (1-18) – Marchant

vs. LOS ANGELES KINGS

RED WINGS (5-21) – Kozlov (2),
Fedorov, Primeau, Sheppard

KINGS (3-14) – Sydor, Tocchet, Zhitnik

vs. SAN JOSE SHARKS

RED WINGS (5-16) – Sheppard (2),
Ciccarelli, Fetisov, Fedorov

SHARKS (2-14) – Dahlen, Friesen

vs. ST. LOUIS BLUES

RED WINGS (8-27) – Fetisov (2),
Sheppard (2), Ciccarelli, Coffey,
Fedorov, McCarty

BLUES (5-19) – Hull (3), Carbonneau,
Laperriere

vs. TORONTO MAPLE LEAFS

RED WINGS (2-10) – Ciccarelli,
Johnson

MAPLE LEAFS (0-14)

vs. VANCOUVER CANUCKS

RED WINGS (4-16) – Lidstrom (2),
Sheppard, Yzerman

CANUCKS (3-25) – Adams, Momesso, Peca

vs. WINNIPEG JETS

RED WINGS (6-24) – Coffey, Fedorov,
Johnson, Kozlov, Lidstrom, Sheppard

JETS (3-22) – Selanne (2), Tkachuk

1995 RED WINGS' RECORDS BY QUARTERS
(12-game quarters)

OVERALL WON-LOST-TIED
1st Quarter: 7-4-1, 15 points
2nd Quarter: 9-2-1, 19 points
3rd Quarter: 10-1-1, 21 points
4th Quarter: 7-4-1, 15 points
Total: 33-11-4, 70 points

HOME WON-LOST-TIED
1st Quarter: 5-2-1, 11 points
2nd Quarter: 4-1-0, 8 points
3rd Quarter: 5-0-1, 11 points
4th Quarter: 3-1-1, 7 points
Total: 17-4-3, 37 points

ROAD WON-LOST-TIED
1st Quarter: 2-2-0, 4 points
2nd Quarter: 5-1-1, 11 points
3rd Quarter: 5-1-0, 10 points
4th Quarter: 4-3-0, 8 points
Total: 16-7-1, 33 points

GOALS FOR
1st Quarter: 45
2nd Quarter: 47
3rd Quarter: 46
4th Quarter: 42
Total: 180

GOALS AGAINST
1st Quarter: 27
2nd Quarter: 25
3rd Quarter: 29
4th Quarter: 36
Total: 117

POWER PLAY
1st Quarter: 12-for-55, 21.8 percent
2nd Quarter: 15-for-54, 27.8 percent
3rd Quarter: 13-for-52, 25.0 percent
4th Quarter: 12-for-54, 22.2 percent
Total: 52-for-215, 24.2 percent

PENALTY KILLING
1st Quarter: 9 goals, 54 short,
               83.3 percent
2nd Quarter: 4 goals, 46 short,
               91.3 percent
3rd Quarter: 5 goals, 48 short,
               89.6 percent
4th Quarter: 10 goals, 58 short,
               82.8 percent
Total: 28 goals, 206 short,
               86.4 percent

SHORTHANDED GOALS FOR
1st Quarter: 2
2nd Quarter: 1
3rd Quarter: 2
4th Quarter: 0
Total: 5

SHORTHANDED GOALS AGAINST
1st Quarter: 2
2nd Quarter: 2
3rd Quarter: 1
4th Quarter: 2
Total: 7

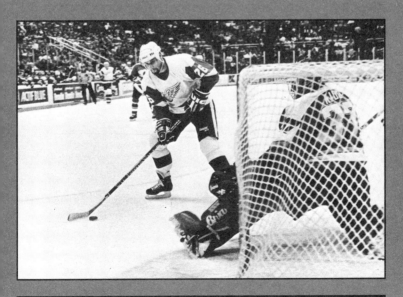

1995 THREE-GOAL OR MORE GAMES

By DETROIT – 2

PLAYER	DATE	OPPONENT	CAREER TOTALS
Fedorov (4)	February 12	Los Angeles	2
Sheppard	January 24	Vancouver	6

By Opponents – 2

Hull (4)	April 16	at St. Louis	23
Tocchet	February 4	at Los Angeles	12

1995 TWO-GOAL GAMES

By DETROIT – 18

Sheppard	5	Errey	1
Yzerman	3	Kozlov	1
Coffey	2	Lidstrom	1
Primeau	2	Sillinger	1
Brown	1		

By Opponents – 9

Kariya, Anaheim	2	Tkachuk, Winnipeg	1
Krugier, Anaheim	1	Corson, Edmonton	1
J. Sacco, Anaheim	1	Oliver, Edmonton	1
Selanne, Winnipeg	1	Todd, Los Angeles	1

1995 SHORTHANDED GOALS

By DETROIT – (5)	By Opponents — (7)	
Fedorov 3 – Los Angeles (2), Edmonton	Hull, St. Louis	2
Brown 1 – Vancouver	Maltby, Edmonton	1
Coffey 1 – Calgary	Buchberger, Edmonton	1
	Titov, Calgary	1
	Amonte, Chicago	1
	Tocchet, Los Angeles	1

PLAYER	*WIN	INS	G-1	D-1	D-0	TIE	LEAD	TOTAL
Sheppard	5 (2)	6	6	7	0	3	8	30
Fedorov	5 (5)	7	2	5	1	2	6	20
Ciccarelli	3 (4)	7	1	1	0	1	1	16
Primeau	3 (3)	4	4	6	1	2	4	15
Coffey	2 (8)	4	1	4	1	2	2	14
Kozlov	3 (4)	2	3	4	0	1	6	13
Yzerman	1 (4)	2	2	3	0	1	2	12
Lidstrom	0 (2)	0	2	5	0	5	3	10
Brown	2 (4)	0	2	3	0	1	4	9
Errey	1 (2)	1	0	0	0	1	2	6
Burr	3 (1)	0	1	1	0	0	4	6
McCarty	2 (1)	1	0	2	0	2	0	5
Lapointe	1 (1)	0	1	1	0	2	2	4
Fetisov	0 (5)	0	1	1	0	1	2	3
Konstantinov	0 (2)	0	1	0	0	0	2	3
Johnson	0 (2)	0	0	1	0	0	0	3
Draper	0 (0)	1	0	0	0	0	0	2
Krushelnyski	0 (1)	1	0	1	1	0	0	2
Sillinger	0 (2)	0	0	0	0	0	0	2
Rouse	1 (1)	1	0	0	0	0	0	1
Howe	1 (1)	0	0	0	0	0	1	1
Carkner	0 (0)	0	0	0	1	0	0	1
Ramsey	0 (0)	0	0	0	0	0	1	1
York	0 (1)	0	1	1	0	0	1	1

WIN–Winning Goal   INS–Insurance Goal   G-1–Game's First Goal   D-1–Detroit's First Goal
D-0–Detroit's Only Goal   TIE–Tying Goal   LEAD–Detroit's Go-Ahead Goal
*-Figure in parentheses denotes assists on winning goals

—————RED WINGS' GOAL-SCORING BREAKDOWN—————

PLAYER	1st	2nd	3rd	OT	HOME	AWAY	MID-YEAR	TOTAL
Sheppard	13	9	8	0	17	13	15	30
Fedorov	7	9	4	0	13	7	13	20
Ciccarelli	3	6	7	0	8	8	10	16
Primeau	7	3	5	0	7	8	5	15
Coffey	6	5	3	0	5	9	4	14
Kozlov	5	3	5	0	8	5	8	13
Yzerman	3	4	5	0	6	6	7	12
Lidstrom	4	5	1	0	5	5	5	10
Brown	3	3	3	0	5	4	7	9
Errey	2	2	2	0	4	2	1	6
Burr	1	5	0	0	4	2	4	6
McCarty	2	2	1	0	3	2	2	5
Lapointe	1	1	2	0	1	3	1	4
Fetisov	1	2	0	0	0	3	0	3
Konstantinov	0	0	3	0	2	1	1	3
Johnson	1	0	2	0	3	0	3	3
Draper	1	0	1	0	2	0	1	2
Krushelnyski	0	0	2	0	1	1	2	2
Sillinger	0	2	0	0	2	0	2	2
Rouse	0	0	1	0	1	0	1	1
Howe	0	0	1	0	0	1	0	1
Carkner	1	0	0	0	1	0	0	1
Ramsey	0	1	0	0	1	0	0	1
York	1	0	0	0	0	1	0	1

DETROIT'S WINNING COMBINATION!

OLYMPIA ARENAS, INC.
and
the DETROIT RED WINGS
DETROIT TIGERS
DETROIT ROCKERS
JOE LOUIS ARENA
COBO ARENA
TIGER STADIUM
FOX THEATRE
THE SECOND CITY

OVER 8 MILLION PEOPLE PASS THROUGH OUR GATES!

The news is getting around that Detroit is doing great business!
Detroit's premier entertainment venues and Pro teams,
make a definitive statement about the City of Detroit
and underscore the talent and experience of the nationally
recognized marketing and promotional staff of
Olympia Arenas, Inc., a full-service management company.

Aside from providing great entertainment, we can also provide
complete services for YOUR entertaining and catering needs.
So host your next function at an OAI venue.

So...the next time you think of entertainment...think

 OLYMPIA ARENAS, INC.
Call for information (313) 396-7600

TEAM HISTORY

The greatest of 'em all — Gordie Howe

Sid Abel's number was retired last April 29, reuniting him with Production Line teammates Gordie Howe and Ted Lindsay, whose Nos. 9 and 7 hang in rafters with No. 10 Alex Delvecchio, No. 1 Terry Sawchuk.

————————RED WINGS' HISTORY————————

This is the 70th anniversary season of NHL hockey in Detroit as the Red Wings continue to soar among the league's elite teams.

Last season was one of the most exciting in years. Detroit won the President's Trophy with the league's best record, posting a 33-11-4 mark for 70 points. The club went on to capture the Clarence Campbell Bowl as Western Conference playoff champions and earned a berth in the Stanley Cup final for the first time since 1966. Being swept by New Jersey in the final was disappointing but took only some luster off an otherwise brilliant season.

It was the second year in a row Detroit paced the Western Conference during regular-season action. In winning the Central Division title, the club finished first in its division for the second consecutive season, the third time in four years and fifth in the previous eight.

The Red Wings remained an offensive powerhouse in 1995, ranking third in the NHL with 180 goals in the lockout-shortened 48-game season after leading the league the previous two years. Detroit's power play was a potent force, tying for second with a 24.2 percentage. Perhaps more impressive was the team's stingy defensive play. The Red Wings were second in the league with a 2.42 goals-against average and second in penalty killing at 86.4 percent.

Detroit fans continued to flock to Joe Louis Arena. Although no attendance records were set in '95 because of the lockout caused by a labor dispute between owners and players, the club drew 474,714 in 24 home games for an average of 19,780 (more than the arena capacity of 19,275). Detroit had set the NHL attendance record in 1993-94 when 812,640 viewed 41 regular-season games for an average of 19,820 per game. Entering this season, including regular season and playoffs, the Red Wings have drawn more than 19,000 for 348 of their last 350 games, including 236 in a row.

One of the most important dates in recent club history was June 22, 1982, when Mike Ilitch purchased a struggling franchise and transformed it into the one of the NHL's best. In Ilitch's 13 years as owner, the club has won five division titles (87-88, 88-89, 91-92, 93-94, 95) and made three trips to the conference playoff final ('87, '88, '95). Ten times the team has made the playoffs in that stretch, including eight of the past nine years.

Detroit's love affair with hockey goes back to the late 1920s and has continued to the present at Joe Louis Arena, which opened for hockey Dec. 27, 1979. The area also has some of North America's finest youth programs, producing future players and cultivating lifelong fans.

Pro hockey arrived in Detroit Sept. 25, 1926, when a group of Detroit businessmen purchased an NHL franchise and stocked it with players from the Victoria Cougars of the Western Hockey League. The club was called the Detroit Cougars but played its inaugural season across the Detroit River in Canada at Windsor's Border Cities Arena.

The Cougars' first NHL game was Nov. 18, 1926, in which they dropped a 2-0 decision to the Boston Bruins. Detroit won the next game, 4-2 against the New York Americans, but finished last with a 12-28-4 record.

The Cougars moved into legendary Olympia Stadium on Grand River Avenue for their second season and played the first game there Nov. 22, 1927. Detroit's Johnny Sheppard scored the first goal, but the Cougars suffered a 2-1 loss to the defending champion Ottawa Senators. Detroit registered its first home victory and shutout Nov. 27 as goaltender "Hap" Holmes posted a 2-0 decision over the Montreal Canadiens.

Arriving in 1927-28 was Jack Adams, whose 35-year career with the club left an indelible mark on hockey in Detroit and earned him a niche in the Hockey Hall of Fame.

In 1928-29, Detroit finished third and made the first of 44 playoff appearances in 69 seasons. The team changed its name to Falcons in 1930 when some Detroit media members thought a change might bring some luck to a club that had missed the playoffs the previous season. No luck, however, as Detroit again missed the playoffs, although the Falcons did gain a berth in 1931-32.

In the summer of 1932, American industrialist James Norris bought the franchise and renamed it Red Wings. He imported the name from Canada, where he had played hockey for a club called the Winged Wheelers in the Montreal Athletic Association. That team's insignia — a winged wheel — struck Norris as a natural for a club representing the Motor City. The logo became an automobile tire with a flying wing attached and has remained the same except for minor artistic variations.

The Red Wings became an NHL power under Norris and Adams. In 1933-34, they won the first of 14 regular-season NHL titles and reached the Stanley Cup final for the first time before bowing to the Chicago Blackhawks, three games to one, in a best-of-five series.

The Red Wings dominated the NHL in 1935-36 and 36-37, winning a pair of regular-season championships and their first two Stanley Cup titles — a prize the club has won seven times. Detroit won its third Cup championship in 1943, but the best was yet to come.

Adams assembled a team in the late '40s that ranks among the NHL's greatest dynasties. Between the 1948-49 and 54-55 seasons, the Red Wings won seven consecutive regular-season titles — still a league record — and four Stanley Cup championships.

Detroit remained strong through the late 1950s and into the '60s, winning two more regular-season titles but bowing four times in the Cup final during that span.

The Norris family retained ownership of the team for 50 years. The elder Norris served as club president until his death in 1952 and was succeeded by his daughter, Marguerite. Norris' son, Bruce, took over as president in 1955 and remained until selling the club to Ilitch in '82.

The Red Wings have featured some of the game's brightest stars — including the greatest of them all, Gordie Howe — and continue to showcase some of the world's best players. Forty-six people associated with the club are in the Hockey Hall of Fame. Detroit players have been voted to postseason NHL All-Star teams 92 times, and club players, coaches and executives have won 51 individual league trophies.

Season	GP	W	L	T	PTS	GF	GA	Position	Coach
1926-27	44	12	28	4	28	76	105	5th×	Art Duncan/Duke Keats*
1927-28	44	19	19	6	44	88	79	4th×	Jack Adams
1928-29	44	19	16	9	47	72	63	3rd	Adams
1929-30	44	14	24	6	34	117	133	4th×	Adams
1930-31	44	16	21	7	39	102	105	4th×	Adams
1931-32	48	18	20	10	46	95	108	3rd	Adams
1932-33	48	25	15	8	58	111	93	2nd	Adams
1933-34	48	24	14	10	58	113	98	1st	Adams
1934-35	48	19	22	7	45	127	114	4th×	Adams
1935-36	48	24	16	8	56	124	103	1st-SC	Adams
1936-37	48	25	14	9	59	128	102	1st-SC	Adams
1937-38	48	12	25	11	35	99	133	4th×	Adams
1938-39	48	18	24	6	42	107	128	5th	Adams
1939-40	48	16	26	6	38	90	126	5th	Adams
1940-41	48	21	16	11	53	112	102	3rd	Adams
1941-42	48	19	25	4	42	140	147	5th	Adams
1942-43	50	25	14	11	61	169	124	1st-SC	Adams
1943-44	50	26	18	6	58	214	177	2nd	Adams
1944-45	50	31	14	5	67	218	161	2nd	Adams
1945-46	50	20	20	10	50	146	159	4th	Adams
1946-47	60	22	27	11	55	190	193	4th	Adams
1947-48	60	30	18	12	72	187	148	2nd	Tom Ivan
1948-49	60	34	19	7	75	195	145	1st	Ivan
1949-50	70	37	19	14	88	229	164	1st-SC	Ivan
1950-51	70	44	13	13	101	236	139	1st	Ivan
1951-52	70	44	14	12	100	215	133	1st-SC	Ivan
1952-53	70	36	16	18	90	222	133	1st	Ivan
1953-54	70	37	19	14	88	191	132	1st-SC	Ivan
1954-55	70	42	17	11	95	204	134	1st-SC	Jimmy Skinner
1955-56	70	30	24	16	76	183	148	2nd	Skinner
1956-57	70	38	20	12	88	198	157	1st	Skinner
1957-58	70	29	29	12	70	176	207	3rd	Skinner/Sid Abel
1958-59	70	25	37	8	58	167	218	6th×	Abel
1959-60	70	26	29	15	67	186	197	4th	Abel
1960-61	70	25	29	16	66	195	215	4th	Abel
1961-62	70	23	33	14	60	184	219	5th×	Abel
1962-63	70	32	25	13	77	200	194	4th	Abel
1963-64	70	30	29	11	71	191	204	4th	Abel
1964-65	70	40	23	7	87	224	175	1st	Abel
1965-66	70	31	27	12	74	221	194	4th	Abel
1966-67	70	27	39	4	58	212	241	5th×	Abel
1967-68	74	27	35	12	66	245	257	6th×	Abel
1968-69	76	33	31	12	78	239	221	5th×	Bill Gadsby
1969-70	76	40	21	15	95	246	199	3rd	Gadsby/Abel
1970-71	78	22	45	11	55	209	308	7th×	Ned Harkness/Doug Barkley
1971-72	78	33	35	10	76	261	262	5th×	Barkley/JohnnyWilson
1972-73	78	37	29	12	86	265	243	5th×	Wilson
1973-74	78	29	39	10	68	255	319	6th×	Ted Garvin/Alex Delvecchio
1974-75	80	23	45	12	58	259	335	4th×	Delvecchio
1975-76	80	26	44	10	62	226	300	4th×	Barkley/Delvecchio/Billy Dea*
1976-77	80	16	55	9	41	183	309	5th×	Dea*/Larry Wilson
1977-78	80	32	34	14	78	252	266	2nd	Bobby Kromm
1978-79	80	23	41	16	62	252	295	5th×	Kromm
1979-80	80	26	43	11	63	268	306	5th×	Kromm/Marcel Pronovost*
1980-81	80	19	43	18	56	252	339	5th×	Ted Lindsay/Wayne Maxner
1981-82	80	21	47	12	54	270	351	6th×	Maxner/Dea
1982-83	80	21	44	15	57	263	344	5th×	Nick Polano
1983-84	80	31	42	7	69	298	323	3rd	Polano
1984-85	80	27	41	12	66	313	357	3rd	Polano
1985-86	80	17	57	6	40	266	415	5th×	Harry Neale/Brad Park
1986-87	80	34	36	10	78	260	274	2nd	Jacques Demers
1987-88	80	41	28	11	93	322	269	1st	Demers
1988-89	80	34	34	12	80	313	316	1st	Demers
1989-90	80	28	38	14	70	288	323	5th×	Demers
1990-91	80	34	38	8	76	273	298	3rd	Bryan Murray
1991-92	80	43	25	12	98	320	256	1st	Murray
1992-93	84	47	28	9	103	369	280	2nd	Murray
1993-94	84	46	30	8	100	356	275	1st	Scotty Bowman
1995	48	33	11	4	70	180	117	1st	Bowman
TOTALS	4582	1928	1936	718	4574	14157	14207		

×-Out of playoffs   **SC**-Won Stanley Cup   *-Interim coach

1st-18   2nd-8   3rd-8   4th-14   5th-16   6th-4   7th-1

——RED WINGS' ALL-TIME HOME-AWAY RECORDS——

HOME						AWAY			
Won	Lost	Tied	Pts	Season	Games	Won	Lost	Tied	Pts
6	16	0	12	1926-27	44	6	12	4	16
9	10	3	21	1927-28	44	10	9	3	23
11	6	5	27	1928-29	44	8	10	4	20
9	10	3	21	1929-30	44	5	14	3	13
10	7	5	25	1930-31	44	6	14	2	14
15	3	6	36	1931-32	48	3	17	4	10
17	3	4	38	1932-33	48	8	12	4	20
15	5	4	34	1933-34	48	9	9	6	24
11	8	5	27	1934-35	48	8	14	2	18
14	5	5	33	1935-46	48	10	11	3	23
14	5	5	33	1936-37	48	11	9	4	26
8	10	6	22	1937-38	48	4	15	5	13
14	8	2	30	1938-39	48	4	16	4	12
11	10	3	25	1939-40	48	5	16	3	13
14	5	5	33	1940-41	48	7	11	6	20
14	7	3	31	1941-42	48	5	18	1	11
16	4	5	37	1942-43	50	9	10	6	24
18	5	2	38	1943-44	50	8	13	4	20
19	5	1	39	1944-45	50	12	9	4	28
16	5	4	36	1945-46	50	4	15	6	14
14	10	6	34	1946-47	60	8	17	5	21
16	9	5	37	1947-48	60	14	9	7	35
21	6	3	45	1948-49	60	13	13	4	30
19	9	7	45	1949-50	70	18	10	7	43
25	3	7	57	1950-51	70	19	10	6	44
24	7	4	52	1951-52	70	20	7	8	48
20	5	10	50	1952-51	70	19	11	8	40
24	4	7	55	1953-54	70	13	15	7	33
25	5	5	55	1954-55	70	17	12	6	40
21	6	8	50	1955-56	70	9	18	8	26
23	7	5	51	1956-57	70	15	13	7	37
16	11	8	40	1957-58	70	12	18	4	30
13	17	5	31	1958-59	70	12	20	3	27
18	14	3	39	1959-60	70	8	15	12	28
15	13	7	37	1960-61	70	10	16	9	29
17	11	7	41	1961-62	70	6	22	7	19
19	10	6	44	1962-63	70	13	15	7	33
23	9	3	49	1963-64	70	7	20	8	22
25	7	3	53	1964-65	70	15	16	4	34
20	8	7	47	1965-66	70	11	19	5	27
21	11	3	45	1966-67	70	6	28	1	13
18	15	4	40	1967-68	74	9	20	8	26
23	8	7	53	1968-69	76	10	23	5	25
20	11	7	47	1969-70	76	20	10	8	48
17	15	7	41	1970-71	78	5	30	4	14
25	11	3	53	1971-72	78	8	24	7	23
22	12	5	49	1972-73	78	15	17	7	37
21	12	6	48	1973-74	78	8	27	4	20
17	17	6	40	1974-75	80	6	28	6	18
17	15	8	42	1975-76	80	9	29	2	20
12	22	6	30	1976-77	80	4	33	3	11
22	11	7	51	1977-78	80	10	23	7	27
15	17	8	38	1978-79	80	8	24	8	24
14	21	5	33	1979-80	80	12	22	6	30
16	15	9	41	1980-81	80	3	28	9	15
15	19	6	36	1981-82	80	6	28	6	18
14	19	7	35	1982-83	80	7	25	8	22
18	20	2	38	1983-84	80	13	22	5	31
19	14	7	45	1984-85	80	8	27	5	21
10	26	4	24	1985-86	80	7	31	2	16
20	14	6	46	1986-87	80	14	22	4	32
24	10	6	54	1987-88	80	17	18	5	39
20	14	6	46	1988-89	80	14	20	6	34
20	14	6	46	1989-90	80	8	24	8	24
26	14	0	52	1990-91	80	8	24	8	24
24	12	4	52	1991-92	80	19	13	8	46
25	14	3	53	1992-93	84	22	14	6	50
23	13	6	52	1993-94	84	23	17	2	48
17	4	3	37	1995	48	16	7	1	33

DETROIT RED WINGS VS. ALL NHL TEAMS

SINCE 1926-27 SEASON

Detroit Red Wings vs.	GP	W	L	T	PTS
Chicago Blackhawks	623	311	236	76	698
Toronto Maple Leafs	607	256	262	89	601
New York Rangers	554	245	206	103	593
Boston Bruins	557	235	227	95	565
Montreal Canadiens	548	187	265	96	470
+Dallas Stars	171	70	75	26	166
St. Louis Blues	171	60	85	26	146
Pittsburgh Penguins	115	50	50	15	115
Vancouver Canucks	95	45	37	13	103
Los Angeles Kings	123	41	62	20	102
Philadelphia Flyers	103	36	47	20	92
*Calgary Flames	83	32	39	12	76
Washington Capitals	78	31	33	14	76
Buffalo Sabres	92	31	49	12	74
New York Islanders	75	33	38	4	70
#New Jersey Devils	65	28	27	10	66
Winnipeg Jets	59	25	22	12	62
Quebec Nordiques	45	20	21	4	44
Edmonton Oilers	52	19	27	6	44
Hartford Whalers	45	17	21	7	41
San Jose Sharks	15	13	1	1	27
Tampa Bay Lightning	10	8	2	0	16
Anaheim Mighty Ducks	8	6	0	2	14
Ottawa Senators	4	3	1	0	6
Florida Panthers	2	2	0	0	4
Defunct Teams (*a*)	282	124	103	55	303
TOTALS	**4582**	**1928**	**1936**	**718**	**4574**

+-Formerly Minnesota North Stars.
*-Formerly Atlanta Flames.
#-Formerly Kansas City Scouts, Colorado Rockies.
(*a*)-Includes records vs. Montreal Maroons, New York Americans, Ottawa Senators (1917-31), Pittsburgh Pirates, Philadelphia Quakers, St. Louis Eagles, California Golden Seals and Cleveland Barons.

HOME

Detroit Red Wings vs.	GP	W	L	T	PTS
Chicago Blackhawks	311	191	92	28	410
Toronto Maple Leafs	304	160	101	45	365
New York Rangers	278	158	75	45	361
Boston Bruins	278	151	76	51	353
Montreal Canadiens	274	125	96	53	303
@ Dallas Stars	85	43	30	12	98
Pittsburgh Penguins	58	36	11	11	83
St. Louis Blues	85	35	37	13	83
Vancouver Canucks	48	29	13	6	64
Los Angeles Kings	61	25	27	9	59
Philadelphia Flyers	51	24	18	9	57
Buffalo Sabres	47	24	18	5	53
★ Calgary Flames	41	21	13	7	49
Washington Capitals	40	17	13	10	44
New York Islanders	37	19	16	2	40
# New Jersey Devils	32	18	12	2	38
Winnipeg Jets	31	17	10	4	38
Hartford Whalers	23	10	7	6	26
Quebec Nordiques	22	12	9	1	25
Edmonton Oilers	26	11	13	2	24
San Jose Sharks	7	7	0	0	14
Anaheim Mighty Ducks	4	3	0	1	7
Tampa Bay Lightning	4	3	1	0	6
Ottawa Senators	2	2	0	0	4
Florida Panthers	2	1	0	0	2
(a)Defunct Teams	141	76	40	25	177
TOTALS	2291	1216	728	347	2779

ROAD

Detroit Red Wings vs.	GP	W	L	T	PTS
Chicago Blackhawks	312	120	144	48	288
Toronto Maple Leafs	303	98	161	44	240
New York Rangers	276	87	131	58	232
Boston Bruins	279	84	151	44	212
Montreal Canadiens	274	62	169	43	167
@ Dallas Stars	86	27	45	14	68
St. Louis Blues	86	25	48	13	63
Los Angeles Kings	62	16	35	11	43
Vancouver Canucks	47	16	24	7	39
Philadelphia Flyers	52	12	29	11	35
Washington Capitals	38	14	20	4	32
Pittsburgh Penguins	57	14	39	4	32
New York Islanders	38	14	22	2	30
# New Jersey Devils	33	10	15	8	28
★ Calgary Flames	42	11	26	5	27
Winnipeg Jets	28	8	12	8	24
Buffalo Sabres	45	7	31	7	21
Edmonton Oilers	26	8	14	4	20
Quebec Nordiques	23	8	12	3	19
Hartford Whalers	22	7	14	1	15
San Jose Sharks	8	6	1	1	13
Tampa Bay Lightning	6	5	1	0	10
Anaheim Mighty Ducks	4	3	0	1	7
Ottawa Senators	2	1	1	0	2
Florida Panthers	1	1	0	0	2
(a)Defunct Teams	141	48	63	30	126
TOTALS	2291	712	1208	371	1795

@ -Formerly Minnesota North Stars.
★ -Formerly Atlanta Flames.
-Formerly Kansas City Scouts, Colorado Rockies.
(a)-Includes records vs. Montreal Maroons, New York Americans, Ottawa Senators (1917-31), Pittsburgh Pirates, Philadelphia Quakers, St. Louis Eagles, California Golden Seals and Cleveland Barons.

	GC	W	L	T
ART DUNCAN, 1926-27 (First 33 games)	33	10	21	2
* DUKE KEATS, 1926-27 (Final 11 games)	11	2	7	2
JACK ADAMS, 1927-28 through 1946-47	964	413	390	161
TOMMY IVAN, 1947-48 through 1953-54	470	262	118	90
JIMMY SKINNER, 1954-55 to 1957-58 (First 38 games)	248	123	79	46
SID ABEL, 1957-58 (Final 32 games) through 1967-68& 1969-70 (Final 74 games)	810	340	338	132
BILL GADSBY, 1968-69 to1969-70 (First 2 games)	78	35	31	12
NED HARKNESS, 1970-71 (First 38 games)	38	12	22	4
DOUG BARKLEY, 1970-71 (Final 40 games), 1971-72 (First 11 games) & 1975-76 (First 26 games)	77	20	46	11
JOHNNY WILSON, 1971-72 (Final 67 games) through 1972-73	145	67	56	22
TED GARVIN, 1973-74 (First 11 games)	11	2	8	1
ALEX DELVECCHIO, 1973-74 (Final 67 games) through 1974-75 & 1975-76 (9 games)	156	53	82	21
**BILLY DEA, 1975-76 (Final 45 games), 1976-77 (First 44 games) & 1981-82 (Final 11 games)	100	32	57	11
LARRY WILSON, 1976-77 (Final 36 games)	36	3	29	4
BOBBY KROMM, 1977-78 through 1978-79, & 1979-80 (First 71 games)	231	79	111	41
***MARCEL PRONOVOST, 1979-80 (Final 9 games)	9	2	7	0
TED LINDSAY, 1980-81 (First 20 games)	20	3	14	3
WAYNE MAXNER, 1980-81 (Final 20 games) & 1981-82 (First 69 games)	129	34	68	27
NICK POLANO, 1982-83 through 1984-85	240	79	127	34
HARRY NEALE, 1985-86 (First 35 games)	35	8	23	4
BRAD PARK, 1985-86 (45 games)	45	9	36	2
JACQUES DEMERS, 1986-87 to 1989-90	320	137	136	47
BRYAN MURRAY, 1990-91 to 1992-93	244	124	91	29
SCOTTY BOWMAN, 1993-94 to present	132	79	41	12
TOTALS	**4582**	**1928**	**1936**	**726**

*-Art Duncan remained general manager/player but gave coaching duties to Duke Keats.

**-Alex Delvecchio officially was head coach late in 75-76 season and early 76-77, but Billy Dea worked behind bench. In 81-82, Dea replaced the fired Wayne Maxner late in season.

***-Ted Lindsay officially was head coach but Marcel Pronovost worked behind bench.

RED WINGS' ALL-TIME GENERAL MANAGERS

ART DUNCAN, 1926-27
JACK ADAMS, 1927-28 through 1962-63
SID ABEL, 1963-64 to 1970-71 (First 38 games)
NED HARKNESS, 1970-71 (Final 40 games) through 1973-74
ALEX DELVECCHIO, 1974-75 to 1976-77 (First 70 games)
TED LINDSAY, 1976-77 (Final 10 games) through 1979-80
JIMMY SKINNER, 1980-81 through 1981-82
JIM DEVELLANO, 1982-83 to 1989-90
BRYAN MURRAY, 1990-91 to 1993-94
JIM DEVELLANO, 1994-95 to present (Senior Vice-President)

RED WINGS' ALL-TIME TEAM CAPTAINS

1926-27 — Art Duncan
1927-28 — Reg Noble
1928-29 — Reg Noble
1929-30 — Reg Noble
1930-31 — George Hay
1931-32 — Carson Cooper
1932-33 — Larry Aurie
1933-34 — Herbie Lewis
1934-35 — Ebbie Goodfellow
1935-36 — Doug Young
1936-37 — Doug Young
1937-38 — Doug Young
1938-39 — Ebbie Goodfellow
1939-40 — Ebbie Goodfellow
1940-41 — Ebbie Goodfellow
1941-42 — Ebbie Goodfellow, Syd Howe
1942-43 — Sid Abel
1943-44 — Mud Bruneteau, Bill Hollett
1944-45 — Bill Hollett
1945-46 — Bill Hollett, Sid Abel
1946-47 — Sid Abel
1947-48 — Sid Abel
1948-49 — Sid Abel
1949-50 — Sid Abel
1950-51 — Sid Abel
1951-52 — Sid Abel
1952-53 — Ted Lindsay
1953-54 — Ted Lindsay
1954-55 — Ted Lindsay
1955-56 — Ted Lindsay
1956-57 — Red Kelly
1957-58 — Red Kelly
1958-59 — Gordie Howe
1959-60 — Gordie Howe
1960-61 — Gordie Howe
1961-62 — Gordie Howe
1962-63 — Alex Delvecchio

1963-64 — Alex Delvecchio
1964-65 — Alex Delvecchio
1965-66 — Alex Delvecchio
1966-67 — Alex Delvecchio
1967-68 — Alex Delvecchio
1968-69 — Alex Delvecchio
1969-70 — Alex Delvecchio
1970-71 — Alex Delvecchio
1971-72 — Alex Delvecchio
1972-73 — Alex Delvecchio
1973-74 — Alex Delvecchio, Nick Libett,
            Red Berenson, Gary Bergman,
            Ted Harris, Mickey Redmond,
            Larry Johnston
1974-75 — Marcel Dionne
1975-76 — Danny Grant, Terry Harper
1976-77 — Danny Grant, Dennis Polonich
1977-78 — Dan Maloney, Dennis Hextall
1978-79 — Dennis Hextall, Nick Libett,
            Paul Woods
1979-80 — Dale McCourt
1980-81 — Errol Thompson, Reed Larson
1981-82 — Reed Larson
1982-83 — Danny Gare
1983-84 — Danny Gare
1984-85 — Danny Gare
1985-86 — Danny Gare
1986-87 — Steve Yzerman
1887-88 — Steve Yzerman
1988-89 — Steve Yzerman
1889-90 — Steve Yzerman
1990-91 — Steve Yzerman
1991-92 — Steve Yzerman
1992-93 — Steve Yzerman
1993-94 — Steve Yzerman
1995   — Steve Yzerman

SEASON

MOST POINTS – 103 – 1992-93
FEWEST POINTS – 28 – 1926-27
MOST WINS – 47 – 1992-93
FEWEST WINS – 12 – 1926-27, 37-38
MOST DEFEATS – 57 – 1985-86
FEWEST DEFEATS – 11 – 1995
MOST TIES – 18 – 1952-53, 80-81
FEWEST TIES – 4 – 1926-27, 66-67. 95
MOST WINS, HOME – 26 – 1990-91
MOST DEFEATS, HOME – 26 – 1985-86
MOST TIES, HOME – 10 – 1952-53
MOST WINS, ROAD – 23 – 1993-94
MOST DEFEATS, ROAD – 33 – 1976-77
MOST GOALS FOR – 369 – 1992-93
MOST GOALS AGAINST – 415 – 1985-86
FEWEST GOALS FOR – 72 – 1928-29
FEWEST GOALS AGAINST – 63 – 1928-29
MOST POWER-PLAY GOALS FOR – 113 – 1992-93
MOST POWER-PLAY GOALS AGAINST – 111 – 1985-86
MOST SHORTHANDED GOALS FOR – 22 – 1993-94
MOST SHORTHANDED GOALS AGAINST – 15 – 1984-85
MOST PENALTY MINUTES – 2393 – 1985-86
MOST SHUTOUTS – 13 – 1953-54
FEWEST SHUTOUTS – 0 – 1980-81, 81-82, 84-85
LONGEST UNBEATEN STREAK – 15 games
(8 wins, 7 ties) – Nov. 27-Dec. 28, 1952
LONGEST WINNING STREAK – 9 games (twice) –
Mar. 3-21, 1951; Feb. 27-Mar. 20, 1955
LONGEST UNBEATEN STREAK, HOME – 18 games
(13 wins, 5 ties) – Dec. 26-Mar. 20, 1955
LONGEST WINNING STREAK, HOME – 14 games –
Jan. 21-Mar. 25, 1965
LONGEST UNBEATEN STREAK, ROAD – 15 games
(10 wins, 5 ties) – Oct. 18-Dec. 26, 1951
LONGEST WINNING STREAK, ROAD – 7 games –
Mar. 25-Apr. 14, 1995
LONGEST UNBEATEN STREAK, START OF SEASON
– 10 games (8 wins, 2 ties) – Oct. 11-Nov. 4, 1962
LONGEST WINNING STREAK, START OF SEASON –
6 games – Oct. 7-22, 1972

LONGEST HOME UNBEATEN STREAK,
START OF SEASON – 17 games (13 wins, 4 ties) –
Oct. 11-Dec. 25, 1956
LONGEST HOME WINNING STREAK,
START OF SEASON – 6 games (twice) –
Oct. 14-Nov. 4, 1962; Oct. 10-26, 1990
LONGEST ROAD UNBEATEN STREAK,
START OF SEASON – 15 games (11 wins, 4 ties) –
Oct. 18-Dec. 20, 1951
LONGEST ROAD WINNING STREAK,
START OF SEASON – 4 games (twice) –
Oct. 27-Nov. 12, 1949; Oct. 18-Nov. 3, 1951
LONGEST WINLESS STREAK – 19 games
(18 losses, 1 tie) – Feb. 26-Apr. 3, 1977
LONGEST LOSING STREAK – 14 games –
Feb. 24-Mar. 25, 1982
Longest Winless Streak, Home – 10 games
(9 losses, 1 tie) – Dec. 11, 1985-Jan. 18, 1986
LONGEST LOSING STREAK, HOME – 7 games –
Feb. 20-Mar. 25, 1982
LONGEST WINLESS STREAK, ROAD – 26 games
(23 losses, 3 ties) – Dec. 15, 1976-Apr. 3, 1977
LONGEST LOSING STREAK, ROAD – 14 games –
Oct. 19-Dec. 21, 1966
LONGEST WINLESS STREAK, START OF SEASON –
10 games (7 losses, 3 ties) – Oct. 8-26, 1975
LONGEST LOSING STREAK, START OF SEASON –
5 games – Oct. 10-18, 1980
LONGEST HOME WINLESS STREAK,
START OF SEASON – 5 games (twice) – Oct. 8-25,
1975 (2 losses, 3 ties); Oct. 10-23, 1985 (1 loss, 4 ties)
LONGEST HOME LOSING STREAK, START OF
SEASON – 3 games (four times) – Nov. 14-26, 1929;
Nov. 6-13, 1938; Oct. 10-17, 1957; Oct. 6-20, 1982
LONGEST ROAD WINLESS STREAK, START OF
SEASON – 19 games (*8 losses, 1 tie) –
Oct. 19, 1966-Jan. 14, 1967
LONGEST ROAD LOSING STREAK, START OF
SEASON – 14 games – Oct. 19-Dec. 21, 1966
MOST PLAYERS – 45 1990-91

GAME

MOST GOALS FOR – 15 vs. N.Y. Rangers at Detroit, Jan. 23, 19(4; Detroit 15, Rangers 0
MOST GOALS AGAINST – 13 by Toronto at Toronto, Jan. 2, 1971; Toronto 13, Detroit 0
MOST POINTS – 37 vs. N.Y. Rangers at Detroit, Jan. 23, 1944
MOST GOALS, ONE PERIOD – 8 vs. N.Y. Rangers at Detroit, Jan. 23, 1944
MOST POINTS, ONE PERIOD – 22 vs. N.Y. Rangers at Detroit, Jan. 23, 1944
FASTEST TWO GOALS, START OF GAME – 37 seconds apart – Dec. 4. 1987 vs. Chicago (Tim Higgins, STEVE YZERMAN)
FASTEST TWO GOALS – 7 seconds apart – Nov. 5, 1936 vs. Toronto (Syd Howe, Larry Aurie); Nov. 25, 1987 vs. Winnipeg (Jeff Sharples, Brent Ashton)
FASTEST THREE GOALS – 28 seconds apart – Nov. 16, 1944 vs. Toronto (Hal Jackson, Steve Wochy, Don Grosso)
FASTEST FOUR GOALS – 2:25 apart – Nov. 7, 1991 vs. St. Louis (Shawn Burr, Jimmy Carson, NICKLAS LIDSTROM, Paul Ysebaert)
FASTEST FIVE GOALS – 4:54 apart – Nov. 25, 1987 vs. Winnipeg (Gerard Gallant, Adam Oates, Mel Bridgman, Jeff Sharples, Brent Ashton)
MOST POWER-PLAY GOALS – 6 vs N.Y. Rangers, Nov. 5, 1942; Detroit 12, Rangers 5

ACTIVE PLAYERS IN CAPITALS

MOST POWER-PLAY GOALS, ONE PERIOD – 4
vs. N.Y. Rangers, Nov. 5, 1942; Detroit 12, Rangers 5
MOST POWER-PLAY GOALS AGAINST – 5 (four times) –
vs. Buffalo, Feb. 1, 1987, Buffalo 6, Detroit 1;
vs. Chicago, Nov. 11, 1987, Chicago 6, Detroit 3;
vs. St. Louis, Jan. 25, 1991, St. Louis 9, Detroit 4;
vs. Toronto, Dec. 9, 1992, Toronto 5, Detroit 3
MOST POWER-PLAY GOALS AGAINST, ONE PERIOD –
3 (several times) – Last time vs. St. Louis, Nov. 25,
1992, Detroit 11, St. Louis 6
MOST SHORTHANDED GOALS – 3 (three times) –
vs. Minnesota, Jan. 9, 1990 (Shawn Burr 2, STEVE
YZERMAN), Detroit 9, Minnesota 0; vs. Minnesota,
Apr. 14, 1992 (STEVE YZERMAN 2, SERGEI
FEDOROV), Detroit 7, Minnesota 4; vs. Philadelphia,
Feb. 11, 1994 (SERGEI FEDOROV, VYACHESLAV
KOZLOV, STEVE YZERMAN), Detroit 6, Philadelphia 3
MOST SHORTHANDED GOALS, ONE PERIOD – 2
(several times) – Last time vs. Philadelphia, Feb. 11,
1994 (SERGEI FEDOROV, VYACHESLAV KOZLOV),
Detroit 6, Philadelphia 3
MOST SHORTHANDED GOALS AGAINST – 2 (several
times) – Last time vs. NY Rangers, Feb. 9, 1992,
Detroit 5, NY Rangers 5
MOST SHORTHANDED GOALS AGAINST, ONE
PERIOD – 2 (several times) – Last time vs. NY
Rangers, Feb. 9, 1992, Detroit 5, NY Rangers 5

RED WINGS' INDIVIDUAL RECORDS

CAREER

MOST GAMES – 1687 – Gordie Howe (25 seasons)
MOST GAMES BY GOALIE – 734 – Terry Sawchuk
MOST CONSECUTIVE GAMES – 548 – Alex Delvecchio
MOST GOALS – 786 – Gordie Howe (25 seasons)
MOST ASSISTS – 1023 – Gordie Howe (25 seasons)
MOST POINTS – 1809 – Gordie Howe (25 seasons)
MOST PENALTY MINUTES – 2090 – Bob Probert
MOST SHUTOUTS – Terry Sawchuk – 85
MOST POWER-PLAY GOALS – 211 – Gordie Howe
MOST POWER-PLAY GOALS BY DEFENSEMAN – 68 – Reed Larson
MOST SEASONS LEADING TEAM IN POWER-PLAY GOALS – 13 – Gordie Howe
MOST SHORTHANDED GOALS – 41 – STEVE YZERMAN
MOST 3-GOAL OR MORE GAMES – 18 – Gordie Howe, STEVE YZERMAN
MOST WINNING GOALS – 121 – Gordie Howe
MOST SEASONS LEADING TEAM IN WINNING GOALS – 12 – Gordie Howe
MOST ASSISTS BY GOALIE – 15 – Tim Cheveldae

SEASON

MOST GOALS – 65 – STEVE YZERMAN (1988-89)
MOST ASSISTS – 90 – STEVE YZERMAN (1988-89)
MOST POINTS – 155 – STEVE YZERMAN (1988-89)
MOST GOALS BY LINE – 140 (1988-89) (STEVE YZERMAN, 65; Gerard Gallant, 39; Paul MacLean, 36)
MOST POINTS BY LINE – 319 (1988-89) (STEVE YZERMAN, 155; Gerard Gallant, 93; Paul MacLean, 71)
MOST GOALS BY CENTER – 65 – STEVE YZERMAN (1988-89)
MOST GOALS BY RIGHT WING – 52 – Mickey Redmond (1972-73); RAY SHEPPARD (1993-94)
MOST GOALS BY LEFT WING – 55 – John Ogrodnick (1984-85)
MOST GOALS BY DEFENSEMAN – 27 – Reed Larson (1980-81)
MOST GOALS BY ROOKIE – 39 – STEVE YZERMAN (1983-84)
MOST GOALS BY ROOKIE DEFENSEMAN – 19 – Reed Larson (1977-78)
MOST ASSISTS BY CENTER – 90 – STEVE YZERMAN (1988-89)
MOST ASSISTS BY RIGHT WING – 59 – Gordie Howe (1968-69)
MOST ASSISTS BY LEFT WING – 55 – Ted Lindsay (1949-50, 56-57)
MOST ASSISTS BY DEFENSEMAN – 63 – PAUL COFFEY (1993-94)
MOST ASSISTS BY GOALTENDER – 5 – Tim Cheveldae (1990-91)
MOST ASSISTS BY ROOKIE – 49 – Marcel Dionne (1971-72); NICKLAS LIDSTROM (1991-92)
MOST ASSISTS BY ROOKIE DEFENSEMAN – 49 – NICKLAS LIDSTROM (1991-92)
MOST POINTS BY CENTER – 155 – STEVE YZERMAN (1988-89)
MOST POINTS BY RIGHT WING – 103 – Gordie Howe (1968-69)
MOST POINTS BY LEFT WING – 105 – John Ogrodnick (1984-85)
MOST POINTS BY DEFENSEMAN – 77 – PAUL COFFEY (1993-94)
MOST POINTS BY ROOKIE – 87 – STEVE YZERMAN (1983-84)
MOST POINTS BY ROOKIE DEFENSEMAN – 60 – Reed Larson (1977-78); NICKLAS LIDSTROM (1991-92)
MOST POWER-PLAY GOALS – 21 – Mickey Redmond (1973-74); DINO CICCARELLI (1992-93)
MOST POWER-PLAY GOALS BY DEFENSEMAN – 11 – Reed Larson (1985-86)
MOST POWER-PLAY GOALS BY ROOKIE – 13 – STEVE YZERMAN (1983-84)
MOST SHORTHANDED GOALS – 10 – Marcel Dionne (1974-75)
MOST WINNING GOALS – 10 – Carson Cooper (1928-29)
MOST WINNING GOALS BY DEFENSEMAN – 5 – Red Kelly (1949-50); Reed Larson (1983-84)
MOST WINNING GOALS BY ROOKIE – 6 – Alex Delvecchio (1951-52)
LONGEST GOAL STREAK – 9 games – STEVE YZERMAN
(12 goals, Nov. 18-Dec. 5, 1988; 14 goals, Jan. 29-Feb. 12, 1992)
LONGEST GOAL STREAK, START OF SEASON – 6 games – STEVE YZERMAN (6 goals, Oct. 6-18, 1989)
LONGEST POINT STREAK – 28 games – STEVE YZERMAN (29 goals, 36 assists, 65 points, Nov. 1-Jan. 4, 1988-89)

MOST SHOTS ON GOAL – 388 – STEVE YZERMAN (1988-89)
MOST PENALTY MINUTES – 398 – Bob Probert (1987-88)
MOST GAMES BY GOALIE – 72 – Tim Cheveldae (1991-92)
MOST MINUTES PLAYED BY GOALIE – 4236 – Tim Cheveldae (1991-92)
MOST WINS BY GOALIE – 44 – Terry Sawchuk (1950-51, 51-52)
LONGEST WINNING STREAK BY GOALIE – 9 (twice) – Terry Sawchuk (Mar. 3-21, 1951; Feb. 27-Mar. 20, 1955)
LONGEST UNBEATEN STREAK BY GOALIE – 16 – Mike Vernon (13 wins, 3 ties, Feb. 12-Apr. 13, 1995)
BEST GOALS-AGAINST AVERAGE BY GOALIE – 1.43 – Dolly Dolson (1928-29)
MOST SHUTOUTS BY GOALIE – 12 – Terry Sawchuk (1951-52, 53-54, 54-55); Glenn Hall (1955-56)
MOST CONSECUTIVE SHUTOUTS BY GOALIE – 3
 – Terry Sawchuk (1954 – 1-0 Nov. 7 vs. N.Y. Rangers, 1-0 Nov. 11 vs. Toronto, 1-0 Nov. 13 at Toronto);
 – Glenn Hall (1955 – 2-0 Dec. 11 vs. N.Y. Rangers, 4-0 Dec. 15 vs. Toronto, 2-0 Dec. 18 vs. Montreal);
 – Jim Rutherford (1975-76 – 4-0 Dec. 31 vs. Washington, 1-0 Jan. 3 at Toronto, 5-0 Jan. 8 vs. Minnesota)
MOST GAMES BY ROOKIE GOALIE – 70 – Terry Sawchuk (1950-51); Glenn Hall (1955-56); Roger Crozier (1964-75)
MOST VICTORIES BY ROOKIE GOALIE – 44 – Terry Sawchuk (1950-51)
MOST MINUTES PLAYED BY ROOKIE GOALIE – 4200 – Terry Sawchuk (1950-51); Glenn Hall (1955-56)
BEST GOALS-AGAINST AVERAGE BY ROOKIE GOALIE – 1.43 – Dolly Dolson (1928-29)
MOST SHUTOUTS BY ROOKIE GOALIE – 11 – Terry Sawchuk (1950-51)

GAME

MOST GOALS – 6 – Syd Howe (Feb. 3, 1944; Detroit 12, N.Y. Rangers 2 at Detroit)
MOST ASSISTS – # 7 – Billy Taylor (Mar. 16, 1947; Detroit 10, Chicago 6 at Chicago)
MOST POINTS – 7 – Carl Liscombe (3 goals, 4 assists) vs. N.Y. Rangers at Detroit, Nov. 5, 1942, Detroit 12, N.Y. 5;
 – Don Grosso (1 goal, 6 assists) vs. N.Y. Rangers at Detroit, Feb. 3, 1944, Detroit 12, N.Y. 2;
 – Billy Taylor (7 assists) at Chicago, March 16, 1947, Detroit 10, Chicago 6.
MOST GOALS, ONE PERIOD – 3 (Several Players) Active Red Wings:
 – STEVE YZERMAN (Mar. 30, 1985, Detroit 6, Vancouver 5);
 – Shawn Burr (Nov. 13, 1986, Philadelphia 7, Detroit 5);
 – YZERMAN (Jan. 3, 1988, Detroit 4, Winnipeg 4);
 – YZERMAN (Nov. 17, 1990, Detroit 8, Toronto 4)
MOST POWER-PLAY GOALS – 3 – Ted Lindsay (vs. Montreal, Mar. 20, 1955, Detroit 6, Montreal 0);
 – Jimmy Carson (vs. Toronto, Dec. 27, 1989, Detroit 7, Toronto 7)
MOST POWER-PLAY GOALS, ONE PERIOD – 3 – Jimmy Carson (Dec. 27, 1989; Detroit 7, Toronto 7)
MOST SHORTHANDED GOALS – 2 – Shawn Burr (Jan. 9, 1990; Detroit 9, Minnesota 0);
 – STEVE YZERMAN (Apr. 14, 1992; Detroit 7, Minnesota 4);
 – YZERMAN (Apr. 8, 1993; Detroit 9, Tampa Bay 1)
MOST SHORTHANDED GOALS, ONE PERIOD – 2 – Shawn Burr (Jan. 9, 1990; Detroit 9, Minnesota 0)
MOST ASSISTS, ONE PERIOD – 4 – Joe Carveth (Jan. 23, 1944; Detroit 15, N.Y. Rangers 0)
MOST POINTS, ONE PERIOD – 4 – Joe Carveth (Jan. 23, 1944; Detroit 15, N.Y. Rangers 0);
 – Mickey Redmond (Oct. 21, 1973; Detroit 11, California 2);
 – John Ogrodnick (Dec. 4, 1984; Detroit 7, Toronto 6);
 – STEVE YZERMAN (Nov. 17, 1990; Detroit 8, Toronto 4);
 – SERGEI FEDOROV (Jan. 21, 1992; Detroit 7, Philadelphia 3)
FASTEST GOAL, START OF GAME & PERIOD – 6 seconds – Henry Boucha (Jan. 28, 1973; Detroit 4, Montreal 2)
FASTEST TWO GOALS – 8 seconds apart – Don Grosso (Mar. 19, 1942; Detroit 6, Chicago 4)
FASTEST THREE GOALS – 1:52 apart – Carl Liscombe (Mar. 13, 1938; Detroit 5, Chicago 1)
MOST GOALS BY ROOKIE, FIRST NHL GAME – 2 – Chris Cichocki (Oct. 10, 1985; Detroit 6, Minnesota 6)
MOST ASSISTS BY ROOKIE, FIRST NHL GAME – # 4 – Earl Reibel (Oct. 8, 1953; Detroit 4, N.Y. Rangers 1)
MOST POINTS BY ROOKIE, FIRST NHL GAME – 4 – Earl Reibel (Oct. 8, 1953; Detroit 4, N.Y. Rangers 1)
MOST PENALTY MINUTES – 42 – Joe Kocur (Nov. 2, 1985; Detroit 5, St. Louis 5)
MOST PENALTIES – 8 – Dennis Polonich (Mar. 24, 1976; Detroit 7, Washington 3);
 – Bob Probert (Dec. 23, 1987; Buffalo 5, Detroit 2)
MOST PENALTY MINUTES, ONE PERIOD – 37 – Joe Kocur (Nov. 2, 1985; Detroit 5, St. Louis 5)
MOST PENALTIES, ONE PERIOD – 6 – Joe Kocur (Nov. 2, 1985; Detroit 5, St. Louis 5)

#-Shares NHL record
ACTIVE PLAYERS IN CAPITALS

RED WINGS' CAREER SCORING LEADERS
(MINIMUM 100 POINTS)

RANK	PLAYER	YEARS	GP	G	A	PTS
1.	Gordie Howe	25	1687	786	1023	1809
2.	Alex Delvecchio	24	1549	456	825	1281
3.	**STEVE YZERMAN**	**12**	**862**	**481**	**679**	**1160**
4.	Norm Ullman	13	875	324	434	758
5.	Ted Lindsay	14	862	335	393	728
6.	Reed Larson	10	708	188	382	570
7.	John Ogrodnick	9	558	265	281	546
8.	Gerard Gallant	9	563	207	260	468
9.	Nick Libett	12	861	217	250	467
10.	Sid Abel	10	571	184	279	463
11.	Red Kelly	13	846	154	297	451
12.	Syd Howe	11	793	202	231	433
13.	**SERGEI FEDOROV**	**5**	**354**	**173**	**249**	**422**
14.	Marcel Dionne	4	309	139	227	366
15.	Shawn Burr	11	659	148	214	362
16.	Dale McCourt	5	341	134	203	337
17.	Bruce MacGregor	11	673	151	184	335
18.	Ebbie Goodfellow	14	575	134	190	324
19.	Herbie Lewis	11	481	148	161	309
	Mickey Redmond	6	317	177	132	309
21.	Gary Bergman	11	706	60	243	303
22.	Marcel Pronovost	15	983	80	217	297
23.	Mud Bruneteau	11	399	139	138	277
	Carl Liscombe	9	378	137	140	277
25.	Larry Aurie	12	490	147	129	276
26.	Steve Chiasson	8	471	67	200	267
27.	**RAY SHEPPARD**	**4**	**239**	**150**	**111**	**261**
28.	Bob Probert	9	474	114	145	259
29.	Walt McKechnie	5	321	89	167	256
30.	Marty Pavelich	10	634	93	159	252
31.	Vaclav Nedomansky	5	364	108	139	247
32.	Joe Carveth	8	325	105	133	238
33.	Petr Klima	5	293	129	93	222
34.	Ron Duguay	3	227	90	127	217
35.	Parker McDonald	7	361	94	122	216
36.	Floyd Smith	6	347	93	122	215
	Dutch Reibel	5	306	74	141	215
38.	Metro Prystai	8	433	91	123	214
39.	Willie Huber	5	372	88	140	208
40.	Red Berenson	5	231	111	91	202
	Jimmy Carson	3	240	100	102	202
42.	Adam Oates	4	246	54	145	199
43.	**DINO CICCARELLI**	**3**	**190**	**85**	**112**	**197**
	Kelly Kisio	4	236	68	129	197
45.	Frank Mahovlich	4	198	108	88	196
	Paul Woods	7	501	72	124	196
47.	**NICKLAS LIDSTROM**	**4**	**291**	**38**	**145**	**183**
48.	Danny Gare	5	306	86	95	181
49.	Johnny Wilson	6	349	79	100	179
50.	**KEITH PRIMEAU**	**5**	**289**	**70**	**108**	**178**

RANK	PLAYER	YEARS	GP	G	A	PTS
51.	John Sorrell 7		347	93	79	172
52.	Don Grosso 7		234	71	99	170
	Paul Ysebaert 3		210	84	86	170
54.	**PAUL COFFEY** **3**		**155**	**32**	**133**	**165**
55.	Ivan Boldirev 3		183	67	95	162
56.	Dave Barr 4		223	64	96	160
	Mike Foligno 3		186	77	83	160
58.	Marty Berry 4		192	60	94	154
59.	Garry Unger 4		216	84	58	152
60.	Dean Prentice 4		230	60	89	149
61.	Paul Henderson 6		269	67	79	146
62.	Bill Hogaboam 6		221	61	84	145
63.	Jim McFadden 4		253	64	78	142
64.	Dennis Polonich 8		390	59	82	141
65.	Guy Charron 5		265	61	78	139
66.	Dan Maloney 3		177	56	81	137
67.	Vic Stasiuk 7		330	52	84	136
68.	Errol Thompson 4		200	76	58	134
	Eddie Wares 6		216	50	84	134
70.	Bill Collins 4		239	54	77	131
71.	Bill Quackenbush 6		313	40	89	129
	Greg Smith 5		352	24	105	129
73.	Danny Grant 4		174	64	62	126
74.	Bill Lochead 5		296	65	60	125
75.	Yves Racine 4		231	22	102	124
76.	Glen Skov 5		301	62	61	123
	Andre St.Laurent 3		172	50	73	123
78.	Lee Norwood 4		238	33	89	122
79.	Dennis Hextall 4		193	39	82	121
80.	Tim Ecclestone 4		191	40	80	120
81.	John Chabot 3		199	24	94	118
82.	Carson Cooper 5		222	68	48	116
83.	Pete Stemkowski 4		170	51	63	114
84.	**VYACHESLAV KOZLOV** **3**		**147**	**51**	**62**	**113**
85.	George Hay 5		204	60	52	112
	Bill Gadsby 5		323	18	94	112
87.	Michel Bergeron 4		174	64	46	110
	Dwight Foster 4		215	48	62	110
	Mark Osborne 2		160	45	65	110
90.	Jack Stewart 10		503	30	79	109
91.	Gary Couture 6		266	61	46	107
92.	Dan Labraaten 3		198	52	54	106
93.	Mike Blaisdell 3		192	44	61	105
94.	Doug Barkley 4		247	24	80	104
95.	**VLADIMIR KONSTANTINOV** . . . **4**		**288**	**28**	**75**	**103**
	Darren Veitch 3		153	20	83	103
	Bob Goldham 6		406	11	92	103
98.	Joe Kocur 6		347	51	51	102
99.	Adam Brown 4		148	58	43	101
	Brad Park 2		147	18	83	101
101.	Tony Leswick 5		291	41	59	100
	Warren Godfrey 12		528	23	77	100

ACTIVE PLAYERS IN BOLD CAPITALS

	GOALS		ASSISTS		POINTS				PENALTIES	
Season	**Player**	**Total**	**Player**	**Total**	**Player**	**G**	**A**	**TP**	**Player**	**TPM**
1926-27	Sheppard	13	Sheppard	8	Sheppard	13	8	21	Sheppard	60
1927-28	Hay	22	Hay	13	Hay	22	13	35	Traub	78
1928-29	Cooper	18	Cooper	9	Cooper	18	9	27	Connors	68
1929-30	Lewis	20	Cooper	18	Cooper	18	18	36	Rockburn	97
1930-31	Goodfellow	25	Goodfellow	23	Goodfellow	25	23	48	Rockburn	118*
1931-32	Goodfellow	14	Goodfellow	16	Goodfellow	14	16	30	Noble	72
1932-33	Lewis	20	Lewis	14	Lewis	20	14	34	Evans	74
1933-34	Sorrell	21	Aurie	19	Aurie	16	19	35	Emms	51
1934-35	S. Howe	22	Aurie	29	S. Howe	22	25	47	Jackson	44
1935-36	Barry	21	Lewis	23	Barry	21	19	40	Goodfellow	44
1936-37	Aurie	23*	Barry	27	Barry	17	27	44	Goodfellow	69
1937-38	Liscombe	14	Barry	20	Lewis	13	18	31	Goodfellow	43
1938-39	S. Howe	16	Barry	28	Barry	13	28	41	Barry	34
1939-40	S. Howe	14	S. Howe	23	S. Howe	14	23	37	Conacher	39
1940-41	S. Howe	20	S. Howe	24	S. Howe	20	24	44	Orlando	54
1941-42	Grosso	23	Abel	31	Grosso	23	30	53	Orlando	99*
1942-43	Bruneteau	23	S. Howe	35	S. Howe	20	35	55	Orlando	111*
1943-44	Liscombe	36	Liscombe	37	Liscombe	36	37	73	Orlando	99*
1944-45	Carveth	26	S. Howe	36	Carveth	26	28	54	Jackson	76
1945-46	Brown	20	Carveth	18	Carveth	17	18	35	Jackson	45
			Armstrong	18					Stewart	73*
1946-47	Conacher	30	Taylor	46*	Taylor	17	46	63	Stewart	83
1947-48	Lindsay	33*	Abel	30	Lindsay	33	19	52	Lindsay	95
1948-49	Abel	28*	Lindsay	28	Abel	28	26	54	Lindsay	97
					Lindsay	26	28	54		
1949-50	G. Howe	35	Lindsay	55*	Lindsay	23	55	78*	Lindsay	141
1950-51	G. Howe	43*	G. Howe	43*	G. Howe	43	43	86*	Lindsay	110
1951-52	G. Howe	47*	G. Howe	39*	G. Howe	47	39	86*	Lindsay	123
1952-53	G. Howe	49*	G. Howe	46*	G. Howe	49	46	95*	Lindsay	111
1953-54	G. Howe	33	G. Howe	48*	G. Howe	33	48	81*	Lindsay	112
1954-55	G. Howe	29	Reibel	41	Reibel	25	41	66	Leswick	137
1955-56	G. Howe	38	G. Howe	41	G. Howe	38	41	79	Lindsay	161
1956-57	G. Howe	44*	Lindsay	55*	G. Howe	44	45	89*	Lindsay	103
									Godfrey	103
1957-58	G. Howe	33	G. Howe	44	G. Howe	33	44	77	Kennedy	135
1958-59	G. Howe	32	G. Howe	46	G. Howe	32	46	78	Goegan	111
1959-60	G. Howe	28	G. Howe	45	G. Howe	28	45	73	Morrison	62
1960-61	Ullman	28	G. Howe	49	G. Howe	23	49	72	Young	108
1961-62	G. Howe	33	G. Howe	44	G. Howe	33	44	77	Gadsby	88
1962-63	G. Howe	38*	G. Howe	48	G. Howe	38	48	86*	Young	273*
1963-64	G. Howe	26	G. Howe	47	G. Howe	26	47	73	Barkley	115
1964-65	Ullman	42	G. Howe	47	Ullman	42	41	83	Lindsay	173
1965-66	Ullman	31	G. Howe	46	G. Howe	29	46	75	Watson	133
	Delvecchio	31								
1966-67	MacGregor	28	Ullman	44	Ullman	26	44	70	Bergman	129
1967-68	G. Howe	39	Delvecchio	48	G. Howe	39	43	82	Douglas	126
1968-69	F. Mahovlich	49	G. Howe	59	G. Howe	44	59	103	Baun	121
1969-70	Unger	42	Delvecchio	47	G. Howe	31	40	71	Bergman	122
1970-71	Webster	30	Webster	37	Webster	30	37	67	Bergman	149
1971-72	Redmond	42	Dionne	49	Dionne	28	49	77	Bergman	138
1972-73	Redmond	52	Delvecchio	53	Redmond	52	41	93	Johnston	169
1973-74	Redmond	51	Dionne	54	Dionne	24	53	78	Johnston	139
1974-75	Grant	50	Dionne	74	Dionne	47	74	121	Watson	238
1975-76	Bergeron	32	McKechnie	56	McKechnie	26	56	82	Watson	322
1976-77	McKechnie	25	McKechnie	34	McKechnie	24	34	59	Polonich	274
1977-78	McCourt	33	Larson	41	McCourt	33	39	72	Polonich	254
1978-79	Nedomansky	38	Larson	49	Nedomansky	38	35	73	Polonich	208
1979-80	Foligno	36	McCourt	51	McCourt	30	51	81	Huber	164
1980-81	Ogrodnick	35	McCourt	56	McCourt	30	56	86	Korn	246
1981-82	Ogrodnick	28	Osborne	41	Osborne	26	41	67	Larson	112
1982-83	Ogrodnick	41	Larson	52	Ogrodnick	41	44	85	Gare	107
1983-84	Ogrodnick	42	Park	53	Yzerman	39	48	87	Paterson	148
1984-85	Ogrodnick	55	Yzerman	59	Ogrodnick	55	50	105	Gare	163
1985-86	Ogrodnick	38	Kisio	48	Shedden	34	37	71	Kocur	377*
1986-87	Ashton	40	Yzerman	59	Yzerman	31	59	90	Kocur	276
1987-88	Yzerman	50	Yzerman	52	Yzerman	50	52	102	Probert	398*
1988-89	Yzerman	65	Yzerman	90	Yzerman	65	90	155	Gallant	230
1989-90	Yzerman	62	Yzerman	65	Yzerman	62	65	127	Kocur	268
1990-91	Yzerman	51	Yzerman	57	Yzerman	51	57	108	Probert	315
1991-92	Yzerman	45	Yzerman	58	Yzerman	45	58	103	Probert	276
1992-93	Yzerman	58	Yzerman	79	Yzerman	58	79	137	Probert	292
1992-93	Yzerman	58	Yzerman	79	Yzerman	58	79	137	Probert	292
1993-94	Fedorov	56	Fedorov	64	Fedorov	56	64	120	Probert	275
1995	Sheppard	30	Coffey	44	Coffey	14	44	58	Grimson	147

*—League leader

RED WINGS' TOP-SCORING SEASONS

GOALS

Total	Player	Season	Total	Player	Season
65	**STEVE YZERMAN**	**88-89**	35	Mud Bruneteau	43-44
62	**STEVE YZERMAN**	**89-90**		Gordie Howe	49-50
58	**STEVE YZERMAN**	**92-93**		Vaclav Nedomansky	79-80
56	**SERGEI FEDOROV**	**93-94**		John Ogrodnick	80-81
55	John Ogrodnick	84-85		Ivan Boldirev	83-84
	STEVE YZERMAN	**90-91**		Errol Thompson	79-80
52	Mickey Redmond	72-73		Paul Ysebaert	91-92
	RAY SHEPPARD	**93-94**	34	Gerard Gallant	87-88
51	Mickey Redmond	73-74		Jim Carson	91-92
50	Danny Grant	74-75		Paul Ysebaert	92-93
	STEVE YZERMAN	**87-88**		**VYACHESLAV KOZLOV**	**93-94**
49	Gordie Howe	52-53	33	Ted Lindsay	47-48
	Frank Mahovlich	68-69		Gordie Howe (3)	53-54
47	Gordie Howe	51-52			57-58
	Marcel Dionne	74-75			61-62
45	**STEVE YZERMAN**	**91-92**		Parker MacDonald	62-63
44	Gordie Howe (2)	56-57		Dale McCourt	77-78
		68-69		Ron Duguay	83-84
43	Gordie Howe	50-51	32	Syd Howe	43-44
42	Norm Ullman	64-65		Ted Lindsay	52-53
	Garry Unger	69-70		Gordie Howe	58-59
	Mickey Redmond	71-72		Michel Bergeron	75-76
	John Ogrodnick	83-84		Petr Klima	85-86
41	John Ogrodnick	82-83		**SERGEI FEDOROV**	**91-92**
	DINO CICCARELLI	**92-93**		**RAY SHEPPARD**	**92-93**
40	Marcel Dionne	72-73	31	Norm Ullman	65-66
39	Gordie Howe	67-68		Alex Delvecchio	65-66
	STEVE YZERMAN	**83-84**		Gordie Howe	69-70
	Gerard Gallant	88-89		Nick Libbett	71-72
38	Gordie Howe (2)	55-56		Andre St. Laurent	77-78
		66-63		**STEVE YZERMAN**	**86-87**
	Frank Mahovlich	69-70		**SERGEI FEDOROV**	**90-91**
	Vaclav Nedomansky	78-79		**KEITH PRIMEAU**	**93-94**
	Ron Duguay	84-85	30	Roy Conacher	46-47
	John Ogrodnick	85-86		Ted Lindsay (2)	51-52
	Gerard Gallant	86-87			56-57
37	Petr Klima	87-88		Norm Ullman	67-68
36	Carl Liscombe	43-44		Tom Webster	70-71
	Mike Foligno	79-80		Dale McCourt	79-80
	Paul MacLean	88-89		Dan Labraaten	79-80
	Gerard Gallant	89-90		Dale McCourt	80-81
	RAY SHEPPARD	**91-92**		**STEVE YZERMAN**	**84-85**
				Petr Klima	86-87
				RAY SHEPPARD	**95**

ASSISTS

Total	Player	Season	Total	Player	Season
90	**STEVE YZERMAN**	**88-89**	51	Dale McCourt	79-89
79	**STEVE YZERMAN**	**92-93**		Ron Duguay	84-85
74	Marcel Dionne	74-75	50	Marcel Dionne	72-73
65	**STEVE YZERMAN**	**89-90**		John Ogrodnick	84-85
64	**SERGEI FEDOROV**	**93-94**		**STEVE CHIASSON**	**92-93**
63	**PAUL COFFEY**	**93-94**	49	Gordie Howe	60-61
62	Adam Oates	88-89		Marcel Dionne	71-72
59	Gordie Howe	68-69		Reed Larson	78-79
	STEVE YZERMAN (2)	**84-85**		Peter Mahovlich	79-80
		86-87		**NICKLAS LIDSTROM**	**91-92**
58	Alex Delvecchio	68-69	48	Gordie Howe	(2) 53-54
	STEVE YZERMAN	**91-92**			62-63
		93-94		Alex Delvecchio	67-68
57	**STEVE YZERMAN**	**90-91**		**STEVE YZERMAN**	**83-84**
56	Walt McKechnie	75-76		Ivan Boldirev	83-84
	Dale McCourt	80-81		Kelly Kisio	85-86
	DINO CICCARELLI	**92-93**		**SERGEI FEDOROV**	**90-91**
55	Ted Lindsay (2)	49-50	47	Gordie Howe (2)	63-64
		56-57			64-65
54	Marcel Dionne	73-74		Alex Delvecchio	69-70
	Gerard Gallant	88-89		Ron Duguay	83-84
	SERGEI FEDOROV	**91-92**		Alex Delvecchio	69-70
53	Alex Delvecchio	72-73	46	Billy Taylor	46-47
	Brad Park	83-84		Gordie Howe (3)	52-53
	SERGEI FEDOROV	**92-93**			58-59
52	Reed Larson	82-83			65-66
	STEVE YZERMAN	**87-88**		**NICKLAS LIDSTROM**	**93-94**

Total	Player	Season
45	Gordie Howe (2)	56-57
		59-60
	Alex Delvecchio	71-72
	Reed Larson	84-85
	Darren Veitch	86-87
44	Gordie Howe (2)	57-58
		61-62
	Alex Delvecchio	62-63
	Norm Ullman	66-67
	Reed Larson	79-80
	John Ogrondick	82-83
	John Chabot	87-88
	Gerard Gallant	89-90
	PAUL COFFEY	**95**
43	Gordie Howe (2)	50-51
		67-68
	Alex Delvecchio (2)	52-53
		61-62
	Dale McCourt	78-79
	Mickey Redmond	72-73
	Red Berenson	71-72
	Reed Larson	77-78
	Mark Osborne	81-82
	Kelly Kisio	84-85

Total	Player	Season
42	Norm Ullman	60-61
	Alex Delvecchio	64-65
	Red Berenson	73-74
	KEITH PRIMEAU	**93-94**
41	Dutch Reibel	54-55
	Gordie Howe	55-56
	Norm Ullman (2)	60-61
		65-66
	RAY SHEPPARD	**93-94**
40	Gordie Howe (2)	66-67
		69-70
	Adam Oates	87-88
	Bernie Federko	89-90
	John Chabot	89-90
	Yves Racine	90-91
	Paul Ysebaert	91-92

POINTS

Total	Player	Season
155	**STEVE YZERMAN**	**88-89**
137	**STEVE YZERMAN**	**92-93**
127	**STEVE YZERMAN**	**89-90**
120	**SERGEI FEDOROV**	**93-94**
121	Marcel Dionne	74-75
108	**STEVE YZERMAN**	**90-91**
105	John Ogrodnick	84-85
103	Gordie Howe	68-69
	STEVE YZERMAN	**91-92**
102	**STEVE YZERMAN**	**87-88**
97	**DINO CICCARELLI**	**92-93**
95	Gordie Howe	52-53
93	Mickey Redmond	72-73
	Gerard Gallant	88-89
	RAY SHEPPARD	**93-94**
90	Marcel Dionne	72-73
	STEVE YZERMAN	**86-87**
89	Gordie Howe	56-57
	Ron Duguay	84-85
	STEVE YZERMAN	**84-85**
87	**STEVE YZERMAN**	**83-84**
87	**SERGEI FEDOROV**	**92-93**
86	Gordie Howe (3)	50-51
		51-52
		62-63
	Danny Grant	74-75
	Dale McCourt	80-81
	SERGEI FEDOROV	**91-92**
85	Ted Lindsay	56-57
	John Ogrodnick	82-83
83	Norm Ullman	64-65
	Alex Delvecchio	68-69
	Ivan Boldirev	83-84
82	Gordie Howe	67-68
	Walt McKechnie	75-76
	STEVE YZERMAN	**93-94**
81	Gordie Howe	53-54
	Dale McCourt	79-80
80	Ron Duguay	83-84
	Gerard Gallant	89-90
79	Gordie Howe	55-56
	SERGEI FEDOROV	**90-91**

Total	Player	Season
78	Ted Lindsay	49-50
	Gordie Howe	58-59
	Frank Mahovlich	68-69
	Marcel Dionne	73-74
	John Ogrodnick	83-84
	Adam Oates	88-89
77	Gordie Howe (2)	57-58
		61-62
	Marcel Dionne	71-72
	Mickey Redmond	73-74
	PAUL COFFEY	**93-94**
76	Gordie Howe	64-65
75	Gordie Howe	65-66
	Paul Ysebaert	91-92
74	Vaclav Nedomansky	79-80
	Reed Larson	82-83
73	Carl Liscombe	43-44
	Gordie Howe (2)	59-60
		63-64
	Vaclav Nedomansky	78-79
	Gerard Gallant	87-88
	VYACHESLAV KOZLOV	**93-94**
	KEITH PRIMEAU	**93-94**
72	Gordie Howe	60-61
	Norm Ullman	65-66
	Dale McCourt	77-78
	Gerard Gallant	86-87
71	Ted Lindsay	52-53
	Gordie Howe	69-70
	Mickey Redmond	71-72
	Alex Delvecchio	72-73
	Dale McCourt	78-79
	Mike Foligno	79-80
	Paul MacLean	88-89
70	Norm Ullman (2)	60-61
		66-67
	Alex Delvecchio	67-68
	Frank Mahovlich	69-70
	Andre St. Laurent	77-78
	John Ogrodnick (2)	80-81
		85-86

ACTIVE PLAYERS IN BOLD CAPITALS

DETROIT RED WINGS
GOALTENDERS' ALL-TIME RECORDS

PLAYER	YRS	GP	WON	LOST	TIED	GA	SO	AVG
Terry Sawchuk	14	734	352	244	130	1782	85	2.46
Harry Lumley	7	324	163	107	54	885	26	2.73
Roger Crozier	7	310	130	119	43	853	20	2.94
Tim Cheveldae	6	264	128	93	30	851	9	3.39
Greg Stefan	9	299	115	127	30	1068	5	3.92
Jim Rutherford	10	314	97	165	43	1112	10	3.68
Roy Edwards	6	221	95	74	34	601	14	2.94
Norm Smith	7	178	76	68	34	417	17	2.34
Glenn Hall	4	148	74	45	29	317	17	2.14
John Mowers	4	152	65	61	26	399	13	2.63
Glen Hanlon	5	186	65	71	26	569	7	3.47
John Ross Roach	3	89	41	37	11	201	11	2.26
CHRIS OSGOOD	**2**	**60**	**37**	**13**	**5**	**146**	**2**	**2.66**
Clarence Dolson	3	93	35	41	17	192	17	2.06
Hank Bassen	6	99	34	39	19	274	3	2.99
Cecil Thompson	2	85	32	41	12	225	7	2.65
Harry Holmes	2	85	30	46	9	179	17	2.11
Rogie Vachon	2	109	30	57	19	398	4	3.74
Corrado Micalef	5	113	26	59	15	409	2	4.23
Connie Dion	2	38	23	11	4	119	1	3.13
Eddie Giacomin	3	71	23	37	7	234	6	3.47
Gilles Gilbert	3	95	21	48	16	365	0	4.18
Mike Vernon	1	30	19	6	4	76	1	2.52
Alex Connell	1	48	18	20	10	108	6	2.25
Al Smith	1	43	18	20	4	135	4	3.24
Doug Grant	3	46	17	22	2	182	1	4.33
Vince Riendeau	3	32	17	8	2	89	0	3.28
Wilf Cude	1	29	15	6	8	47	4	1.62
Bill Beveridge	1	39	14	20	5	109	2	2.79
Joe Daly	1	29	11	10	5	85	0	3.15
Bob Sauve	1	41	11	25	4	165	0	4.19
Ed Mio	3	49	10	20	5	205	1	5.00
Ron Low	1	32	9	12	9	102	1	3.37
Denis Dejordy	2	25	8	12	3	87	1	3.86
George Gardner	3	24	7	7	3	69	0	3.59
Jim Franks	2	18	7	8	3	72	1	4.00
Andy Brown	2	17	6	6	3	57	0	3.80
Mark Laforest	2	33	6	22	0	126	1	4.71
Larry Lozinski	1	30	6	11	7	105	0	4.32
Sam St. Laurent	4	30	5	11	4	79	0	3.76
Dennis Riggin	2	18	5	9	2	54	1	3.27
Bill McKenzie	2	26	5	13	6	101	1	4.16
BOB ESSENSA	**1**	**13**	**4**	**7**	**2**	**34**	**1**	**2.62**
Terry Richardson	4	19	3	10	0	75	0	5.31
Don McLeod	1	14	3	7	0	60	0	5.15
Greg Millen	1	10	3	2	3	22	0	2.71
Dave Gatherum	1	3	2	1	0	3	1	1.00
Bob Perrault	1	3	2	1	0	9	1	3.00
Harvey Teno	1	5	2	3	0	15	0	3.00
Herb Stuart	1	3	1	2	0	5	0	1.60
Gerry Gray	1	7	1	4	1	30	0	4.73
Peter Ing	1	3	1	2	0	15	0	5.29
Abbie Cox	1	1	0	0	1	4	0	4.00
Joe Turner	1	1	0	0	1	3	0	3.00
Ralph Almas	2	2	0	1	1	8	0	4.00
Ken Holland	1	3	0	1	1	11	0	4.11
Claude Legris	2	4	0	1	1	4	0	2.66

Pete McDuffe	1	4	0	3	1	22	0	5.50
Allan Bester	2	4	0	3	0	15	0	4.31
Darren Eliot	1	3	0	0	1	9	0	5.57
Alain Chevrier	1	3	0	3	0	11	0	6.11
Carl Wetzel	1	2	0	1	0	4	0	8.00
Claude Bourque	1	1	0	1	0	3	0	3.00
Alf Moore	1	1	0	1	0	3	0	3.00
Pat Rupp	1	1	0	1	0	4	0	4.00
Harrison Gray	1	1	0	1	0	5	0	7.50
Al Jensen	1	1	0	1	0	7	0	7.00
Gillies Boisvert	1	3	0	3	0	9	0	3.00
Dave Gagnon	1	2	0	1	0	6	0	10.29
Scott King	2	2	0	0	0	3	0	2.95
Chris Pusey	1	1	0	0	0	3	0	4.50
Tom McGratton	1	1	0	0	0	1	0	7.50
Lefty Wilson	1	1	0	0	0	0	0	0.00

ACTIVE PLAYERS IN BOLD CAPITALS

———DETROIT NHL GOALTENDING LEADERS———

REGULAR SEASON

SHUTOUTS

T. Sawchuk – 12 ......51-52, 53-54, 54-55
G. Hall – 12 55-56
H. Holmes – 11 27-28
T. Sawchuk – 11 50-51
J.R. Roach – 10 32-33
C. Dolson – 10 28-29
T. Sawchuk – 9 52-53
H. Lumley – 7 ....47-48, 49-50
R. Crozier – 7 65-66
H. Holmes – 6 26-27
C. Dolson – 6 30-31
A. Connell – 6 31-32
N. Smith – 6 ....35-36, *36-37
H. Lumley – 6 48-49
R. Crozier – 6 64-65
R. Edwards – 6 ....*72-73
G. Hanlon – 4 ....*87-88
T. Cheveldae – 4 92-93

*-Shared lead

WINS

T. Sawchuk – 44 ....50-51, 51-52
T. Sawchuk – 40 54-55
R. Crozier – 40 64-65
G. Hall – 38 56-57
T. Chevedlae – 38 91-92
T. Sawchuk – 35 53-54
H. Lumley – 34 48-49
H. Lumley – 33 49-50
T. Sawchuk – 32 52-53
H. Lumley – 30 47-48
G. Hall – 30 55-56

RED WINGS' ALL-STARS

GOAL

Coach	No. Times Selected	Season and Team
John Ross Roach	1	1933 (1st Team)
Normie Smith	1	1937 (1st)
John Mowers	1	1943 (1st)
Glenn Hall	2	1956 (2nd), 1957 (1st)
Terry Sawchuk	7	1951 (1st), 1952 (1st), 1953 (1st), 1954 (2nd), 1955 (2nd), 1959 (2nd), 1963 (2nd)
Roger Crozier	1	1965 (1st)

DEFENSE

Coach	No. Times Selected	Season and Team
Ebbie Goodfellow	3	1936 (2nd), 1937 (1st), 1940 (1st)
Jack Stewart	5	1943 (1st), 1946 (2nd), 1947 (2nd), 1948 (1st), 1949 (1st)
Flash Hollett	1	1945 (1st)
Bill Quackenbush	3	1947 (2nd), 1948 (1st), 1949 (1st)
Leo Reise	2	1950 (2nd), 1951 (2nd)
Bob Goldham	1	1955 (2nd)
Red Kelly	8	1950 (2nd), 1951 (1st), 1952 (1st), 1953 (1st), 1954 (1st), 1955 (1st), 1956 (2nd), 1957 (1st)
Marcel Pronovost	4	1958 (2nd), 1959 (2nd), 1960 (1st), 1961 (1st)
Bill Gadsby	1	1965 (2nd)
Carl Brewer	1	1970 (2nd)
PAUL COFFEY	**1**	**1995 (1st)**

LEFT WING

Coach	No. Times Selected	Season and Team
Sid Abel	1	1942 (2nd)
Syd Howe	1	1945 (2nd)
Ted Lindsay	9	1948 (1st), 1949 (2nd), 1950 (1st), 1951 (1st), 1952 (1st), 1953 (1st), 1954 (1st), 1956 (1st), 1957 (1st)
Alex Delvecchio	1	1959 (2nd)
Frank Mahovlich	2	1969 (2nd), 1970 (2nd)
John Ogrodnick	1	1985 (1st)
Gerard Gallant	1	1989 (2nd)

CENTER

Coach	No. Times Selected	Season and Team
Cooney Weiland	1	1935 (2nd)
Marty Barry	1	1937 (1st)
Sid Abel	3	1949 (1st, 1950 (1st), 1951 (2nd)
Alex Delvecchio	1	1953 (2nd)
Norm Ullman	2	1965 (1st), 1967 (2nd)
SERGEI FEDOROV	**1**	**1994 (1st)**

RIGHT WING

Coach	No. Times Selected	Season and Team
Larry Aurie	1	1937 (1st)
Gordie Howe	*21	1949 (2nd), 1950 (2nd), 1951 (1st), 1952 (1st), 1953 (1st), 1954 (1st), 1956 (2nd), 1957 (1st), 1958 (1st), 1959 (2nd), 1960 (1st), 1961 (2nd), 1962 (2nd), 1962 (2nd), 1963 (1st), 1964 (2nd), 1965 (2nd), 1966 (1st), 1967 (2nd), 1968 (1st), 1969 (1st), 1970 (1st)
Mickey Redmond	2	1973 (1st), 1974 (2nd)

COACH

Coach	No. Times Selected	Season and Team
Jack Adams	3	1937 (1st), 1943 (1st), 1945 (2nd)
Bobby Kromm	1	Jack Adams Trophy 1978
Jacques Demers	2	Jack Adms Trophy 1987, 1988

*-NHL Record
ACTIVE PLAYERS IN BOLD CAPITALS

RED WINGS' NHL TROPHY WINNERS

ART ROSS TROPHY
(Leading Point-scorer)

Ted Lindsay.............................1949-50
Gordie Howe 1950-51
Gordie Howe 1951-52
Gordie Howe 1952-53
Gordie Howe 1953-54
Gordie Howe 1956-57
Gordie Howe 1962-63

HART TROPHY
(Most Valuable Player)

Ebbie Goodfellow.....................1939-40
Sid Abel.....................................1948-49
Gordie Howe 1951-52
Gordie Howe 1952-53
Gordie Howe 1956-57
Gordie Howe 1957-58
Gordie Howe 1959-60
Gordie Howe 1962-63
SERGEI FEDOROV.................1993-94

VEZINA TROPHY
(Best Goalie)

Norm Smith................................1936-37
John Mowers.............................1942-43
Terry Sawchuk...........................1951-52
Terry Sawchuk 1952-53
Terry Sawchuk 1954-55

NORRIS TROPHY
(Best Defenseman)

Red Kelly...................................1953-54
PAUL COFFEY 1995

CALDER TROPHY
(Rookie of the Year)

Carl Voss...................................1932-33
Jim McFadden...........................1947-48
Terry Sawchuk...........................1950-51
Glenn Hall 1955-56
Roger Crozier............................1964-65

FRANK J. SELKE TROPHY
(Best Defensive Forward)
SERGEI FEDOROV.................1993-94

LADY BYNG TROPHY
(Sportsmanship & Ability)

Marty Barry 1936-37
Bill Quackenbush......................1948-49
Red Kelly...................................1950-51
Red Kelly...................................1952-53
Red Kelly...................................1953-54
Dutch Reibel 1955-56
Alex Delvecchio 1958-59
Alex Delvecchio 1965-66
Alex Delvecchio 1968-69
Marcel Dionne 1974-75

LESTER B. PEARSON AWARD
(Oustanding Performer
Selected by Players' Assn.)
STEVE YZERMAN 1988-89
SERGEI FEDOROV.................1993-94

PLUS-MINUS AWARD
(Plus-Minus Leader)
Paul Ysebaert............................1991-92

CONN SMYTHE TROPHY
(Playoff MVP)
Roger Crozier.................................1966

JACK ADAMS AWARD
(Coach of the Year)
Bobby Kromm 1977-78
Jacques Demers.......................1986-87
Jacques Demers 1987-88

BILL MASTERTON TROPHY
(Perseverance, Sportsmanship and
Dedication to Hockey)
Brad Park 1983-84

LESTER PATRICK TROPHY
(Outstanding Service
to U.S. Hockey)
Jack Adams 1965-66
Gordie Howe 1966-67
Alex Delvecchio 1973-74
Bruce A. Norris 1974-75
MIKE ILITCH 1990-91

ACTIVE PLAYER/OWNER IN BOLD CAPITALS

RED WINGS IN HOCKEY HALL OF FAME

Sid Abel 1969
Jack Adams 1959
Marty Barry 1965
Andy Bathgate 1978
Leo Boivin 1986
Scotty Bowman 1991
John Bucyk 1981
Charlie Conacher 1961
Alex Connell 1958
Alex Delvecchio 1977
Marcel Dionne 1992
Frank Fosyton 1958
Frank Frederickson 1958
Bill Gadsby 1970
Ed Giacomin 1987
Ebbie Goodfellow 1963
Glenn Hall 1975
Doug Harvey 1973
George Hay 1958
Hap Holmes 1972
Gordie Howe 1972
Syd Howe 1965
Tommy Ivan 1974
Duke Keats 1958
Red Kelly 1969

Herbie Lewis 1989
Ted Lindsay 1966
Harry Lumley 1980
Budd Lynch 1985
Frank Mahovlich 1981
Bruce Martyn 1991
Reg Noble 1962
Bruce A. Norris 1969
James Norris 1958
James D. Norris 1962
Brad Park 1988
Bud Poile 1990
Marcel Pronovost 1978
Bill Quackenbush 1976
Terry Sawchuk 1971
Earl Seibert 1964
Darryl Sittler 1989
Jack Stewart 1964
Cecil "Tiny" Thompson 1959
Norm Ullman 1982
Carl Voss 1974
Jack Walker 1960
Cooney Weiland 1971
John A. Ziegler Jr. 1987

MEMBERS OF RED WINGS HALL OF FAME

Sid Abel 1944
Jack Adams 1945
Larry Aurie 1944
Marty Barry 1944
Mud Bruneteau 1944
Joe Carveth 1978
Carson Cooper 1949
Alex Delvecchio 1978
Bill Gadsby 1978
Ebbie Goodfellow 1944
Don Grosso 1947
George Hay 1944
Gordie Howe 1985
Syd Howe 1944
Tommy Ivan 1977
Red Kelly 1978
Herb Lewis 1944
Ted Lindsay 1962

Carl Liscombe 1964
Carl Mattson 1978
Bucko McDonald 1961
John Mowers 1946
Reg Noble 1944
Bruce A. Norris 1968
James Norris 1959
James D. Norris 1968
Jimmy Orlando 1962
Marcel Pronovost 1978
Bill Quackenbush 1961
Marguerite Norris 1977
Terry Sawchuk 1971
Jimmy Skinner 1977
Norm Smith 1963
Jack Stewart 1944
Frank "Honey" Walker 1954
Doug Young 1951

RED WINGS' BIGGEST VICTORIES
(Scoring 10 Goals or More)

SEASON	DATE	OPPONENT	SCORE
1930-31	Dec. 25	Toronto	10-1
1934-35	Dec. 13	at St. Louis	11-2
1941-42	Jan. 4	Montreal	10-0
1942-43	Nov. 5	NY Rangers	12-5
1943-44	Jan. 23	NY Rangers	15-0
1943-44	Feb. 3	NY Rangers	12-2
1943-44	Mar. 16	Boston	10-9
1944-45	Nov. 2	NY Rangers	10-3
1944-45	Dec. 27	NY Rangers	11-3
1944-45	Mar. 4	Boston	10-4
1946-47	Mar. 16	at Chicago	10-6
1948-49	Dec. 29	Boston	10-2
1950-51	Feb. 7	Chicago	11-3
1952-53	Nov. 22	Chicago	10-1
1952-53	Dec. 11	at Boston	10-1
1952-53	Mar. 2	Boston	10-2
1964-65	Mar. 18	Boston	10-3
1965-66	Dec. 2	Boston	10-2
1973-74	Oct. 21	California	11-2
1977-78	Nov. 16	St. Louis	10-1
1981-82	Oct. 29	Calgary	12-4
1981-82	Nov. 5	Los Angeles	10-2
1984-85	Feb. 27	Vancouver	11-5
1987-88	Nov. 25	Winnipeg	10-8
1987-88	Dec. 4	Chicago	12-0
1991-92	Nov. 7	St. Louis	10-3
1991-92	Feb. 15	San Jose	11-1
1992-93	Nov. 23	Tampa Bay	10-5
1992-93	Nov. 25	St. Louis	11-6
1993-94	Nov. 27	Dallas	10-4
1993-94	Jan. 6	at San Jose	10-3

RED WINGS' BIGGEST DEFEATS
(Allowing 10 Goals or More)

SEASON	DATE	OPPONENT	SCORE
1939-40	Feb. 13	at Boston	10-3
1941-42	Jan. 25	at NY Rangers	11-2
1945-46	Mar. 17	Toronto	11-7
1958-59	Mar. 7	at Montreal	10-2
1964-65	Dec. 5	at Toronto	10-2
1966-67	Apr. 1	at NY Rangers	10-5
1970-71	Jan. 2	at Toronto	13-0
1970-71	Mar. 16	Boston	11-4
1973-74	Feb. 2	at Philadelphia	12-2
1974-75	Oct. 23	at Atlanta	10-1
1979-80	Mar. 27	at Buffalo	10-1
1980-81	Jan. 15	at Calgary	10-0
1980-81	Jan. 20	at Los Angeles	11-4
1984-85	Dec. 1	at St. Louis	10-5
1985-86	Oct. 17	at Minnesota	10-1
1985-86	Nov. 30	at Montreal	10-1
1985-86	Dec. 11	Minnesota	10-2
1985-86	Dec. 23	at NY Rangers	10-2
1987-88	Feb. 23	Philadelphia	11-6
1988-89	Jan. 20	at Pittsburgh	10-5
1989-90	Oct. 5	at Calgary	10-7
1992-93	Feb. 24	at Buffalo	10-7
1993-94	Oct. 9	at Los Angeles	10-3

RED WINGS' HISTORY OF SCORELESS TIES

SEASON	DATE	OPPONENT SITE	GOALIES DETROIT	OPPONENT
1927-28	Nov. 26	at Chicago	Hap Holmes	Chuck Gardiner
	Feb. 23	OTTAWA	Hap Holmes	Alex Connell
	Feb. 26	NY Rangers	Hap Holmes	Lorne Chabot
1928-29	Feb. 23	CHICAGO	Dolly Dolson	Chuck Gardiner
1931-32	Jan. 7	BOSTON	Alex Connell	Tiny Thompson
	Feb. 18	BOSTON	Alex Connelll	Tiny Thompson
1934-35	Dec. 30	NY Americans	John Ross Roach	Roy Worters
	Jan. 26	at Toronto	John Ross Roach	George Hainsworth
1934-35	Nov. 14	CHICAGO	Normie Smith	Mike Karakas
	Nov. 28	MONTREAL	Normie Smith	Wilf Cude
1936-37	Feb. 28	MONTREAL	Normie Smith	Wilf Cude
1939-40	Dec. 17	NY RANGERS	Tiny Thompson	Dave Kerr
1946-47	Dec. 4	at Chicago	Harry Lumley	Paul Bibeault
1947-48	Mar. 17	at Boston	Harry Lumley	Frank Brimsek
1948-49	Oct. 23	at Montreal	Harry Lumley	Bill Durnan
1050-51	Jan. 21	TORONTO	Terry Sawchuk	Turk Broda
1951-52	Nov. 6	at Boston	Terry Sawchuk	Jim Henry
1952-53	Dec. 14	MONTREAL	Terry Sawchuk	Gerry McNeil
	Mar. 15	at Chicago	Terry Sawchuk	Al Rollins
1953-54	Jan. 3	TORONTO	Terry Sawchuk	Harry Lumley
	Feb. 17	at Toronto	Terry Sawchuk	Harry Lumley
1955-56	Oct. 22	BOSTON	Glenn Hall	Terry Sawchuk
	Nov. 13	at Boston	Glenn Hall	Terry Sawchuk
1962-63	Oct. 13	at Chicago	Terry Sawchuk	Glenn Hall
1976-77	Nov. 7	ATLANTA	Eddie Giacomin	Phil Myre

PENALTY SHOTS INVOLVING RED WINGS
(RULE INSTITUTED IN 1934-35) (GOOD UNLESS NG)

DATE	PLAYER	TEAM	GOALIE	TEAM
Nov. 15, 1934	Ebbie Goodfellow–NG	at DETROIT	Percy Jackson	NY Rangers
Nov. 22, 1934	Bill Cook–NG	at NY Rangers	Norm Smith	DETROIT
Nov. 22, 1934	Ebbie Goodfellow–NG	DETROIT	Andy Aitkenhead	at NY Rangers
Nov. 24, 1934	Bill Thomas–NG	at Toronto	Norm Smith	DETROIT
Dec. 13, 1934	Ebbie Goodfellow	DETROIT	Bill Beveridge	at St. Louis
Dec. 20, 1934	Ebbie Goodfellow–NG	at DETROIT	Alex Connell	Mon. Maroons
Feb. 10, 1935	Ebbie Goodfellow–NG	at DETROIT	Alex Connell	Mon. Marrons
Feb. 17, 1935	Ebbie Goodfellow–NG	at DETROIT	Dave Kerr	NY Rangers
Feb. 21, 1935	Earl Robinson–NG	Mon. Maroons	John Roach	at DETROIT
Mar. 3, 1935	Charlie McVeigh–NG	NY Americans	Norm Smith	at DETROIT
Mar. 9, 1935	Armand Mondou–NG	at Mon. Canadiens	Norm Smith	DETROIT
Nov.14, 1935	Art Coulter–NG	NY Rangers	Norm Smith	at DETROIT
Nov. 24, 1935	Ebbie Goodfellow–NG	at DETROIT	George Hainsworth	Toronto
Dec. 19, 1935	Dave Schriner–NG	at NY Americans	Norm Smith	DETROIT
Dec. 29, 1935	Ebbie Goodfellow–NG	at DETROIT	Cecil Thompson	Boston
Jan. 1, 1936	Paul Thompson	at Chicago	Norm Smith	DETROIT
Nov. 22, 1936	King Clancy–NG	Toronto	Norm Smith	at DETROIT
Dec. 3, 1936	Neil Colvilli–NG	NY Rangers	Norm Smith	at DETROIT
Dec. 25, 1936	John Sorrell–NG	at DETROIT	Mike Karakas	Chicago
Dec. 31, 1936	Mud Bruneteau–NG	at DETROIT	Roy Wortors	NY Americans
Jan. 7, 1937	Hap Emms–NG	at NY Americans	Norm Smith	DETROIT
Feb. 7, 1937	John Sorrell	at DETROIT	Cecil Thompson	Boston
Mar. 4, 1937*	John Sorrell–NG	at DETROIT	Dave Kerr	NY Rangers
Mar. 4, 1937*	Alex Shibicky–NG	NY Rangers	Norm Smith	at DETROIT
Dec. 25, 1937	George Parsons–NG	at Toronto	Norm Smith	DETROIT
Nov. 6, 1938	Charlie Conacher–NG	at DETROIT	Frank Brimsek	Boston
Nov. 24, 1938	Mud Bruneteau–NG	at DETROIT	Mike Karakas	Chicago
Jan. 22, 1939	Woody Dumart	Boston	Cecil Thompson	at DETROIT
Jan. 28, 1939	Nick Metz–NG	at Toronto	Cecil Thompson	DETROIT
Dec. 17, 1939	Ebbie Goodfellow–NG	at DETROIT	Dave Kerr	NY Rangers
Feb. 13, 1940	Ebbie Goodfellow	DETROIT	Frank Brimsek	at Boston
Feb. 29, 1940	Syd Howe–NG	DETROIT	Turk Broda	at Toronto
Mar. 3, 1940	Mud Bruneteau	DETROIT	Frank Brimsek	Boston
Nov. 19, 1940	Roy Conacher–NG	at Boston	John Mowers	DETROIT
Dec. 5, 1940	Earl Siebert–NG	at Chicago	John Mowers	DETROIT
Dec. 17, 1940	Archie Wilder–NG	DETROIT	Earl Robertson	at NY Americans
Jan. 24, 1941	Charlie Conacher	NY Americans	John Mowers	at DETROIT
Dec. 4, 1941	Don Grosso–NG	at DETROIT	Charlie Rayner	NY Americans
Dec. 25, 1941	Jack Stewart–NG	at DETROIT	Charlie Rayner	NY Americans
Jan. 3, 1942	Sid Abel–NG	DETROIT	Paul Bibeault	Mon. Canadiens
Feb. 22, 1942	Eddie Bush–NG	at DETROIT	Turk Broda	Toronto
Feb. 25, 1942	Sid Abel	DETROIT	Jim Henry	at NY Rangers
Mar. 24, 1942*	Charlie Sands–NG	at Mon. Canadiens	John Mowers	DETROIT
Nov. 21, 1943	Syd Howe	at DETROIT	Hec Highton	Chicago

Date	Player	Team	Goalie	Team
Jan. 18, 1945	Fred Thurier	NY Rangers	Harry Lumley	at DETROIT
Jan. 21, 1945	Ray Getliffe	Mon. Canadiens	Harry Lumley	at DETROIT
Nov. 25, 1945	Alex Shibicky	NY Rangers	Harry Lumley	at DETROIT
Jan. 12, 1946	Carl Liscombe–NG	DETROIT	Frank McCool	at Toronto
Mar. 9, 1947	Pat Lundy–NG	DETROIT	Frank Brimsek	at Boston
Nov. 19, 1947	Buddy O'Connell–NG	NY Rangers	Harry Lumley	at DETROIT
Mar. 5, 1953	Gordie Howe	at DETROIT	Gump Worsley	NY Rangers
Dec. 31, 1961	Gordie Howe	at DETROIT	John Bower	Toronto
Jan. 31, 1962	Bruce MacGregor–NG	DETROIT	Glenn Hall	at Chicago
Feb. 4, 1962	Alex Delvecchio–NG	DETROIT	Bruce Gamble	at Boston
Mar. 14, 1962	Andy Bathgate	NY Rangers	Hank Bassen	at DETROIT
Nov. 20, 1963	Doug Barkley	DETROIT	Glenn Hall	at Chicago
Nov. 27, 1963	Rod Gilbert	at NY Rangers	Terry Sawchuk	DETROIT
Dec. 8, 1963	Claude LaForge	at DETROIT	Don Simmons	Toronto
Jan. 5, 1967	Norm Ullman	at DETROIT	Glenn Hall	Chicago
Feb. 8, 1967	Pete Stemkowski–NG	at Toronto	Roger Crozier	DETROIT
Jan. 28, 1968	Wayne Connelly–NG	at Minnesota	Roger Crozier	DETROIT
Mar. 9, 1968	Mike Walton	at Toronto	Roger Crozier	DETROIT
Oct. 28, 1968	Claude Provost–NG	Montreal	Roger Crozier	at DETROIT
Dec. 6, 1969	Andre Boudrias–NG	at St. Louis	Roger Crozier	DETROIT
Jan. 14, 1971	Jean Pronovost	Pittsburgh	Roy Edwards	at DETROIT
Feb. 29, 1972	Guy Charron–NG	at DETROIT	Ed Dyke	Vancouver
Jan. 10, 1973	Ron Schock–NG	at Pittsburgh	Roy Edwards	at DETROIT
Jan. 28, 1973	Jacques Lemaire–NG	at Montreal	Denis DeJordy	DETROIT
Mar. 7, 1974	Bill Clement	at Philadelphia	Jim Rutherford	DETROIT
Jan. 23, 1975	Pierre Jarry–NG	DETROIT	Roger Crozier	at Buffalo
Feb. 1, 1975	Lorne Henning	NY Islanders	Jim Rutherford	at DETROIT
Dec. 4, 1976	Dennis Polonich–NG	DETROIT	Rogatien Vachon	at Los Angeles
Dec. 12, 1976	Bill Lochead–NG	DETROIT	Gilles Gilbert	at Boston
Jan. 6, 1977	Dean Talafous–NG	Minnesota	Ed Giacomin	at DETROIT
Mar. 12, 1977	Lanny McDonald–NG	Toronto	Jim Rutherford	at DETROIT
Nov. 5, 1977	Reed Larson–NG	at DETROIT	Gilles Meloche	Cleveland
Mar. 5, 1978	Andre St. Laurent–NG	at DETROIT	Gary Smith	Minnesota
Nov. 22, 1978	Dale McCourt–NG	DETROIT	Mario Lessard	at Los Angeles
Jan. 30,1980	Mike Foligno	DETROIT	Paul Harrison	at Toronto
Mar. 26, 1980	Mike Foligno–NG	at DETROIT	Ron Low	Edmonton
Mar. 14, 1981	Bernie Federko	at St. Louis	Larry Lozinski	DETROIT
Feb. 11, 1982	Tom Gradin	at DETROIT	Gilles Gilbert	Vancouver
Feb. 11, 1982	Ivan Hlinka	at DETROIT	Gilles Gilbert	Vancouver
Dec. 8, 1982	Clark Gillies–NG	NY Islanders	Corrado Miclaef	at DETROIT
Dec. 10, 1983	Alain Lemieux	at St. Louis	Greg Stefan	DETROIT
Jan. 9, 1984	Ron Duguay–NG	at DETROIT	Grant Fuhr	Edmonton
Jan. 14, 1984	Brent Peterson	Buffalo	Greg Stefan	at DETROIT
Feb. 1, 1984	Bob Crawford	Hartford	Ken Holland	at DETROIT
Feb. 7, 1985	Dwight Foster	at DETROIT	Rick Wamsley	St. Louis
Oct. 8, 1985	Bo Berglund	Minnesota	Corrado Micalef	at DETROIT
Oct. 16, 1985	Gerard Gallant	at DETROIT	Brian Hayward	Winnipeg
Dec. 15, 1985	Denis Savard	at Chicago	Greg Stefan	DETROIT
Feb. 16, 1986	Pierre LaRouche–NG	at NY Rangers	Corrado Micalef	DETROIT
Feb. 16, 1986	Mike Ridley–NG	at NY Rangers	Corrado Micalef	DETROIT
Feb. 17, 1987	Petr Klima–NG	DETROIT	John Vanbiesbrouck	at NY Rangers
Mar. 5, 1987	Bob Probert	at DETROIT	Kari Takko	Minnesota
Mar. 25, 1987	Mel Bridgman	at DETROIT	Roland Melanson	Los Angeles
Nov. 22, 1987	Steve Yzerman–NG	at DETROIT	Doug Kerns	Boston
Feb. 3, 1988	Denis Savard–NG	at Chicago	Glen Hanlon	DETROIT
Apr. 9, 1988*	Petr Klima	DETROIT	Alan Bester	at Toronto
Oct. 28, 1988	Miroslav Frycer–NG	at DETROIT	Don Beaupre	Minnesota
Feb. 13, 1989	Steve Yzerman	at DETROIT	Bob Essensa	Winnipeg
Feb. 19, 1989	Mike Foligno–NG	at Buffalo	Glen Hanlon	DETROIT
Mar. 20, 1989	Petr Klima–NG	at DETROIT	Jon Casey	Minnesota
Nov. 3, 1989	Jimmy Carson–NG	at DETROIT	Mike Liut	Hartford
Feb. 19, 1990	Russ Courtnall	Montreal	Tim Cheveldae	at DETROIT
Nov. 23, 1990	Rich Sutter—NG	St. Louis	Tim Cheveldae	at DETROIT
Nov. 29, 1990	Joe Kocur	at DETROIT	Jacques Cloutier	at Chicago
Jan. 9, 1991	Ken Linseman–NG	Edmonton	Tim Cheveldae	at DETROIT
Jan. 25, 1991	Brent Fedyk–NG	at DETROIT	Vince Riendeau	St. Louis
Oct. 30, 1991	Kevin Miller	at DETROIT	Patrick Roy	Montreal
Nov. 2, 1991	Wes Walz–NG	at Boston	Tim Cheveldae	DETROIT
Jan. 3, 1992	Steve Yzerman	at DETROIT	Grant Fuhr	Toronto
Jan. 29, 1992	Steve Yzerman	at DETROIT	Darren Puppa	Buffalo
Nov. 27, 1992	Paul Ysebaert	at DETROIT	Rob Stauber	Los Angeles
Mar. 18, 1993	Steve Yzerman–NG	at DETROIT	Darcy Wakaluk	Minnesota
Dec. 27, 1993	Sergei Fedorov	DETROIT	Andy Moog	at Dallas
Mar. 4, 1994	Peter Zezel–NG	Toronto	Chris Osgood	at DETROIT
Mar. 22, 1994	Mark Howe–NG	at DETROIT	Ed Belfour	Chicago
Feb. 12, 1995	Sergei Fedorov–NG	at DETROIT	Kelly Hrudey	Los Angeles
Mar. 22, 1995	Bob Errey–NG	at DETROIT	Nikolai Khabibulin	Winnipeg
Apr. 1, 1995	Dave Gagner–NG	at Dallas	Chris Osgood	DETROIT

*Playoffs

DETROIT RED WINGS
ALL-TIME DETROIT HAT TRICKS
(Regular Season and Playoffs)

1926-27 — Duke Keats vs. Pittsburgh, March 10, 1927.

1927-28 — Larry Aurie vs. N.Y. Rangers, Jan. 3, 1928
George Hay vs. Chicago, March 6, 1928

1928-29 — NONE

1929-30 — Carson Cooper vs. Montreal Maroons, Nov. 28, 1929
Herbie Lewis (4) vs. Pittsburgh, Feb. 10, 1930

1930-31 — Larry Aurie vs. N.Y. Americans, Dec. 21, 1930
Ebbie Goodfellow (4) vs. Toronto, Dec. 25, 1930

1931-32 — NONE

1932-33 — Johnny Sorrell vs. N.Y. Americans, Nov. 15, 1932

1933-34 — Johnny Sorrell (4) vs. N.Y. Americans, Nov. 13, 1933

1934-35 — Cooney Weiland vs. St. Louis, Dec. 13, 1934

1935-36 — Marty Barry vs. Canadiens, Jan. 5, 1936
Syd Howe vs. N.Y. Americans, March 22, 1936

1936-37 — Larry Aurie vs. N.Y. Rangers, Feb. 2, 1937
Johnny Sorrell vs. Boston, Feb. 7, 1937
Syd Howe vs. Chicago, Feb. 21, 1937
Marty Barry vs. Montreal Maroons, March 2, 1937

1937-38 — Herbie Lewis vs. Boston, March 6, 1938
Carl Liscombe vs. Chicago, March 13, 1938

1938-39 — Gus Geisbrecht vs. N.Y. Americans, Feb. 5, 1939
Syd Howe vs. N.Y. Americans, March 2, 1939
*Syd Howe vs. Canadiens, March 23, 1939

1939-40 — Syd Howe vs. Canadiens, Dec. 25, 1939

1940-41 — Mud Bruneteau (4) vs. N.Y. Americans, March 6, 1941

1941-42 — NONE

1942-43 — Carl Liscombe vs. N.Y. Rangers, Nov. 5, 1942
Syd Howe vs. Toronto, Dec. 12, 1942
Carl Liscombe vs. N.Y. Rangers, Jan. 24, 1943
*Mud Bruneteau vs. Boston, April 1, 1943
*Don Grosso vs. Boston, April 7, 1943

1943-44 — Mud Bruneteau (4) vs. Boston, Nov. 7, 1943
Mud Bruneteau vs. Chicago, Nov. 21, 1943
Syd Howe vs. N.Y. Rangers, Jan. 23, 1944
Syd Howe (6) vs. N.Y. Rangers, Feb. 3, 1944
Joe Carveth vs. N.Y. Rangers, Feb. 10, 1944
Adam Brown vs. N.Y. Rangers, March 2, 1944
Mud Bruneteau vs. Toronto, March 12, 1944
Carl Liscombe vs. Boston, March 16, 1944
*Carl Liscombe (4) vs. Boston, April 3, 1944

1944-45 — Jud McAtee vs. N.Y. Rangers, Nov. 2, 1944
Flash Hollett vs. N.Y. Rangers, Dec. 21, 1944
Joe Carveth vs. Boston, March 4, 1945

1945-46 — Adam Brown vs. Boston, Oct. 28, 1945

1946-47 — Pete Horeck (4) vs. Chicago, Jan. 23, 1947
Roy Conacher vs. Canadiens, Feb. 22, 1947
Roy Conacher (4) vs. Chicago, March 16, 1947
Ted Lindsay vs. Chicago, March 16, 1947

1947-48 — Jim McFadden vs. Chicago, Nov. 22, 1947

1948-49 — Gerry Couture vs. Chicago, Nov. 28, 1948
Ted Lindsay vs. Chicago, Feb. 2, 1949

1949-50 — Sid Abel vs. Boston, Nov. 2, 1949
Gerry Couture (4) vs. Boston, Feb. 11, 1950
Gordie Howe vs. Boston, Feb. 11, 1950
Gordie Howe vs. Toronto, March 19, 1950

1950-51 — Gordie Howe vs. Chicago, Jan. 16, 1951
Gordie Howe vs. Chicago, Jan. 23, 1951
George Gee vs. Chicago, March 11, 1951
Gordie Howe vs. Chicago, March 17, 1951

1951-52 — Gordie Howe vs. Canadiens, Dec. 31, 1951
Gordie Howe vs. Canadiens, March 23, 1952

1952-53 — Gordie Howe vs. Toronto, Jan. 11, 1953
Gordie Howe vs. Toronto, Jan. 29, 1953
Ted Lindsay (4) vs. Boston, March 2, 1953

1953-54 — NONE

1954-55 — Red Kelly vs. Boston, Oct. 21, 1954
Dutch Reibel vs. Chicago, Jan. 9, 1955
Dutch Reibel vs. Toronto, March 13, 1955
Ted Lindsay vs. Montreal, March 20, 1955
*Ted Lindsay vs. Montreal, April 5, 1955
*Gordie Howe vs. Montreal, April 10, 1955

1955-56 — Gordie Howe vs. Boston, Jan. 19, 1956

1956-57 — Ted Lindsay vs. Montreal, Nov. 18, 1956
Gordie Howe vs. N.Y. Rangers, Dec. 25, 1956
Lorne Ferguson vs. N.Y. Rangers, Feb. 2, 1957

1957-58 — Jack McIntyre vs. Boston, Feb. 22, 1958

1958-59 — Alex Delvecchio vs. Chicago, Oct. 18, 1958
Johnny Wilson vs. Boston, Nov. 18, 1958

1959-60 — Norm Ullman vs. Boston, Jan. 21, 1960

1960-61 — Howie Glover vs. Toronto, Jan. 4, 1961
Norm Ullman (4) vs. N.Y. Rangers, March 14, 1961

1961-62 — Vic Stasiuk vs. Boston, Oct. 19, 1961
Norm Ullman vs. Toronto, Dec. 3, 1961
Gordie Howe vs. Toronto, Dec. 31, 1961

1962-63 — Norm Ullman vs. N.Y. Rangers, March 14, 1963

1963-64 — Norm Ullman vs. Boston, March 8, 1964
Floyd Smith vs. Chicago, March 15, 1964
*Norm Ullman vs. Chicago, March 29, 1964
*Norm Ullman vs. Chicago, April 7, 1964

1964-65 — Norm Ullman vs. Montreal, Feb. 28, 1965
Norm Ullman vs. N.Y. Rangers, March 19, 1965
Gordie Howe vs. Chicago, March 21, 1965
Alex Delvecchio vs. N.Y. Rangers, March 25, 1965
*Norm Ullman vs. Chicago, April 11, 1965

1965-66 — Norm Ullman vs. Boston, Dec. 2, 1965
Gordie Howe vs. Boston, Dec. 12, 1965
Bruce MacGregor vs. Chicago, Dec. 19, 1965
Norm Ullman vs. Toronto, Jan. 16, 1966

1966-67 — Paul Henderson (4) vs. N.Y. Rangers, Oct. 27, 1966
Dean Prentice vs. N.Y. Rangers, Jan. 22, 1967
Norm Ullman vs. Toronto, Feb. 8, 1967

1967-68 — Norm Ullman vs. Montreal, Dec. 17, 1967
Floyd Smith vs. Los Angeles, Feb. 1, 1968
Gordie Howe vs. St. Louis, March 16, 1968

1968-69 — Frank Mahovlich vs. Boston, Oct. 31, 1968
Garry Unger vs. Minnesota, Dec. 15, 1968
Frank Mahovlich vs. Minnesota, Dec. 31, 1968
Pete Stemkowski vs. Los Angeles, Feb. 9, 1969
Frank Mahovlich (4) vs. Oakland, Jan. 12, 1969
Gordie Howe vs. Chicago, Feb. 6, 1969
Frank Mahovlich vs. Los Angeles, Feb. 9, 1969
Gordie Howe vs. Los Angeles, Feb. 16, 1969

1969-70 — Gordie Howe vs. Pittsburgh, Nov. 2, 1969
Frank Mahovlich vs. Montreal, Nov. 19, 1969
Garry Unger vs. Oakland, Dec. 28, 1969
Alex Delvecchio vs. Philadelphia, Jan. 3, 1970

1970-71 — NONE

1971-72 — Nick Libett vs. Buffalo, Jan. 27, 1972
Mickey Redmond vs. California, Feb. 6, 1972
Marcel Dionne vs. Montreal, March 19, 1972

1972-73 — Mickey Redmond vs. Vancouver, Jan. 12, 1973
Marcel Dionne vs. Montreal, Feb. 22, 1973

1973-74 — Guy Charron vs. California, Oct. 21, 1973
Guy Charron vs. Toronto, Nov. 11, 1973
Red Berenson vs. Los Angeles, Jan. 12, 1974
Mickey Redmond vs. N.Y. Islanders, Feb. 24, 1974

1974-75 — Mickey Redmond vs. Washington, Oct. 19, 1974
Marcel Dionne vs. N.Y. Rangers, Nov. 20, 1974
Marcel Dionne vs. Boston, Dec. 5, 1974
Phil Roberto vs. Toronto, Feb. 9, 1975
Danny Grant vs. Vancouver, Feb. 14, 1975
Mickey Redmond vs. N.Y. Rangers, March 22, 1975

1975-76 — Michel Bergeron vs. Washington, Dec. 12, 1975
Michel Bergeron (4) vs. St. Louis, March 18, 1976

1976-77 — Dan Maloney vs. Cleveland, Nov. 19, 1976
Dennis Hextall vs. Atlanta, Dec. 18, 1976

1977-78 — Dale McCourt vs. Washington, Jan. 22, 1978
Paul Woods vs. Vancouver, Feb. 12, 1978
Dale McCourt vs. Atlanta, Feb. 16, 1978
Dale McCourt vs. Atlanta, March 22, 1978

1978-79 — Vaclav Nedomansky vs. Chicago, Oct. 28, 1978
Errol Thompson vs. Boston, Dec. 7, 1978
Dale McCourt vs. Vancouver, Dec. 20, 1978
Dale McCourt vs. Pittsburgh, Feb. 18, 1979
Vaclav Nedomansky vs. Colorado, Feb. 25, 1979
Vaclav Nedomansky vs. St. Louis, Feb. 28, 1979

1979-80 — Vaclav Nedomansky vs. Winnipeg, Oct. 17, 1979
Errol Thompson vs. Chicago, Dec. 16, 1979
Mike Foligno vs. Quebec, Jan. 27, 1980
Mike Foligno vs. Pittsburgh, Jan. 31, 1980

1980-81 — Dale McCourt vs. Colorado, Dec. 20, 1980
Reed Larson vs. Pittsburgh, Jan. 3, 1981
Dale McCourt vs. N.Y. Rangers, Jan. 19, 1981

1981-82 — Mike Foligno vs. Calgary, Oct. 29, 1981
John Ogrodnick vs. Calgary, Oct. 29, 1981
John Ogrodnick vs. Los Angeles, Nov. 5, 1981
Mark Osborne vs. St. Louis, Dec. 1, 1981

1982-83 — John Ogrodnick vs. Calgary, Dec. 12, 1982
Reed Larson vs. Pittsburgh, Feb. 15, 1983
Ivan Boldirev vs. Hartford, Feb. 20, 1983

1983-84 — Ron Duguay vs. Chicago, Nov. 3, 1983
STEVE YZERMAN vs. Toronto, Dec. 23, 1983
John Ogrodnick vs. Toronto, Dec. 23, 1983
Ivan Boldirev vs. Toronto, Feb. 19, 1984
Ivan Boldirev (4) vs. Los Angeles, March 24, 1984

1984-85 — John Ogrodnick vs. Toronto, Dec. 4, 1984
Lane Lambert vs. Calgary, Dec. 28, 1984
Ron Duguay vs. Chicago, Dec. 17, 1985
Danny Gare vs. Vancouver, Feb. 27, 1985
Reed Larson vs. Vancouver, Feb. 27, 1985
Ron Duguay vs. Minnesota, March 1, 1985
John Ogrodnick vs. Edmonton, March 13, 1985
Ron Duguay vs. Vancouver, March 15, 1985
STEVE YZERMAN vs. Toronto, March 30, 1985

1985-86 — Danny Gare vs. Pittsburgh, Oct. 30, 1985
Warren Young vs. St. Louis, Dec. 7, 1985
Petr Klima vs. Chicago, March 5, 1986
Petr Klima vs. Chicago, March 22, 1986

1986-87 — Shawn Burr vs. Philadelphia, Nov. 13, 1986
Petr Klima vs. Boston, March 2, 1987

1987-88 — Tim Higgins vs. Chicago, Dec. 4, 1987
Gerard Gallant vs. Minnesota, Dec. 18, 1987
Bob Probert vs. St. Louis, Dec. 31, 1987
STEVE YZERMAN vs. Winnipeg, Jan. 3, 1988
STEVE YZERMAN vs. Montreal, Feb. 6, 1988
Gerard Gallant vs. New Jersey, Feb. 12, 1988
Gerard Gallant vs. N.Y. Rangers, March 26, 1988
*Petr Klima vs. Toronto, April 7, 1988
*Petr Klima vs. St. Louis, April 21, 1988

1988-89 — STEVE YZERMAN vs. Philadelphia, Nov. 4, 1988
STEVE YZERMAN vs. Philadelphia, Nov. 12, 1988
Gerard Gallant vs. St. Louis, Jan. 4, 1989
Dave Barr vs. N.Y. Islanders, Feb. 21, 1989
*STEVE YZERMAN vs. Chicago, April 6, 1989

1989-90 — STEVE YZERMAN vs. Chicago, Dec. 15, 1989
Jimmy Carson vs. Toronto, Dec. 27, 1989
Shawn Burr vs. Minnesota, Jan. 9, 1990
STEVE YZERMAN (4) vs. Edmonton, Jan. 31, 1990
STEVE YZERMAN vs. Los Angeles, Feb. 14, 1990

1990-91 — STEVE YZERMAN vs Toronto, Nov. 17, 1990
Johan Garpenlov (4) vs. St. Louis, Nov. 23, 1990
STEVE YZERMAN vs vs. Winnipeg, Dec. 22, 1990
STEVE YZERMAN vs. St. Louis, Jan. 26, 1991
Jimmy Carson vs. Quebec, March 5, 1991
*STEVE YZERMAN vs. St. Louis, April 4, 1991

1991-92 — RAY SHEPPARD vs. Calgary, Nov. 12, 1991
STEVE YZERMAN vs. Calgary, Dec. 3, 1991
Paul Ysebaert vs. Toronto, Jan. 3, 1992
STEVE YZERMAN vs. Buffalo, Jan 29, 1992
Kevin Miller vs. Buffalo, Feb. 12, 1992
Jimmy Carson vs. St. Louis, Feb. 15, 1992
STEVE YZERMAN vs. Minnesota, Apr. 14, 1992
*RAY SHEPPARD vs. Minnesota, Apr. 24, 1992

1992-93 — STEVE YZERMAN vs. St. Louis, Oct. 25, 1992
Jimmy Carson vs. Pittsburgh, Nov. 13, 1992
STEVE YZERMAN vs. Calgary, Jan. 26, 1993
STEVE YZERMAN vs. Chicago, Feb. 14, 1993
*DINO CICCARELLI vs. Toronto, Apr. 29, 1993

1993-94 — Shawn Burr vs. Buffalo, Oct. 18, 1993
RAY SHEPPARD vs. San Jose, Jan. 6, 1994
VYACHESLAV KOZLOV vs. San Jose, Jan. 6, 1994
RAY SHEPPARD vs. Winnipeg, Jan. 29, 1994
SERGEI FEDOROV vs. Calgary, Mar. 1, 1994
DINO CICCARELLI (4) vs. Vancouver, Apr. 4, 1994

1995 — RAY SHEPPARD vs. Vancouver, Jan. 24, 1995
SERGEI FEDOROV (4) vs. Los Angeles, Feb. 12, 1995
*DINO CICCARELLI vs. Dallas, May 11, 1995

*-Playoffs
ACTIVE PLAYERS IN CAPITALS

REGULAR-SEASON HAT TRICKS: 206	FOUR-GOAL GAMES: 19 (Includes 1 in playoffs)
PLAYOFF HAT TRICKS: 16	FIVE-GOAL GAMES: 0
TOTAL HAT TRICKS: 222	SIX-GOAL GAMES: 1
THREE-GOAL GAMES: 202 (Includes 16 in playoffs)	

Times in Playoffs 44	Games Played 369
Times in Finals 19	Games Won 180
Times Won Cup 7	Games Lost 188
Total Series 76	Games Tied...1#
Series Won-Lost 39-37	Goals For-Against 1021-1005

DETROIT VS. ATLANTA FLAMES

Series Played 1   Won by Detroit 1, by Atlanta 0
Games Played 2   Won by Detroit 2, by Atlanta 0   Goals For-Against 8-5
1978 — Detroit won 2 games to 0

DETROIT VS. BOSTON BRUINS

Series Played 7   Won by Boston 4, by Detroit 3
Games Played 33   Won by Boston 19, by Detroit 14   Goals For-Against 98-96

1941* — Boston won 4 games to 0	1946 — Boston won 4 games to 1
1942 — Detroit won 2 games to 0	1953 — Boston won 4 games to 2
1943* — Detroit won 4 games to 0	1957 — Boston won 4 games to 1
1945 — Detroit won 4 games to 3	

DETROIT VS. CHICAGO BLACKHAWKS

Series Played...........14   Won by Chicago 8, by Detroit 6
Games Played 69   Won by Chicago 38, by Detroit 31   Goals For-Against...190-210

1934* — Chicago won 3 games to 1	1966 — Detroit won 4 games to 2
1941 — Detroit won 2 games to 0	1970 — Chicago won 4 games to 0
1944 — Chicago won 4 games to 1	1985 — Chicago won 3 games to 0
1961* — Chicago won 4 games to 2	1987 — Detroit won 4 games to 0
1963 — Detroit won 4 games to 2	1989 — Chicago won 4 games to 2
1964 — Detroit won 4 games to 3	1992 — Chicago won 4 games to 0
1965 — Chicago won 4 games to 3	1995 — Detroit won 4 games to 1

DETROIT VS. EDMONTON OILERS

Series Played 2   Won by Edmonton 2, by Detroit 0
Games Played 10   Won by Edmonton 8, by Detroit 2   Goals For-Against 26-39
1987 — Edmonton won 4 games to 1   1988 — Edmonton won 4 games to 1

DETROIT VS. DALLAS STARS/MINNESOTA NORTH STARS

Series Played 2   Won by Detroit 2, by Stars 0
Games Played 12   Won by Detroit 8, by Stars 4   Goals For-Against 40-29
1992 — Detroit won 4 games to 3   1995 — Detroit won 4 games to 1

DETROIT VS. MONTREAL CANADIENS

Series Played..........12   Won by Detroit 7, by Montreal 5
Games Played 62   Won by Montreal 33, by Detroit 29   Goals For-Against ...149-161

1937 — Detroit won 3 games to 2	1949 — Detroit won 4 games to 3
1939 — Detroit won 2 games to 1	1951 — Montreal won 4 games to 2
1942 — Detroit won 2 games to 1	1952* — Detroit won 4 games to 0
1954* — Detroit won 4 games to 3	1958 — Montreal won 4 games to 0
1955* — Detroit won 4 games to 3	1966* — Montreal won 4 games to 2
1956* — Montreal won 4 games to 1	1978 — Montreal won 4 games to 1

DETROIT VS. MONTREAL MAROONS

Series Played 3   Won by Detroit 2, by Montreal 1
Games Played 7   Won by Detroit 5, by Montreal 1#   Goals For-Against........12-6
1932 — Montreal won 1 game# (total goals)   1936 — Detroit won 3 games to 0
1933 — Detroit won 2 games (total goals)

#-Tie game 1-1 vs. Montreal Maroons March 27, 1932, at Detroit

DETROIT VS. NEW JERSEY DEVILS

Series Played 1   Won by New Jersey 1, by Detroit 0
Games Played 4   Won by New Jersey 4, by Detroit 0   Goals For-Against.........7-16
1995* — New Jersey won 4 games to 0

DETROIT VS. NEW YORK AMERICANS

Series Played 1   Won by Detroit 1, by Americans 0
Games Played 3   Won by Detroit 2, by Americans 1   Goals For-Against...........9-7
1940 — Detroit won 2 games to 1

DETROIT VS. NEW YORK RANGERS

Series Played 5   Won by Detroit 4, by Rangers 1
Games Played 23   Won by Detroit 13, by Rangers 10   Goals For-Against......57-49
1933 — Rangers won 2 games (total goals)   1941 — Detroit won 2 games to 1
1937* — Detroit won 3 games to 2   1948 — Detroit won 4 games to 2
    1950* — Detroit won 4 games to 3

DETROIT VS. ST. LOUIS BLUES

Series Played 3   Won by Detroit 1, by St. Louis 2
Games Played 16   Won by Detroit 8, by St. Louis 8   Goals For-Against 53-51
1984 — St. Louis won 3 games to 1   1991 —St. Louis won 4 games to 3
1988 — Detroit won 4 games to 1

DETROIT VS. SAN JOSE SHARKS

Series Played 2   Won by Detroit 1, by San Jose 1
Games Played 11   Won by Detroit 7, by San Jose 4   Goals For-Against.......51-27
1994 — San Jose won 4 games to 3   1995 — Detroit won 4 games to 0

DETROIT VS. TORONTO MAPLE LEAFS

Series Played 23   Won by Detroit 11, by Toronto 12
Games Played........117   Won by Detroit 59, by Toronto 58   Goals For-Against...321-311

1929 — Toronto won 2 games (total goals)	1949* — Toronto won 4 games to 0
1934 — Detroit won 3 games to 2	1952 — Detroit won 4 games to 0
1936* — Detroit won 3 games to 1	1954 — Detroit won 4 games to 1
1939 — Toronto won 2 games to 1	1955 — Detroit won 4 games to 0
1940 — Toronto won 2 games to 0	1956 — Detroit won 4 games to 1
1942* — Toronto won 4 games to 3	1960 — Toronto won 4 games to 2
1943 — Detroit won 4 games to 2	1961 — Detroit won 4 games to 1
1945* — Toronto won 4 games to 3	1963* — Toronto won 4 games to 1
1947 — Toronto won 4 games to 1	1964* — Toronto won 4 games to 3
1948* — Toronto won 4 games to 0	1987 — Detroit won 4 games to 3
1950 — Detroit won 4 games to 3	1988 — Detroit won 4 games to 2
	1993 — Toronto won 4 games to 3

*-Final series.
#-Tie game 1-1 vs. Montreal Maroons March 27, 1932, at Detroit.

RED WINGS' TEAM PLAYOFF RECORDS

MOST GOALS FOR, ONE GAME: 9 – vs. Toronto, Apr. 7, 1936, Detroit 9, Toronto 4;
vs. Toronto, Mar. 29, 1947, Detroit 9, Toronto 1
MOST GOALS FOR, ONE YEAR: 69 – 1988 (32 vs. Toronto, 21 vs. St. Louis, 16 vs. Edmonton)
MOST GOALS AGAINST, ONE YEAR: 57 – 1987 (20 vs. Chicago, 14 vs. Toronto, 23 vs. Edmonton)
MOST GOALS FOR, ONE SERIES: 32 – vs. Toronto, 1988
MOST GOALS AGAINST, ONE SERIES: 25 – vs. Toronto, 1942; Chicago, 1989
MOST GOALS FOR, ONE HOME GAME: 9 – vs. Toronto Apr. 7, 1936, Detroit 9, Toronto 4
MOST GOALS AGAINST, ONE HOME GAME: 8 – vs. Montreal, Apr. 23, 1978, Montreal 8, Detroit 0;
vs. Chicago, April 13, 1985, Chicago 8, Detroit 2
MOST GOALS FOR, ONE ROAD GAME: 9 – vs. Toronto, Mar. 29, 1947, Detroit 9, Toronto 1
MOST GOALS AGAINST, ONE ROAD GAME: 9 – vs. Toronto, Apr. 14, 1942, Toronto 9, Detroit 3;
vs. Chicago, April 10, 1985, Chicago 9, Detroit 5
FASTEST TWO GOALS: •5 seconds – Apr. 11, 1965, second period vs. Chicago
(both by Norm Ullman, 17:35, 17:40 against Glenn Hall), Detroit 4, Chicago 2
FASTEST THREE GOALS: 1:30 – Mar. 29, 1947, third period at Toronto
(Jim Conacher, 17:30, Roy Conacher, 18:30; Ed Bruneteau, 19:00), Detroit 9, Toronto 1
FASTEST FOUR GOALS: 4:46 – Mar. 23, 1939, third period vs. Montreal Canadiens
(Syd Howe, 13:44; Syd Howe, 14:39; Sid Abel, 17:02; Ed Wares, 18:30), Detroit 7, Montreal 3
MOST POWER-PLAY GOALS, ONE YEAR: 22 – 1995 vs. Dallas, San Jose, Chicago, New Jersey
MOST POWER-PLAY GOALS, ONE SERIES: 11 – vs. Toronto, 1988
MOST POWER-PLAY GOALS FOR, ONE GAME: 4 – vs. Montreal Canadiens Mar. 23, 1939, Detroit 7, Montreal 3;
vs. Chicago Apr. 4, 1965, Detroit 6, Chicago 3;
vs. Chicago Apr. 10, 1966, Detroit 7, Chicago 0;
vs. Toronto, Apr. 29, 1993, Detroit 7, Toronto 3
MOST POWER-PLAY GOALS FOR, ONE PERIOD: 3 – vs. Atlanta Apr. 11, 1978, Detroit 5, Atlanta 3
MOST POWER-PLAY GOALS AGAINST, ONE YEAR: 20 – 1988 vs. Toronto, St. Louis, Edmonton
MOST POWER-PLAY GOALS AGAINST, ONE SERIES: – 10 vs. Chicago, 1989
MOST POWER-PLAY GOALS AGAINST, ONE GAME: 4 – vs. Chicago, Mar. 28, 1963, Chicago 5, Detroit 2
MOST SHORTHANDED GOALS FOR, ONE GAME: 2
– vs. Toronto, Apr. 5, 1936 (Syd Howe, Bucko McDonald), Detroit 3, Toronto 1;
– vs. Toronto, Apr. 29, 1993 (STEVE YZERMAN, Paul Ysebaert), Detroit 7, Toronto 3
MOST SHORTHANDED GOALS, ONE PERIOD: 2
– vs. Toronto, Apr. 29, 1993 (STEVE YZERMAN, Paul Ysebaert), Detroit 7, Toronto 3
MOST SHORTHANDED GOALS, ONE YEAR: 4 – 1964 vs. Chicago, Toronto; 1993 vs. Toronto
MOST SHORTHANDED GOALS AGAINST, ONE GAME: 2 – vs. Montreal, Apr. 23, 1978, Montreal 8, Detroit 0;
– vs. Chicago, Apr. 11, 1989, Detroit 6, Chicago 4
MOST SHORTHANDED GOALS AGAINST, ONE PERIOD: 2 – vs. Montreal, Apr. 23, 1978, Montreal 8, Detroit 0
MOST SHORTHANDED GOALS AGAINST, ONE PERIOD: 2 – vs. Montreal, Apr. 23, 1978, Montreal 8, Detroit 0
MOST SHORTHANDED GOALS AGAINST, ONE YEAR: 4 – vs. Chicago, 1989
MOST PENALTY MINUTES, ONE GAME: •152 – vs. St. Louis, Apr. 12, 1991
MOST PENALTY MINUTES, ONE PERIOD: 114 – vs. St. Louis, Apr. 12, 1991
MOST PENALTIES, ONE GAME: 33# – vs. St. Louis, Apr. 12, 1991
MOST PENALTIES, ONE PERIOD: 20 – vs. St. Louis, Apr. 12, 1991
MOST CONSECUTIVE VICTORIES, ONE YEAR: 8 – 1952 vs. Toronto, Montreal;
1995 vs. Dallas, San Jose, Chicago
MOST CONSECUTIVE VICTORIES: 9 – Eight straight in 1952, first in '53
MOST CONSECUTIVE DEFEATS: 8 – Final four games of 1966 final vs. Montreal; first four in '70 vs. Chicago
MOST CONSECUTIVE HOME VICTORIES: 11 – Apr. 16, 1954, vs. Montreal; Mar. 22-24, 1955, vs. Toronto; Apr. 3-5-10-14,
1955, vs. Montreal; Mar. 20-22-29, 1956, vs. Toronto; April 5, 1956, vs. Montreal
MOST CONSECUTIVE HOME DEFEATS: 5 – Apr. 22, 1945, vs. Toronto; Mar. 24-26, 1946, vs. Boston;
Apr. 1-3, 1947, vs. Toronto; Apr. 28-May 1-5, 1966, vs. Montreal; Apr. 11-12, 1970, vs. Chicago
MOST CONSECUTIVE ROAD VICTORIES: 4 – Mar. 29-Apr. 1, 1952, vs. Toronto; Apr. 10-12, 1952, vs. Montreal; Mar. 27-30,
1954, vs. Toronto; Apr. 8-10, 1954, vs. Montreal; Apr. 10-17, 1966, vs. Chicago; Apr. 24-26, 1966, vs. Montreal
MOST CONSECUTIVE ROAD DEFEATS: 8 – Mar. 27, 1956, vs. Toronto; Mar. 31, 1956, vs. Montreal;
Apr. 3-10, 1956, vs. Montreal; Mar. 31-Apr. 10, 1957, vs. Boston; Mar. 25-27, 1958, vs. Montreal
MOST CONSECUTIVE SEASONS QUALIFYING FOR PLAYOFFS: 20 – 1939 through '58
MOST CONSECUTIVE SEASONS NOT QUALIFYING FOR PLAYOFFS: 7 – 1971 through '77
EARLIEST PLAYOFF DATE: Mar. 19 – 1929 vs. Toronto; 1940 vs. New York Americans;
1946 vs. Boston
LATEST PLAYOFF DATE: June 24 – 1995 vs. New Jersey

*-NHL record
#-Shares NHL record
ACTIVE PLAYERS IN CAPITALS

──RED WINGS' INDIVIDUAL PLAYOFF RECORDS──

MOST YEARS IN PLAYOFFS: 19 – Gordie Howe
MOST CONSECUTIVE YEARS IN PLAYOFFS: 13 – Ted Lindsay (1945-57)
MOST GAMES, CAREER: 154 – Gordie Howe
MOST POINTS, CAREER: 158 – Gordie Howe
MOST GOALS, CAREER: 67 – Gordie Howe
MOST ASSISTS, CAREER: 91 – Gordie Howe
MOST GAMES, ONE YEAR: 18 – 11 Players on 1995 team
MOST POINTS, ONE YEAR: 24 – SERGEI FEDOROV, 7 goals, 17 assists, 1995, 17 games
MOST GOALS, ONE YEAR: 10 – Petr Klima, 1988, 12 games
MOST ASSISTS, ONE YEAR: 17 – SERGEI FEDOROV, 1995, 17 games
MOST POINTS, ONE GAME: 5 – Norm Ullman (twice), 2 goals, 3 assists Apr. 7, 1963,
        and 3 goals, 2 assists Apr. 7, 1964, both vs. Chicago
MOST GOALS, ONE GAME: 4 – Carl Liscombe (Apr. 3, 1945, vs. Boston); Ted Lindsay (Apr. 5, 1955, vs. Montreal)
MOST ASSISTS, ONE GAME: 4 – Dutch Reibel, Apr. 5, 1955, vs. Montreal
MOST POINTS BY ROOKIE: 9 – Shawn Burr, 1987
MOST GOALS BY ROOKIE: 7 – Shawn Burr, 1987
MOST ASSISTS BY ROOKIE: 5 – Paul Woods, 1978; SERGEI FEDOROV, 1991
LONGEST POINT STREAK: 12 games – Gordie Howe, 1964
LONGEST GOAL STREAK: 5 games – Gordie Howe, 1949, '64; Ted Lindsay, 1952
MOST POINTS BY ONE LINE, ONE YEAR: 51 – 1955 vs. Toronto, Montreal, 11 games
        (Gordie Howe, 9-11–20; Dutch Reibel, 5-7–12; Ted Lindsay, 7-12–19)
MOST THREE-GOAL GAMES, CAREER: 3 – Norm Ullman, 2 in 1964, 1 in 1965
MOST THREE-GOAL GAMES, ONE YEAR: 2 – Norm Ullman, 1964; Petr Klima, 1988
MOST THREE-GOAL GAMES, ONE SERIES: 2 – Norm Ullman, 1964 vs. Chicago
MOST POWER-PLAY GOALS, CAREER: 13 – Gordie Howe; Alex Delvecchio
MOST POWER-PLAY GOALS, ONE YEAR: 6 – Andy Bathgate, 1966, 12 games; DINO CICCARELLI, 1995, 16 games
MOST POWER-PLAY GOALS, ONE SERIES: 5# – Andy Bathgate, 1966, vs. Chicago, 6 games
MOST POWER-PLAY GOALS, ONE GAME: 3# – Syd Howe, Mar. 23, 1939, vs. Montreal;
        DINO CICCARELLI (twice), Apr. 29, 1993, at Toronto, May 11, 1995, at Dallas
MOST POWER-PLAY GOALS, ONE PERIOD: 2 – Syd Howe, Mar. 23, 1939, third period vs. Montreal;
        Floyd Smith, Apr. 10, 1966, first period at Chicago;
        DINO CICCARELLI, Apr. 29, 1993, second period at Toronto
MOST POINTS, ONE PERIOD: 3 – Ted Lindsay, 3 goals, Apr. 5, 1955, second period vs. Montreal;
        Alex Delvecchio, 3 assists, Apr. 14, 1966, third period vs. Chicago;
        VYACHESLAV KOZLOV, 3 assists, May 21, 1995, third period vs. San Jose
MOST GOALS, ONE PERIOD: 3 – Ted Lindsay, Apr. 5, 1955, second period vs. Montreal
MOST ASSISTS, ONE PERIOD: 3# – Alex Delvecchio, Apr. 14, 1966, third period vs. Chicago;
        VYACHESLAV KOZLOV, May 21, 1995, third period vs. San Jose
MOST POINTS BY DEFENSEMAN, ONE YEAR: 18 – PAUL COFFEY, 1995, 18 games
MOST POINTS BY DEFENSEMAN, ONE GAME: 5 – Eddie Bush, Apr. 9, 1942, at Toronto
        (1 goal, 4 assists)
MOST GOALS BY DEFENSEMAN, ONE YEAR: 6 – PAUL COFFEY, 1995, 18 games
MOST ASSISTS BY DEFENSEMAN, ONE YEAR: 12 – PAUL COFFEY, 1995;
        NICKLAS LIDSTROM, 1995, 18 games each
MOST ASSISTS BY DEFENSEMAN, ONE GAME: 4 – Eddie Bush, Apr. 9, 1942, at Toronto
MOST GAME-WINNING GOALS, CAREER: 11 – Gordie Howe
MOST GAME-WINNING GOALS, ONE YEAR: 4 – Petr Klima, 1988; VYACHESLAV KOZLOV, 1995
MOST SHORTHANDED GOALS, CAREER: 4 – Gordie Howe
MOST SHORTHANDED GOALS, GAME: 1 (several times) – Recent PAUL COFFEY, June 24, 1995, at New Jersey
MOST OVERTIME GOALS, CAREER: 2 – Leo Reise, Mud Bruneteau, Syd Howe, Ted Lindsay
MOST OVERTIME GOALS, ONE YEAR: 2 – Leo Reise, 1950
FASTEST GOAL FROM START OF GAME: 9 seconds – Gordie Howe, Apr. 1, 1954, vs. Toronto against Harry Lumley
FASTEST TWO GOALS: *5 seconds – Norm Ullman, Apr. 11, 1965, second period vs. Chicago, 17:35, 17:40 against Glenn Hall
MOST PENALTY MINUTES, CAREER: 218 – Gordie Howe
MOST PENALTY MINUTES, ONE YEAR: 71 – Joe Kocur, 1987, 16 games
MOST PENALTY MINUTES, ONE GAME: 29 – Randy McKay, Apr. 12, 1991, vs. St. Louis, 2 minors, 3 majors, game misconduct
MOST GAMES BY GOALTENDER, CAREER: 84 – Terry Sawchuk
MOST GAMES BY GOALTENDER, ONE YEAR: 18 – Mike Vernon, 1995
MOST MINUTES BY GOALTENDER, ONE YEAR: 1063 – Mike Vernon, 1995, 18 games
MOST SHUTOUTS, CAREER: 11 – Terry Sawchuk
MOST SHUTOUTS, ONE YEAR: 4# – Terry Sawchuk, 1952 vs. Toronto, Montreal, 8 games
LONGEST SHUTOUT SEQUENCE, ONE YEAR: *248 minutes, 32 seconds – Norm Smith, 1936, vs. Montreal Maroons
LONGEST SHUTOUT SEQUENCE, ONE GAME: 8176 minutes, 30 seconds – Norm Smith, Mar. 24-25, 1936, at Montreal;
        Detroit 1, Montreal Maroons 0; winning goal by Mud Bruneteau
SHUTOUT BY DETROIT GOALIE IN PLAYOFF DEBUT: Norm Smith, Mar. 24-25, 1936, at Montreal;
        Detroit 1, Montreal Maroons 0, 6 OTs;
*-NHL record #-Shares NHL record   CHRIS OSGOOD, Apr. 20, 1994, vs. San Jose; Detroit 4, San Jose 0
ACTIVE PLAYERS IN CAPITALS

─── RED WINGS' PLAYOFF SCORING LEADERS ───

	GP	G	A	PTS
Gordie Howe	154	67	91	158
Alex Delvecchio	121	35	69	104
Ted Lindsay	123	46	44	90
STEVE YZERMAN	**75**	**31**	**47**	**78**
Norm Ullman	80	27	47	74
SERGEI FEDOROV	**49**	**17**	**40**	**57**
Sid Abel	93	28	28	56
Syd Howe	68	17	27	44
Bob Probert	63	14	29	43
Carl Liscombe	57	22	18	40
Gerard Gallant	57	18	21	39
Adam Oates	38	12	27	39
Mud Bruneteau	72	23	14	37
Red Kelly	74	16	21	37
PAUL COFFEY	**32**	**9**	**27**	**36**
Joe Carveth	60	19	15	34
Shawn Burr	79	16	17	33
VYACHESLAV KOZLOV	**36**	**13**	**19**	**32**
Marcel Pronovost	117	7	23	30
Don Grosso	45	15	14	29
Marty Pavelich	91	13	15	28
Petr Klima	31	13	14	27
Steve Chiasson	46	12	14	26
Metro Prystai	43	12	14	26
Brent Ashton	32	11	14	25
NICKLAS LIDSTROM	**43**	**9**	**16**	**25**
DINO CICCARELLI	**30**	**18**	**6**	**24**
RAY SHEPPARD	**42**	**14**	**9**	**23**
Herbie Lewis	38	13	10	23
Floyd Smith	44	12	11	23
Bruce MacGregor	56	9	14	23
Marty Berry	23	9	12	21
John Chabot	22	5	16	21
John Wilson	50	11	9	20
Vic Stasiuk	38	10	10	20
John Sorrell	31	8	12	20
Dutch Reibel	32	6	14	20

ACTIVE PLAYERS IN BOLD CAPITALS

─── DETROIT GOALTENDERS' ALL-TIME PLAYOFF RECORDS ───

PLAYER	YRS	GP	W	L	T	GA	SO	AVG
Terry Sawchuk	10	84	47	37		209	11	2.51
Harry Lumley	5	54	24	30		129	6	2.26
John Mowers	4	32	19	13		80	2	2.45
Greg Stefan	5	30	12	17		99	1	3.53
Mike Vernon	1	18	12	6		41	1	2.31
Tim Cheveldae	3	25	9	15		71	0	3.00
Roger Crozier	4	23	9	12		57	1	2.59
Glen Hanlon	3	18	9	6		42	3	2.58
Norm Smith	2	12	9	2		18	3	1.28
Glenn Hall	2	15	6	9		43	0	2.86
Cecil Thompson	2	11	5	6		27	1	2.32
Wilf Cude	1	9	4	5		21	1	2.21
CHRIS OSGOOD	**2**	**8**	**3**	**2**		**14**	**1**	**2.24**
Earl Robertson	1	6	3	2		8	2	1.71
John Ross Roach	1	4	2	2		8	1	2.00
Jim Rutherford	1	3	2	1		12	0	4.00
Ralph Almas	1	5	1	3		13	0	3.00
Hank Bassen	2	5	1	3		11	0	2.44
Bob Champoux	1	1	1	0		4	0	4.00
Connie Dion	1	5	1	4		17	0	3.40
Ron Low	1	4	1	3		17	0	4.25
Vince Riendeau	1	2	1	0		4	0	3.29
BOB ESSENSA	**1**	**4**	**0**	**2**		**9**	**0**	**4.95**
Allan Bester	1	1	0	0		1	0	3.00
Alex Connell	1	2	0	1	1	3	0	1.50
Clarence Dolson	1	2	0	2		7	0	3.50
Roy Edwards	1	4	0	3		11	0	3.14
Jim Franks	1	1	0	1		2	0	3.00
Corrado Micalef	1	3	0	0		8	0	9.80
Ed Mio	1	1	0	1		3	0	2.86
Sam St. Laurent	1	1	0	0		1	0	6.00

ACTIVE PLAYERS IN BOLD CAPITALS

SKATERS	GP	YEARS
* Gordie Howe	22	48, 49, 50, 51, 52, 53, 54, 55, 57, 58, 59, 60, 61, 62, 63, 64, 65, 67, 68, 69, 70, 71
* Alex Delvecchio	13	53, 54, 55, 56, 57, 58, 59, 61, 62, 63, 64, 65, 67
* Ted Lindsay	10	57, 48, 49, 50, 51, 52, 53, 54, 55, 56
* Red Kelly	9	50, 51, 52, 53, 54, 55, 56, 57, 58
* Marcel Pronovost	9	50, 54, 55, 57, 58, 59, 60, 61, 63
* Norm Ullman	8	55, 60, 61, 62, 63, 64, 67, 68
STEVE YZERMAN	7	84, 88, 89, 90, 91, 92, 93
John Ogrodnick	5	81, 82, 84, 85, 86
* Marty Pavelich	4	50, 52, 54, 55
* Bob Goldham	4	50, 52, 54, 55
Jack Stewart	3	47, 48, 49
* Sid Abel	3	49, 50, 51
* Metro Prystai	3	50, 53, 54
Reed Larson	3	78, 80, 81
+Ebbie Goodfellow	2	37, 39
* Leo Reise	2	50, 51
* Tony Leswick	2	52, 54
Bill Quackenbush	2	69, 70
Red Berenson	2	72, 74
SERGEI FEDOROV	2	92, 94
PAUL COFFEY	2	93, 94
+Herbie Lewis	1	34
+Syd Howe	1	39
+Marty Barry	1	37
+Larry Aurie	1	34
Bud Poile	1	48
Reg Sinclair	1	52
Bill Gadsby	1	65
Carl Brewer	1	70
Gary Bergman	1	72
Mickey Redmond	1	74
Marcel Dionne	1	75
Dan Maloney	1	76
Nick Libett	1	77
Willie Huber	1	83
Bob Probert	1	88
Steve Chiasson	1	93

> *Includes games as member of defending Stanley Cup champions in '50, '54 or '55.
>
> +Appeared in Bailey ('34), Morenz ('37), Seibert ('39) benefit All-Star games.
>
> 24 other Red Wings appeared in All-Star games, but only as members of defending Stanley Cup champions in '50, '54 or '55.
>
> ACTIVE PLAYERS IN CAPITALS

GOALTENDERS	GP	YEARS
* Terry Sawchuk	7	50, 51, 52, 53, 54, 59, 63
* Glenn Hall	2	55, 56
+Norm Smith	1	37
Tim Cheveldae	1	92

COACHES	GC	YEARS
* Tommy Ivan	4	48, 49, 50, 52
Sid Abel	4	61, 63, 64, 67
* Jimmy Skinner	2	54, 55
+Jack Adams	1	37

DETROIT CHAMPIONSHIPS, STANLEY CUP FINALS

STANLEY CUP: 1936, 37, 43, 50, 52, 54, 55
LEAGUE CHAMPIONS/BEST REGULAR-SEASON RECORD: 1933-34, 35-36, 36-37, 42-43, 48-49, 49-50, 50-51, 51-52, 52-53, 53-54, 54-55, 56-57, 64-65, 95
DIVISION CHAMPIONS (REGULAR SEASON): American Division: 1934-35, 35-36, 36-37; Norris Division: 87-88, 88-89, 91-92; Central Division: 93-94, 95
DIVISION CHAMPIONS (PLAYOFFS): Norris Division: 1987, 88
STANLEY CUP FINALISTS: 1934, 36, 37, 41, 42, 43, 45, 48, 49, 50, 52, 54, 55, 56, 61, 63, 64, 66, 95

RED WINGS' ENTRY DRAFT SELECTIONS
(Since inception in 1963)

Round	Overall
1963	
1 Pete Mahovlich	2
2 Bill Cosburn	8
1964	
1 Claude Gauthier	1
2 Brian Watts	7
3 Ralph Buchanan	13
4 Ronald LeClerc	19
1965	
1 George Forge	3
2 Bob Birdsell	8
1966	
1 Steve Atkinson	6
2 Jim Whitaker	12
3 Lee Carpenter	18
4 Grant Cole	24
1967	
1 Ron Barkwell	9
2 Alan Karlander	17
1968	
1 Steve Adrascik	11
2 Herb Boxer	17
1969	
1 Jim Rutherford	10
2 Ron Garwasiuk	21
3 Wayne Hawrysh	33
4 Warren Chernecki	45
5 Wally Olds	57
1970	
1 Serge Lageunesse	12
2 Bob Guindon	26
3 Yvon Lambert	40
4 Tom Johnstone	54
5 Tom Mellor	68
6 Bernard McNeil	82
7 Ed Hays	95
1971	
1 Marcel Dionne	2
2 Henry Boucha	16
3 Ralph Hosiavouri	30
4 George Hulme	44
5 Earl Anderson	58
6 Charlie Shaw	72
7 Jim Nahrgang	86
8 Bob Boyd	100
1972	
2 Pierre Guite	26
3 Bob Kreiger	42
4 Danny Gruen	68
5 Dennis Johnson	74
6 Bill Miller	90
7 Glen Seperich	106
8 Mike Ford	122
9 George Kuzmicz	138
12 Dave Arundel	150

1973	
1 Terry Richardson	11
3 Nelson Pyatt	39
3 Robbie Neale	43
4 Mike Korney	59
5 Blair Stewart	75
6 Glen Cikello	91
7 Brian Middleton	107
8 Dennis Polonich	123
9 Dennis O'Brien	135
9 Tom Newman	138
9 Ray Bibeau	139
10 Kevin Neville	151
10 Ken Gibb	154
10 Mitch Brandt	155
1974	
1 Bill Lochead	9
2 Dan Mandryk	44
3 Bill Evo	45
4 Michel Bergeron	63
5 John Taft	81
6 Don Dufek	99
7 Jack Carlson	117
8 Gregg Steele	134
9 Glen McLeod	151
1975	
1 Rick LaPointe	5
2 Jerry Rollins	23
3 Al Cameron	37
3 Blair Davidson	45
3 Clark Hamilton	50
4 Mike Wirachowski	59
5 Mike Wong	77
6 Mike Harazny	95
7 Jean-Luc Phaneuf	113
8 Steve Carlson	131
9 Gary Vaughn	148
10 Jean Thibodeau	164
11 Dave Hanson	176
11 Robin Larson	178
1976	
1 Fred Williams	4
2 Reed Larson	22
3 Fred Berry	40
4 Kevin Schameborn	58
5 Dwight Schofield	76
6 Tony Horvath	94
7 Fern LeBlanc	111
8 Claude Legris	120
1977	
1 Dale McCourt	1
3 Rick Vasko	37
4 John Hilworth	55
5 Jim Korn	73
6 Jim Baxter	91
7 Randy Wilson	109
8 Ray Roy	125
9 Kip Churchill	141
10 Lance Gatoni	155
11 Rob Plumb	163
12 Alan Belanger	170
13 Dean Willers	175
14 Roland Cloutier	178

15 Ed Hill	181
16 Val James	184
17 Grant Morin	185
1978	
1 Willie Huber	9
1 Brent Peterson	12
2 Glen Hicks	28
2 Al Jensen	31
3 Doug Derkson	53
4 Bjorn Skaare	62
5 Ted Nolan	78
6 Sylvain Locas	95
7 Wes George	112
8 John Barrett	129
9 Jim Malazdrewicz	146
10 Geoff Shaw	163
11 Carl VanHarrewyn	178
12 Ladislav Svozil	194
13 Tom Bailey	208
14 Larry Lozinski	219
15 Randy Betty	224
16 Brian Crawley	226
17 Doug Feasby	228
1979	
1 Mike Foligno	3
3 Jody Gage	45
3 Boris Fistric	46
4 John Ogrodnick	66
5 Joe Paterson	87
6 Carmine Cirella	108
1980	
1 Mike Blaisdell	11
3 Mark Osborne	46
3 Mike Corrigan	88
6 Wayne Crawford	109
7 Mike Braun	130
8 John Beukeboom	151
9 Dave Miles	172
10 Brian Rorabeck	193
1981	
2 Claude Loiselle	23
2 Corrado Micalef	44
5 Larry Trader	86
6 Gerard Gallant	107
7 Greg Stefan	128
8 Rick Zombo	149
9 Don LeBlanc	170
10 Robert Nordmark	191
1982	
1 Murray Craven	17
2 Yves Courteau	23
3 Carmine Vani	44
4 Craig Coxe	66
5 Brad Shaw	86
6 Claude Vilgrain	107
7 Greg Hudas	128
8 Pat Lahey	149
9 Gary Cullen	170
10 Brent Meckling	191
11 Mike Stern	212
12 Shaun Reagan	233

1983

1	Steve Yzerman	4
2	Lane Lambert	25
3	Bob Probert	46
4	Dave Korol	70
5	Petr Klima	88
6	Joe Kocur	91
6	Chris Pusey	109
7	Bob Pierson	130
8	Craig Butz	151
9	Dave Sikorski	172
10	Stu Grimson	193
11	Jeff Frank	214
12	Chuck Chiatto	235

1984

1	Shawn Burr	7
2	Doug Houda	28
3	Milan Chalupa	49
5	Mats Lundstrom	91
6	Randy Hansch	112
7	Stefan Larsson	133
8	Lars Karlsson	152
8	Urban Nordin	154
9	Bill Shibicky	175
10	Jay Rose	195
11	Tim Kaiser	216
12	Tom Nickolau	236

1985

1	Brent Fedyk	8
2	Jeff Sharples	29
3	Steve Chiasson	50
4	Mark Gowans	71
5	Chris Luongo	92
6	Randy McKay	113
7	Thomas Bjuhr	134
8	Mike Luckraft	155
9	Rob Schenna	176
10	Eerik Hamalainen	197
11	Bo Svanberg	218
12	Mikael Lindman	239

1986

1	Joe Murphy	1
2	Adam Graves	22
3	Derek Mayer	43
4	Tim Cheveldae	64
5	Johan Garpenlov	85
6	Jay Stark	106
7	Per Djoos	127
8	Dean Morton	148
9	Marc Potvin	169
10	Scott King	190
11	Tom Bissett	211
12	Peter Ekroth	232

1987

1	Yves Racine	11
2	Gord Kruppke	32
2	Bob Wilkie	41
3	Dennis Holland	52
4	Mark Reimer	74
5	Radomir Brazda	95
6	Sean Clifford	116
7	Mike Gober	137
8	Kevin Scott	158
9	Mikko Haapakoski	179
10	Darin Bannister	200
11	Craig Quinlan	221
12	Tomas Jansson	242

1988

1	Kory Kocur	17
2	Serge Anglehart	38
3	Guy Dupuis	47
3	Petr Hrbek	59
4	Sheldon Kennedy	80
7	Kelly Hurd	143
8	Brian McCormack	164
9	Jody Praznik	185
10	Glenn Goodall	206
11	Darren Colbourne	227
12	Don Stone	248

1989

1	Mike Sillinger	11
2	Bob Boughner	32
3	Niklas Lidstrom	53
4	Sergei Fedorov	74
5	Shawn McCosh	95
6	Dallas Drake	116
7	Scott Zygulski	137
8	Andy Suhy	158
9	Bob Jones	179
10	Greg Bignell	200
10	Rick Judson	204
11	Vladimir Konstantinov	221
12	Joseph Frederick	242
12	Jason Glickman	246

1990

1	Keith Primeau	3
3	Viacheslav Kozlov	45
4	Stewart Malgunas	66
5	Tony Burns	87
6	Claude Barthe	108
7	Jason York	129
8	Wes McCauley	150
9	Anthony Gruba	171
10	Travis Tucker	192
11	Brett Larson	213
12	John Hendry	234

1991

1	Martin Lapointe	10
2	Jamie Pushor	32
3	Chris Osgood	54
4	Michael Knuble	76
5	Dimitri Motkov	98
7	Igor Malykhin	142
9	Jim Bermingham	186
10	Jason Firth	208
11	Bart Turner	230
12	Andrew Miller	252

1992

1	Curtis Bowen	22
2	Darren McCarty	46
3	Sylvain Cloutier	70
5	Mike Sullivan	118
6	Jason MacDonald	142
7	Greg Scott	166
8	Justin Krall	183
8	C.J. Denomme	189
9	Jeff Walker	214
10	Dan McGillis	238
11	Ryan Bach	262

1993

1	Anders Eriksson	22
2	Jon Coleman	48
3	Kevin Hilton	74
4	John Jakopin	97
4	Benoit Larose	100
5	Norm Maracle	126
6	Tim Spitzig	152
7	Yuri Yeresko	178
8	Viteslav Skuta	204
9	Ryan Shanahan	230
10	Jim Kosecki	256
11	Gord Hunt	282

1994

1	Yan Golubovsky	23
2	Mathieu Dandenault	49
3	Sean Gilliam	75
4	Frederic Deschenes	114
5	Doug Battaglia	127
6	Paval Agarkov	153
8	Jason Elliot	205
9	Jeff Mikesch	231
10	Tomas Holstrom	257
11	Toivo Suursoo	283

1995

1	Maxim Kuznetsov	26
2	Philippe Audet	52
3	Darryl Laplante	58
4	Anatoly Ustugov	104
5	Chad Wilchynski	125
5	David Arsenault	126
7	Tyler Perry	156
7	Per Eklund	182
8	Andrei Samokvalov	208
9	David Engblom	234

SUPPLEMENTAL DRAFT

1987 — Mike LaMoine
1988 — Gary Shuchuk
1989 — Brad Kreick
1990 — Mike Casselman;
      Don Oliver
1991 — Kelly Sorensen

──RED WINGS' ALL-TIME PLAYER TRANSACTIONS──

────────1926-27 SEASON THROUGH 1929────────
ACQUIRED:

1927 DUKE KEATS and ARCHIE BRIDEN from Boston for Frank Frederickson and Harry Meeking.

1927 RUSS OATMAN sold to Montreal Maroons for $9,500

1927 PETE BELLEFEUILLE from Toronto for Slim Halderson

1927 GEORGE HAY and PERCY TRAUB from Chicago for $15,000

1927 BILL BRYDGE from Toronto for Art Duncan

1927 CARSON COOPER from Boston for Fred Gordon

1927 REG NOBLE from Montreal Maroons for $7,500

1927 STAN BROWN from New York Rangers for Archie Briden

1927 LARRY AURIE from London (Canadian Pro League) for cash

1927 GORD FRASER from Chicago for Duke Keats

1928 JIM HERBERTS from Toronto for Jack Arbour and $12,500

1928 BOB CONNORS and rights to EBBIE GOODFELLOW from New York Americans for John Sheppard

1928 HERB LEWIS from Duluth (U.S. Hockey League) for $5,000

1928 CLARENCE "DOLLY" DOLSON from London (Canadian Pro League) for cash

1929 HAROLD HICKS from Montreal Maronns for cash

1929 BILL BEVERIDGE from Ottawa Senators on loan

────────────────1930s────────────────

1930 JOHN SORRELL from London (International League) for cash

1931 LEROY GOLDSWORTHY from London (International League) for Harold Hicks

1931 ALEX CONNELL, HEC KILREA, ALEX SMITH, DANNY COX and ART GAGNE on loan from Ottawa, which folded after 31-32 season

1931 DOUG YOUNG from Cleveland (International League) in inter-league draft

1931 FRANK CARSON and HAP EMMS from New York Americans for Bert McInenly and Tom Filmore

1932 JOHN ROSS ROACH from New York Rangers for $11,000

1932 CARL VOSS from New York Rangers for $5,500

1933 GORD PETTINGER from New York Rangers for cash

1933 FRED ROBERTSON from Toronto for $6,500

1933 COONEY WEILAND from Ottawa for Carl Voss

1934 TED GRAHAM from Montreal Maroons for Stu Evans

1934 WILF CUDE from Montreal Canadiens on loan for season

1934 LLOYD GROSS from Boston for $2,500

1934 TOM ANDERSON and YANK BOYD from Philadelphia (Canadian-American League) for cash

1934 WALLY KILREA from Montreal Maroons for Gus Marker

1934 GEORGE PATTTERSON from Boston for Gene Carrigan

1934 NORMIE SMITH from St. Louis Eagles for Burr Williams

1935 BUCKO McDONALD, DESSE ROCHE and EARL ROCHE from Buffalo (International League) for George Patterson and Lloyd Gross

1935 SYD HOWE and SCOTTY BOWMAN from St. Louis Eagles for Ted Graham and $50,000

1935 MARTY BARRY and ART GIROUX from Boston for Cooney Weiland and Walt Buswell

1935 HEC KILREA from Toronto for $7,500

1935 PETE KELLY from St. Louis Eagles in dispersal draft

1937 KEN DORATY from Cleveland (International League) for cash

1937 RED BEATTIE from Boston for Gord Pettinger

1937 ALEX MOTTER from Boston for Clarence Drouillard

1938 EDDIE WARES from New York Rangers for John Sherf and $12,500

1938 JOE LAMB from New York Americans for Red Beattie

1938 CHARLIE CONACHER from Toronto for $16,000

1938 CHARLIE MASON from New York Rangers for cash

1938 CECIL THOMPSON from Boston for Jim Franks and $15,000
1938 BILL THOMSON and $10,000 from Toronto for Bucko McDonald
1939 PHIL BESLER from Chicago for Charlie Mason
1939 CECIL DILLON from New York Rangers for cash

1940s

1940 HAROLD JACKSON from Providence (American League) for Cecil Dillon and Eddie Bush
1941 DUTCH HILLER from New York Rangers for $5,000
1942 PAT McREAVY from Boston for Dutch Hiller
1942 EDDIE BUSH from Providence (American League) for Bob Whitelaw and Buck Jones
1942 PAT EGAN, MURRAY ARMSTRONG and HARRY WATSON from New York Americans for $35,000 after that club folded
1944 BILL HOLLETT from Boston for Pat Egan
1945 EARL SIEBERT from Chicago for Don Grosso, Byron McDonald and Cully Simon
1945 FERN GAUTHIER and ROLLIE ROSSINGNOL from Montreal Canadiens for Billy Reay
1946 BILLY TAYLOR from Toronto for Harry Watson.
1946 DOUG BALDWIN and RAY POWELL from Toronto for Gerry Brown
1946 ROY CONACHER from Boston for Joe Carvath
1946 PETE HORECK and LEO REISE from Chicago for Adam Brown and Ray Powell
1947 JIM McFADDEN from Buffalo (American League) for Les Douglas and Hal Jackson
1947 BEP GUIDOLIN from Boston for Billy Taylor
1948 GEORGE GEE and BUD POILE from Chicago for Jim Conacher, Bep Guidolin and Doug McCaig
1949 Steve Black from St. Louis (American League) for cash
1949 PETE BABANDO, PETE DURHAM, CLARE MARTIN and JIM PETERS from Boston for Pete Horeck and Bill Quackenbush
1949 JOE CARVETH from Montreal for Calum Mackay and cash

1950s

1950 BOB GOLDHAM, JIM HENRY, METRO PRYSTAI and GAYE STEWART from Chicago for Pete Babando, Al Dewsbury, Harry Lumley, Don Morrison and Jack Stewart
1950 BERT OLMSTEAD and VIC STASIUK from Chicago for Lee Fogolin and Steve Black
1950 LEO GRAVELLE and cash from Montreal for Bert Olmstead
1951 TONY LESWICK from New York for Gaye Stewart
1951 $75,000 from Chicago for George Gee, Clare Martin, Jim McFadden, Max McNab, Jim Peters and Clare Raglan
1952 RED SINCLAIR from New York for Leo Reise
1954 LORNE DAVIS and cash from Chicago for Metro Prystai
1955 DAVE CREIGHTON, BUCKY HOLLINGWORTH and JERRY TOPPAZZINI from Chicago for Tony Leswick, Glen Skov, Johnny Wilson and Benny Woit
1955 BILLY DEA and DOLPH KUKOLOWICZ from New York for Dave Creighton and Bronco Horvath
1955 GILLES BOISVERT, REAL CHEVREFILS, NORM CORCORAN, WARREN GODFREY and ED SANFORD from Boston for Marcel Bonin, Lorne Davis, Terry Sawchuk and Vic Stasiuk
1955 MURRAY COSTELLO and LORNE FERGUSON from Boston for Real Chevrefils and Jerry Toppazzini
1955 METRO PRYSTAI from Chicago for Ed Sanford
1957 TERRY SAWCHUK from Boston for John Bucyk and cash
1957 HANK BASSEN, FORBES KENNEDY, BILL PRESTON and JOHNNY WILSON from Chicago for Glenn Hall and Ted Lindsay
1957 BOB BAILEY, HEC LALANDE, JACK McINTYRE and NICK MICKOSKI from Chicago for Billy Dea, Bill Dineen, Lorne Ferguson and Dutch Reibel
1959 BARRY CULLEN from Toronto for Johnny Wilson
1959 JIM MORRISON from Boston for Nick Mickoski

1960s

1960 MARC REAUME from Toronto for Red Kelly
1960 HOWIE GLOVER from Chicago for Jim Morrison
1960 ALLAN JOHNSON from Montreal for cash
1960 PETE CONACHER from Buffalo (American League) for Barry Cullen
1961 HOWIE YOUNG from Hershey (American League for Marc Reaume
1961 LEO LABINE and VIC STASIUK from Boston for Gary Aldcorn, Tom McCarthy and Murray Oliver
1961 BILL GADSBY from New York for Les Hunt and cash
1961 ED LITZENBERGER from Chicago for Gerry Melnyk and Brian Smith
1961 NOEL PRICE from New York for Pete Goegan and cash
1962 DOUG BARKLEY from Chicago for Len Lunde and John McKenzie
1962 PETE GOEGAN from New York for Noel Price
1962 ANDRE PRONOVOST from Boston for Forbes Kennedy
1963 ROGER CROZIER and RON INGRAM from Chicago for Howie Young
1963 WARREN GODFREY from Boston for Gerry Odrowski
1964 AL LANGLOIS from New York for Ron Ingram
1964 AUTRY ERICKSON and RON MURPHY from Chicago for Ian Cushenan, John Miszuk and Art Stratton
1965 ANDY BATHGATE, BILLY HARRIS and GARRY JARRETT from Toronto for Autry Erickson, Larry Jeffrey, Eddie Joyal, Lowell MacDonald and Marcel Pronovost
1965 BOB McCORD, AB McDONALD and KEN STEPHANSON from Boston for Bob Dillabough, Ron Harris, Al Langlois and Parker MacDonald
1965 PARKER MacDONALD from Boston for Pit Martin
1966 LEO BOIVIN and DEAN PRENTICE from Boston for Gary Doak, Ron Murphy, Bill Lesuk and Rick Smith
1966 HOWIE YOUNG from Chicago for Murray Hall, Al LeBrun and Rick Morris
1967 JOHN BRENNEMAN from St.Louis for Craig Cameron, Don Giesebrecht and Larry Hornung
1967 JEAN GUY TALBOT and DAVE RICHARDSON from Minnesota for Duke Harris and Bob McCord
1968 KENT DOUGLAS from Oakland for John Brenneman, Ted Hampson and Bert Marshall
1968 CARL BREWER, PETE STEMKOWSKI, FRANK MAHOVLICH and GARRY UNGER from Toronto for Floyd Smith, Norm Ullman and Paul Henderson
1968 BOB BAUN and RON HARRIS from Oakland for Gary Jarrett, Doug Roberts, Chris Worthy and Howie Young
1968 TERRY SAWCHUK from Los Angeles for Jimmy Peters Jr.
1968 POUL POPIEL from Los Angeles for Ron Anderson
1969 WAYNE CONNELLY from Minnesota for Danny Lawson
1969 GARRY MONAHAN and DOUG PIPER from Montreal for Bart Crashley and Pete Mahovlich
1969 LARRY JEFFREY from New York for Terry Sawchuk and Sandy Snow
1969 BILLY DEA from Pittsburgh for Mike McMahon

1970s

1970 DALE ROLFE, GARY CROTEAU and LARRY JOHNSON from Los Angeles for Garry Monahan, Matt Ravlich and Brian Gibbons
1970 TOM WEBSTER from Buffalo for Roger Crozier
1970 LARRY BROWN and DON LUCE from New York for Pete Stemkowski and Steve Andrascik
1970 $30,000 waiver price from Buffalo for Bob Baun
1971 BILL COLLINS, GUY CHARRON and MICKEY REDMOND from Montreal for Frank Mahovlich
1971 ARNIE BROWN, MIKE ROBITAILLE and TOM MILLER from New York for Larry Brown and Bruce MacGregor
1971 RED BERENSON and TIM ECCLESTONE from St. Louis for Garry Unger and Wayne Connelly

1971 JOE DALEY from Buffalo for Mike Robitaille and Don Luce

1971 LEON ROCHEFORT from Montreal for Kerry Ketter

1971 AB McDONALD, BOB WALL and MIKE LOWE from St. Louis for Carl Brewer

1971 RON STACKHOUSE from California for Tom Webster

1971 ART STRATTON from Seattle (Western League) for cash

1971 BILL SUTHERLAND from St. Louis for cash

1971 BOB COOK from Vancouver for cash

1971 JIM KRULICKI from NY Rangers for Dale Rolfe

1972 RALPH STEWART from Vancouver for Jim Niekamp

1972 RICK NEWELL and GARY DOAK from New York Rangers for first-round pick in 1972 Entry Draft

1972 DENIS DeJORDY and DONN McLAUGHLIN from New York Islanders for Arnie Brown and Gerry Gray

1973 ROY EDWARDS from Pittsburgh for second-round pick in 1973 and '74 entry drafts

1973 BILL HOGABOAM from Atlanta for Leon Rochefort

1973 BRIAN LAVENDER and KEN MURRAY from New York Islanders for Ralph Stewart and Bob Cook

1973 Third-round pick in 1973 Entry Draft and cash from Pittsburgh for Andy Brown

1973 ACE BAILEY and MURRAY WING from Boston for Gary Daok

1973 RICK FOLEY from Philadelphia for Serge Lajeunesse

1973 BRENT HUGHTS from St. Louis for cash

1973 TED HARRIS from Minnesota for Gary Bergman

1973 DOUG ROBERTS from Boston for cash

1973 PIERRE JARRY from Toronto for Tim Ecclestone

1973 MIKE JAKUBO from St. Louis for Dan McPherson

1974 JIM RUTHERFORD and JACK LYNCH from Pittsburgh for Ron Stackhouse

1974 BRYAN WATSON, CHRIS EVANS and JEAN HAMEL from St. Louis for Billy Collins, Ace Bailey and Ted Harris

1974 CLAUDE HOUDE from NY Rangers for Brian Lavender

1974 HENRY NOWAK and third-round pick in 1974 Entry Draft from Pittsburgh for Nelson DeBenedet

1974 DANNY GRANT from Minnesota for Henry Boucha

1974 BRIAN MURPHY from Baltimore (American League) for cash

1974 TED SNELL, BART CRASHLEY and LARRY GIROUX from Kansas City for Guy Charron and Claude Houde

1974 PHIL ROBERTO and third-round pick in 1975 Entry Draft from St. Louis for Red Berenson.

1975 DAVE KRYSKOW from Washington for Jack Lynch.

1975 WALT McKECHNIE from Boston for Earl Anderson, Hank Nowak and third-round pick in 1975 Entry Draft

1975 MIKE BLOOM from Washington for Blair Stewart

1975 Third-round pick in 1975 Entry Draft from Washington for Nelson Pyatt

1975 DAN MALONEY, TERRY HARPER and second round amateur 1976 NHL draft choice from Los Angeles for Marcel Dionne and Bart Crashley

1975 BRIAN HEXTALL from Atlanta for Dave Kryskow

1975 PETER McDUFFE and GLEN BURDON from Kansas City for Gary Bergman and Bill McKenzie

1975 ED GIACOMIN from New York Rangers on waivers

1975 J.P. LeBLANC from Denver (WHA) for cash and second-round pick in 1977 Entry Draft (to Chicago for his rights)

1975 RICK CHINNICK from Minnesota for Bryan Hextall

1975 DON MARTINEAU from Minnesota for Pierre Jarry

1976 BUSTER HARVEY from Kansas City for Phil Roberto

1976 DENNIS HEXTALL from Minnesota for Bill Hogaboam and second-round pick in 1976 Entry Draft

1976 RICK WILSON from St. Louis for Doug Grant

1976 GREG JOLY from Washington for Bryan Watson

1977 TERRY MURRAY, STEVE COATES, BOB RITCHIE and DAVE KELLY from Philadelphia for Mike Korney and Rick Lapointe

1977 RICK BOWNESS from Atlanta for cash
1977 RON LOW from Washington for Walt McKechnie and future considerations
1977 ANDRE ST.LAURENT from New York Islanders for Michel Bergeron
1977 TIM SHEEHY and VACLAV NEDOMANKSY from Birmingham (WHA) for Dave Hanson, Steve Durbano and future considerations
1977 DENNIS HULL from Chicago for future considerations
1978 Third-round pick in 1978 Entry Draft and future considerations from Los Angeles for Danny Grant
1978 ERROL THOMPSON with first-round 1978 and '80 entry drafts, and second-round pick in '78 draft from Toronto for Dan Maloney and second-round draft pick in '80.
1978 ROGIE VACHON from Los Angeles as free agent (Dale McCourt to Los Angeles as equalization)
1979 DALE McCOURT from Los Angeles for Andre St. Laurent and first-round picks in 1980 and '81 entry drafts
1979 GREG CARROLL from Washington on waivers
1979 BILL HOGABOAM from Minnesota on waivers
1979 BARRY LONG from Washington reclaimed prior to 1979 expansion draft
1979 PETE MAHOVLICH from Pittsburgh for Nick Libett
1979 DENNIS SOBCHUK from Philadelphia for third or fourth-round choice in 1981 Entry Draft

---
1980s

1980 GILLES GILBERT from Boston for Rogie Vachon
1980 Cash from Winnipeg for Barry Long
1980 RICK SMITH from Boston on waivers
1980 MARK KIRTON from Toronto for Jim Rutherford
1981 GARY McADAM from Pittsburgh for Errol Thompson
1981 EARL INGARFIELD from Calgary for Dan Labraaten
1981 BRAD SMITH from Calgary for Rick Vasko
1981 MARK LOFTHOUSE from Washington for Al Jensen
1981 WALT McKECHNIE from Colorado as a free agent
1981 DON MURDOCH, GREG SMITH and first-round pick in 1982 Entry Draft from Minnesota for Detroit's first-round pick in '82
1981 ERIC VAIL from Calgary for Gary McAdam and fourth-round picks in 1982 and '83 entry drafts
1981 DEREK SMITH, DANNY GARE and JIM SCHOENFELD from Buffalo for Dale McCourt, Mike Foligno and Brent Peterson
1981 BOB SAUVE from Buffalo for future considerations
1982 CRAIG COXE, a fourth-round pick in 1982 Entry Draft and fifth-round pick in '83 draft from Toronto for Jim Korn
1982 REGGIE LEACH from Philadelphia as free agent
1982 COLIN CAMPBELL from Vancouver as free agent
1982 TOM ROWE from Vancouver as free agent
1982 STAN WEIR from Edmonton for cash
1982 DWIGHT FOSTER from New Jersey for cash
1982 BOBBY FRANCIS from Calgary for Yves Courteau
1983 IVAN BOLDIREV from Vancouver for Mark Kirton
1983 KEN SOLHEIM from Minnesota for player to be named later
1983 ED JOHNSTONE, ED MIO and RON DUGUAY from New York Rangers for Mark Osborne, Mike Blaisdell and Willie Huber
1983 BARRY MELROSE from Toronto as free agent
1983 BOB MANNO from Toronto as free agent
1983 BRAD PARK from Boston as free agent
1983 ANDRE ST.LAURENT from Pittsburgh for future considerations
1983 BLAKE DUNLOP from St. Louis as free agent
1984 RICK MacLEISH from Philadelphia for future considerations
1984 PIERRE AUBRY from Quebec for cash
1984 ROB McCLANAHAN from NY Rangers for future considerations
1984 DAVE "TIGER" WILLIAMS from Vancouver for Rob McClanahan

1984 FRANTISEK CERNIK from Quebec as free agent
1984 DARRYL SITTLER from Philadelphia for Murray Craven and Joe Patterson
1984 TODD BIDNER from Edmonton for Rejean Cloutier
1984 DAVE SILK from Boston on waivers
1985 WARREN YOUNG from Pittsburgh as free agent
1985 MIKE McEWEN from Washington as free agent
1985 HAROLD SNEPSTS from Minnesota as free agent
1985 STEVE RICHMOND from New York Rangers for Mike McEwen
1985 BILLY CARROLL from Edmonton for Bruce Eakin
1986 DARREN VEITCH from Washington for Greg Smith and John Barrett
1986 MIKE O'CONNELL from Boston for Reed Larson
1986 DOUG SHEDDEN from Pittsburgh for Ron Duguay
1986 DAVE DONNELLY from Boston for Dwight Foster
1986 TIM HIGGINS from New Jersey for Claude Loiselle
1986 DAVE LEWIS from New Jersey as free agent
1986 GLEN HANLON and third-round picks in 1987 and '88 entry drafts from New York
     Rangers for Kelly Kisio, Lane Lambert, Jim Leavins and fifth-round pick in '88 draft
1986 LEE NORWOOD from St. Louis for Larry Trader
1986 SAM ST. LAURENT from New Jersey for Steve Richmond
1986 DOUG HALWARD from Vancouver for future considerations
1987 DAVE BARR from Hartford for Randy Ladouceur
1987 BRENT ASHTON, GILBERT DELORME and MARK KUMPEL from Quebec for John
     Ogrodnick, Basil McRae and Doug Shedden
1987 MEL BRIDGMAN from New Jersey for CHRIS CICHOCKI and third-round pick in 1987
     Entry Draft
1987 Second-round pick in 1987 Entry Draft from Philadelphia for Mark Laforest
1987 JOHN CHABOT from Pittsburgh as free agent
1987 DARREN ELIOT from Los Angeles as free agent
1988 JIM NILL from Winnipeg for Mark Kumpel
1988 JIM PAVESE from New York Rangers for a fourth-round pick in 1989 Enrty Draft
1988 PAUL MacLEAN from Winnipeg for Brent Aston
1988 MIROSLAV FRYCER from Toronto for Darren Veitch
1988 JOHN BLUM from Boston as free agent
1988 BRUCE BELL from Quebec claimed on waivers
1989 Tenth-round pick in the 1989 Entry Draft from Edmonton for Miroslav Frycer
1989 Twelfth-round pick in the 1989 Entry Draft from Edmonton for Doug Halward
1989 TORRIE ROBERTSON from Hartford for Jim Pavese
1989 MARK HABSCHEID from Minnesota as free agent
1989 BORJE SALMING from Toronto as free agent
1989 BERNIE FEDERKO and TONY McKEGNEY from St. Louis for Adam Oates and Paul
     MacLean
1989 CHRIS KOTSOPOULOS from Toronto as free agent
1989 JIMMY CARSON, KEVIN McCLELLAND and fifth-round pick in the 1991 Entry Draft from
     Edmonton for Petr Klima, Joe Murphy, Adam Graves and Jeff Sharples
1989 ROBERT PICARD and GREG ADAMS from Quebec for Tony McKegney

1990s

1990 RICK GREEN from Montreal for fifth-round pick in the 1991 Entry Draft
1990 BRAD McCRIMMON from Calgary for second-round pick in the 1990 Entry Draft
1990 PAUL YSEBAERT from New Jersey for Lee Norwood
1991 BRAD MARSH from Toronto for eighth-round pick in the 1991 Entry Draft
1991 DOUG CROSSMAN from Hartford for Doug Houda
1991 ALLAN BESTER form Toronto for sixth-round pick in 1991 Entry Draft
1991 DENNIS VIAL, JIM CUMMINS and KEVIN MILLER from NY Rangers for Joe Kocur and
     Per Djoos
1991 ALAN KERR from NY Islanders for Rich Green
1991 BRIAN MacLELLAN from Calgary for Marc Habscheid
1991 RAY SHEPPARD from NY Rangers as free agent

1991 TROY CROWDER from New Jersey as free agent (Dave Barr and Randy McKay as compensation)

1991 VINCENT RIENDEAU from St. Louis for Rick Zombo

1992 GREG MILLEN from NY Rangers for future consideration.

1992 CHRIS TANCILL from Hartford for Daniel Shank

1992 BOB McGILL from San Jose for Johan Garpenlov

1992 DINO CICCARELLI from Washington for Kevin Miller

1992 Future considerations from Quebec for Dennis Vial and Doug Crossman

1992 MARK HOWE from Philadelphia as free agent

1992 DENNIS VIAL from Quebec for future consideration

1992 Fourth-round pick in 1993 Entry Draft from Philadelphia for Brent Fedyk

1993 PAUL COFFEY, JIM HILLER and SYLVAIN COUTURIER from Los Angeles for Jimmy Carson, Mark Potvin and Gary Shuchuk

1993 Future considerations from Philadelphia for Bob Wilkie

1993 STEVE KONROYD from Hartford for sixth-round pick in 1993 Entry Draft

1993 Sixth-round selection in 1993 Entry Draft (Detroit's) from Hartford for Brad McCrimmon

1993 STEVE MALTAIS from Tampa Bay for Dennis Vial

1993 AARON WARD and a fourth-round pick in 1993 Entry Draft from Winnipeg for Paul Ysebaert

1993 GREG JOHNSON and future considerations from Philadelphia for Jim Cummins and fourth-round pick (Philadelphia's) in 1993 Entry Draft

1993 KRIS DRAPER from Winnipeg for future considerations

1993 MARK PEDERSON from San Jose as free agent

1993 BOB HALKIDIS from Toronto as free agent

1993 PETER ING from Edmonton for future consideration

1993 TERRY CARKNER from Philadelphia for Yves Racine

1993 Future considerations from Boston for Vincent Riendeau

1994 BOB ESSENSA and SERGEI BAUTIN from Winnipeg for Tim Cheveldae and Dallas Drake

1994 Future consideration from Ottawa for Steve Konroyd

1994 Third-round selection from Winnipeg in 1995 NHL Entry Draft for Sheldon Kennedy

1994 Mike Vernon from Calgary for Steve Chiasson

1994 MIKE KRUSHELNYSKI from Toronto as free agent

1994 MIKE RAMSEY from Pittsburgh as free agent

1994 BOB ROUSE from Toronto as free agent

1995 BOB ERREY from San Jose for fifth-round pick in 1995 Entry Draft

1995 VIACHESLAV FETISOV from New Jersey for third-round pick in 1995 Entry Draft

1995 STU GRIMSON, MARK FERNER and sixth-round pick in 1996 Entry Draft from Anaheim for Mike Sillinger and Jason York

1995 MARC BERGEVIN, BEN HANKINSON from Tampa Bay for Shawn Burr and third-round pick in 1996 Entry Draft

1995 WES WALZ from Calgary as free agent

A

Gerry Abel, C.....................................1966-67
Sid Abel, C-LW................1938-39 to 42-43;
45-46 to 51-52
Gene Achtymichuk, C.....................1957-58
Greg C. Adams, LW........................1989-90
Micah Aivazoff, LW.........................1993-94
Gary Aldcorn, LW...............1959-60 to 60-61
Keith Allen, D.....................1953-54 to 54-55
Ralph Almas, G................1946-47; 52-53
Dave Amadio, D...............................1957-58
Dale Anderson, D............................1956-57
Earl Anderson, RW..........................1974-75
Ron Anderson, RW..............1967-68 to 68-69
Tom Anderson, C..............................1934-35
Al Arbour, D.............1953-54; 55-56 to 57-58
Jack Arbour, D-LW..........................1926-27
Murray Armstrong, C.........1943-44 to 45-46
Brent Ashton, LW..............1986-87 to 87-88
Ossie Asmundson, RW....................1934-35
Pierre Aubry, C-LW.............1983-84 to 84-85
Larry Aurie, RW................1927-28 to 38-39

B

Pete Babando, LW............................1949-50
Ace Bailey, LW...................1972-73 to 73-74
Bob Bailey, RW...................1956-57 to 57-58
Doug Baldwin, D...............................1946-47
Doug Barkley, D.................1962-63 to 65-66
David Barr, RW...................1986-87 to 90-91
John Barrett, D....................1980-81 to 85-86
Marty Barry, C....................1935-36 to 38-39
Hank Bassen, G...............1960-61 to 63-64;
65-66 to 66-67
Frank Bathe, D....................1974-75 to 75-76
Andy Bathgate, C-RW.........1965-66 to 66-67
Bob Baun, D........................1968-69 to 70-71
Sergei Bautin, D...............................1993-94
Red Beattie, LW................................1937-38
Clarence Behling, D............1940-41 to 42-43
Pete Bellefeuille, RW.....................1926-27;
28-29 to 29-30
Frank Bennett, C..............................1943-44
Red Berenson, C.................1970-71 to 74-75
Michel Bergeron, RW...........1974-75 to 77-78
Gary Bergman, D.................1964-65 to 74-75
Thommie Bergman, D........1972-73 to 74-75;
77-78 to 79-80
Fred Berry, C.....................................1976-77
Phil Besler, RW.................................1938-39
Pete Bessone, D...............................1937-38
Allan Bester, G....................1990-91 to 91-92
Bill Beveridge, G...............................1929-30
Tim Bissett, C...................................1990-91
Steve Black, LW.................1949-50 to 50-51
Tom Bladon, D...................................1980-81
Mike Blaisdell, RW.............1980-81 to 82-83
Mike Bloom, LW..................1974-75 to 76-77
John Blum, D......................................1988-89
Marc Boileau, C................................1961-62
Gilles Boisvert, G.............................1959-60
Leo Boivin, D......................1965-66 to 66-67
Ivan Boldirev, C-LW...........1982-83 to 84-85
Dan Bolduc, RW..................1978-79 to 79-80
Marcel Bonin, LW................1952-53 to 54-55
Henry Boucha, LW..............1971-72 to 73-74
Claude Bourque, G............................1939-40
Scotty Bowman, D...............1934-35 to 39-40

Rick Bowness, RW............................1977-78
Yank Boyd, RW..................................1934-35
John Brenneman, LW.......................1967-68
Carl Brewer, D...................................1969-70
Archie Briden, LW.............................1926-27
Mel Bridgman, LW-C..........1987-88 to 87-88
Bernie Brophy, C.................1928-29 to 29-30
Adam Brown, LW................1941-42 to 43-44;
45-46 to 46-47
Andy Brown, G....................1971-72 to 72-73
Arnie Brown, D....................1970-71 to 71-72
Connie Brown, C.................1938-39 to 42-43
Doug Brown, RW/LW........................1995
Gerry Brown, LW................1941-42; 45-46
Larry Brown, D...................................1970-71
Stan Brown, D....................................1927-28
Jeff Brubaker, C................................1988-89
Ed Bruneteau, RW.............................1941-42;
43-44 to 48-49
Mud Bruneteau, RW............1935-36 to 45-46
Bill Brydge, D.....................................1928-29
John Buyck, LW...................1955-56 to 56-57
Tony Bukovich, LW..............1943-44 to 44-45
Hy Buller, D........................1943-44 to 44-45
Charlie Burns, C................................1958-59
Shawn Burr, C.....................1984-85 to 95
Cummy Burton, LW.............1955-56;
57-58 to 58-59
Eddie Bush, D....................1938-39; 41-42
Walter Buswell, D...............1932-33 to 34-35

C

Al Cameron, D.....................1975-76 to 78-79
Craig Cameron, RW..........................1966-67
Colin Campbell, D...............1982-83 to 84-85
Terry Carkner, D..................1993-94 to 95
Gene Carrigan, D.................1932-33 to 33-34
Billy Carroll, C.....................1985-86 to 86-87
Greg Carroll, C..................................1978-79
Dwight Carruthers, D........................1965-66
Frank Carson, RW...............1931-32 to 33-34
Jimmy Carson, C.................1989-90 to 92-93
Joe Carveth, RW-C..............1940-41 to 45-46;
49-50 to 50-51
Frank Cernik, LW..............................1984-85
John Chabot, C....................1987-88 to 90-91
Milan Chalupa, D..............................1984-85
Bob Champoux, G.............................1963-64
Guy Charron, C-LW.............1970-71 to 74-75
Lude Check, LW.................................1943-44
Real Chevrefils, LW..........................1955-56
Tim Cheveldae, G................1988-89 to 93-94
Alain Chevrier, G...............................1990-91
Steve Chiasson, D...............1987-88 to 93-94
Dino Ciccarelli, RW.............1992-93 to 95
Chris Cichocki, RW.............1985-86 to 86-87
Rejean Cloutier, D...............1979-80 to 81-82
Roland Cloutier, C...............1977-78 to 78-79
Steve Coates, RW.............................1976-77
Paul Coffey, D......................1992-93 to 95
Bill Collins, RW...................1970-71 to 73-74
Brian Conacher, C.............................1971-72
Charlie Conacher, RW.......................1938-39
Jim Conacher, LW................1945-46 to 48-49
Roy Conacher, LW.............................1946-47
Alex Connell, G..................................1931-32
Wayne Connelly, RW...........1968-69 to 70-71
Bob Connors, C....................1928-29 to 29-30

Bob Cook, RW 1972-73
Carson Cooper, RW ....1927-28 to 31-32
Norm Corcoran, RW.........................1955-56
Murray Costello, C............1955-56 to 56-57
Gerry Couture, RW ....1944-45 to 50-51
Abbie Cox, G 1933-34
Danny Cox, LW 1931-32
Bart Cashley, D...........1965-66 to 68-69; 74-75
Murray Craven, LW-C.........1982-83 to 83-84
Bobby Crawford, C 1982-83
Jim Creighton, C...........1930-31 to 31-32
Troy Crowder, RW 1991-92
Gary Croteau, LW 1969-70
Doug Crossman, D ....1990-91 to 91-92
Roger Crozier, G ....1963-64 to 69-70
Wilf Cude, G 1933-34
Barry Cullen, RW.............................1959-60
Ray Cullen, C 1966-67
Jim Cummins, LW...............1991-92 to 92-93
Ian Cushenan, D 1963-64

D

Frank Daley, D-LW 1928-29
Joe Daley, G 1971-72
Lorne Davis, RW..............................1954-55
Bob Davis, D...................................1932-33
Mal Davis, RW ....1978-79 to 80-81
Billy Dea, LW ....1956-57 to 57-58; 69-70 to 70-71
Don Deacon, C ....1936-37; 38-39 to 39-40
Nelson DeBenedet, LW.....................1973-74
Denis Dejordy, G...............1972-73 to 73-74
Gilbert Delorme, D.............1987-88 to 88-89
Alex Delvecchio, C-LW ....1950-51 to 73-74
Al Dewsbury, D ...1946-47 to 47-48; 49-50
Per Djoos, D 1990-91
Ed Diachuk, LW 1960-61
Bob Dillabough, LW............1961-62 to 64-65
Cecil Dilon, RW 1939-40
Bill Dineen, RW ....1953-54 to 57-58
Peter Dineen, D 1989-90
Connie Dion, G.................1943-44 to 44-45
Marcel Dionne, C ....1971-72 to 74-75
Gary Doak, D 1965-66; 1972-73
Dolly Dolson, G ....1928-29 to 30-31
Bobby Dollas, D.................1990-91 to 92-93
Lloyd Doran, C 1946-47
Red Doran, D 1937-38
Ken Doraty, RW 1937-38
Kent Douglas, D.................1967-68 to 68-69
Les Douglas, C..........1940-41; 42-43; 46-47
Dallas Drake, C-LW ....1992-93 to 93-94
Kris Draper, D ....1993-94 to 95
Rene Drolet, RW 1974-75
Clarence Drouillard, C.......................1937-38
Gilles Dube, LW...............................1953-54
Ron Duguay, RW-C ....1983-84 to 85-86
Lorne Duguid, LW ....1934-35 to 35-36
Art Duncan, D 1926-27
Blake Dunlop, C 1983-84

E

Bruce Eakin, C 1985-86
Murray Eaves, C 1987-88; 1989-90
Tim Ecclestone, RW............1970-71 to 73-74
Roy Edwards, G ....1967-68 to 70-71; 72-73 to 73-74
Pat Egan, D 1943-44
Gerry Ehman, RW 1958-59
Bo Elik, LW......................................1962-63
Darren Eliot, G 1987-88
Hap Emms, LW..................1931-32 to 33-34

Bob Errey, LW 1995
Bob Essensa, G 1993-94
Chris Evans, D 1973-74
Stu Evans, D ....1930-31; 32-33 to 33-34

F

Bob Falkenberg, D ....1966-67 to 68-69; 70-71 to 71-72
Alex Faulkner, C ....1962-63 to 63-64
Bernie Federko, C.............................1989-90
Lorne Ferguson, LW ....1955-56 to 57-58
Sergei Fedorov, C ....1990-91 to 95
Brent Fedyk, D ....1987-88 to 91-92
Mark Ferner, D 1995
Viacheslav Fetisov, D.........................1995
Guyle Fielder, C.................1952-53; 57-58
Tom Filmore, RW ....1930-31 to 31-32
Dunc Fisher, RW...............................1958-59
Joe Fisher, RW..................1939-40 to 42-43
Lee Fogolin, D...................1947-48 to 50-51
Rick Foley, D 1973-74
Mike Foligno, RW...............1979-80 to 81-82
Bill Folk, D.......................1951-52 to 52-53
Len Fontaine, RW...............1972-73 to 73-74
Val Fonteyne, C-LW ....1959-60 to 62-63; 64-65 to 66-67
Dwight Foster, C ....1982-83 to 85-86
Yip Foster, D ....1933-34 to 34-35
Frank Foyston, C.................1926-27 to 27-28
Bobby Francis, C 1982-83
Jimmy Franks, G .....1936-37 to 37-38; 43-44
Gord Fraser, D ....1927-28 to 28-29
Frank Frederickson, C 1926-27; 30-31
Tim Friday, D 1985-86
Miroslav Frycer, RW 1988-89
Robbie Ftorek, C ....1972-73 to 73-74

G

Bill Gadsby, D ....1961-62 to 65-66
Jody Gage, RW ....1980-81 to 81-82; 83-84
Art Gagne, RW..................................1931-32
Johnny Gallagher, D.............1932-33; 36-37
Gerard Gallant, LW ....1984-85 to 92-93
Dave Gagner, G 1990-91
George Gardner, G ....1965-66 to 67-68
Danny Gare, RW ....1981-82 to 85-86
Johan Garpenlov, LW..........1990-91 to 91-92
Dave Gatherum, G 1953-54
Fern Gauthier, RW...............1945-46 to 48-49
George Gee, C ....1948-49 to 50-51
Ed Giacomin, G ....1975-76 to 77-78
Gus Giesebrecht, C ....1938-39 to 41-42
Gilles Gilbert, G ....1980-81 to 82-83
Art Giroux, RW 1935-36
Larry Giroux, D ....1974-75 to 77-78
Lorry Gloeckner, D............................1978-79
Fred Glover, RW ....1948-49 to 51-52
Howie Glover, RW ....1960-61 to 61-62
Warren Godfrey, D ....1955-56 to 61-62; 63-64 to 67-68
Pete Goegan, D ....1957-58 to 66-67
Bob Goldham, D..................1950-51 to 55-56
Leroy Goldsworthy, RW 1930-31; 32-33
Ebbie Goodfellow, C-D ....1929-30 to 42-43
Fred Gordon, RW 1926-27
Ted Graham, D....................1933-34 to 34-35
Danny Grant, LW ....1974-75 to 77-78
Doug Grant, G ....1973-74 to 75-76
Leo Gravelle, RW...............................1950-51
Adam Graves, C ....1987-88 to 89-90
Gerry Gray, G 1970-71
Harrison Gray, G...............................1963-64

Red Green, LW 1928-29
Rick Green, D...................................1990-91
Stu Grimson, LW 1995
Lloyd Gross, LW ....1933-34 to 34-35
Don Grosso, C.....................1938-39; 44-45
Danny Gruen, LW...............1972-73 to 73-74
Bep Guidolin, LW...............1947-48 to 48-49

H

Marc Habscheid, C/RW......1989-90 to 90-91
Lloyd Haddon, D..............................1959-60
Gord Haidy, RW................................1949-50
Slim Halderson, D............................1926-27
Len Haley, RW ....1959-60 to 60-61
Bob Halkidis, D.......................1993-94 to 95
Glenn Hall, G ....1952-53; 54-55 to 56-57
Murray Hall, C ....1964-65 to 66-67
Doug Halward, D................1986-87 to 88-89
Jean Hamel, D ....1973-74 to 80-81
Ted Hampson, C ....1963-64 to 64-65;
                                            66-67 to 67-68
Glen Hanlon, G ....1986-87 to 90-91
Dave Hanson, D...............................1978-79
Emil Hanson, D 1932-33
Terry Harper, D..................1975-76 to 78-79
Billy Harris, C...................................1965-66
Ron Harris, D.....................1962-63 to 63-64;
                                            68-69 to 71-72
Ted Harris, D.....................................1973-74
Gerry Hart, D......................1968-69 to 71-72
Harold Hart, LW 1926-27
Buster Harvey, RW.............1975-76 to 76-77
Doug Harvey, D 1966-67
Ed Hatoum, RW..................1968-69 to 69-70
George Hay, C-LW ...1927-28 to 30-31; 32-33
Jim Hay, D ....1952-53 to 54-55
Galen Head, RW................................1967-68
Rich Healey, D 1960-61
Paul Henderson, LW ....1962-63 to 67-68
Jack Hendrickson, D ....1957-58 to 58-59;
                                            61-62
Jim Herberts, C ....1928-29 to 29-30
Art Herchenratter, C 1940-41
Bryan Hextall, L................................1975-76
Dennis Hextall, C ....1975-76 to 78-79
Glenn Hicks, LW.................1979-80 to 80-81
Harold Hicks, D..................1929-30 to 30-31
Tim Higgins, RW ....1986-88 to 88-89
Dutch Hiller, LW................................1941-42
Jim Hiller, LW...................................1992-93
Larry Hillman, D ....1954-55 to 56-57
John Hilworth, D ....1977-78 to 79-80
Bill Hogaboam, C ....1972-73 to 75-76;
                                            78-79 to 79-80
Ken Holland, G 1983-84
Flash Hollett, D...................1943-44 to 45-46
Bucky Hollingworth, D.........1955-56 to 57-58
Chuck Holmes, RW 1958-59; 61-62
Hap Holmes, G...................1926-27 to 27-28
John Holota, C 1942-43; 45-46
Pete Horeck, RW-LW..........1946-47 to 48-49
Doug Houda, D....1985-86; 1987-88 to 90-91
Gordie Howe, RW ....1946-47 to 70-71
Mark Howe, D ....1992-93 to 95
Syd Howe, C-LW ....1934-35 to 45-46
Steve Hrymnak, D 1952-53
Willie Huber, D...................1978-79 to 82-83
Ron Hudson, RW..................1937-38; 39-40
Brent Hughes, D................................1973-74
Rusty Hughes, D 1929-30
Dennis Hull, LW................................1977-78

I

Miroslav Ihnacak, LW 1988-89
Peter Ing, G 1993-94
Earl Ingarfield, C-LW 1980-81
Ron Ingram, D 1963-64

J

Hal Jackson, D........1940-41; 42-43 to 46-47
Lou Jankowski, RW 1950-51; 52-53
Gary Jarrett, LW ....1966-67 to 67-68
Pierre Jarry, LW ....1973-74 to 74-75
Larry Jeffrey, LW ....1961-62 to 64-65
Bill Jennings, RW ....1940-41 to 43-44
Al Jensen, G.....................................1980-81
Al Johnson, RW..................1960-61 to 62-63
Brian Johnson, RW 1983-84
Danny Johnson, C.............................1971-72
Earl Johnson, C................................1953-54
Greg Johnson, C ....1993-94 to 95
Larry Johnston, D...............1971-72 to 73-74
Ed Johnstone, RW............................1983-84;
                                            85-86 to 85-87
Greg Joly, D ....1976-77 to 82-83
Buck Jones, D ....1938-39 to 39-40; 41-42
Ed Joyal, C ....1962-63 to 64-65

K

Red Kane, D......................................1943-44
Al Karlander, C-LW ....1969-70 to 72-73
Jack Keating, LW................1938-39 to 39-40
Duke Keats, C ....1926-27 to 27-28
Dave Kelly, RW.................................1976-77
Pete Kelly, RW ....1935-36 to 38-39
Red Kelly, D ....1947-48 to 59-60
Forbes Kennedy, C...1957-58 to 59-60; 61-62
Sheldon Kennedy, RW........1989-90 to 93-94
Alan Kerr, RW 1991-92
Brian Kilrea, LW................................1957-58
Hec Kilrea, LW.........1931-32; 35-36 to 39-40
Ken Kilrea, C-LW ...1939-40 to 41-42; 43-44
Wally Kilrea, C....................1934-35 to 37-38
Kris King, RW ....1987-88 to 88-89
Scott King, G ....1990-91 to 91-92
Mark Kirton, D ....1980-81 to 82-83
Kelly Kisio, C ....1982-83 to 85-86
Hobie Kitchen, D...............................1926-27
Petr Klima, LW....................1985-86 to 89-90
Joe Kocur, RW....................1984-85 to 90-91
Steve Konroyd, D................1992-93 to 93-94
Vladimir Konstantinov, D ....1991-92 to 95
Jim Korn, D ....1979-80 to 81-82
Mike Korney, RW ....1973-74 to 75-76
Chris Kotsopoulos, D.........................1989-90
Vyacheslav Kozlov, C ....1991-92 to 95
Dale Krentz, LW ....1986-87 to 88-89
Jim Krulicki, LW.................................1970-71
Gord Kruppke, D .....1990-91; 92-93 to 93-94
Mike Krushelnyski, LW/C.....................1995
Dave Kryskow, LW............................1974-75
Mark Kumpel, RW ....1986-87 to 87-88

L

Leo Labine, RW ....1960-61 to 61-62
Dan Labraaten, LW.............1978-79 to 80-81
Randy Ladouceur, D ....1982-83 to 86-87
Mark Laforest, G ....1985-86 to 86-87
Claude Laforge, LW...........................1958-59;
                                60-61 to 61-62; 63-64 to 64-65
Roger Lafreniere, D 1962-63
Serge Lajeunesse, D..........1970-71 to 72-73
Hec Lalande, C 1957-58
Joe Lamb, LW...................................1937-38

Mark Lamb, C.....................................1986-87
Lane Lambert, RW............1983-84 to 85-86
Al Langlois, D...................1963-64 to 64-65
Rick LaPointe, D...............1975-76 to 76-77
Martin Lapointe, RW..............1991-92 to 95
Reed Larson, D..................1976-77 to 85-86
Brian Lavender, LW.........1972-73 to 73-74
Dan Lawson, RW................1967-68 to 68-69
Reggie Leach, RW...........................1982-83
Jim Leavins, D.................................1985-86
Fernand Leblanc, RW.........1976-77 to 78-79
J.P. Leblanc, C................1975-76 to 78-79
Rene Leclerc, RW...............1968-69; 70-71
Claude Legris, G.................1980-81 to 81-82
Real Lemieux, LW.............................1966-67
Tony Leswick, RW....1951-52 to 54-55; 57-58
Dave Lewis, D..................1986-87 to 87-88
Herb Lewis, LW................1928-29 to 38-39
Nick Libett, LW..................1967-68 to 78-79
Tony Licari, RW................................1946-47
Nicklas Lidstrom, D............1991-92 to 95
Ted Lindsay, LW....1944-45 to 56-57; 64-65
Carl Liscombe, LW............1937-38 to 45-46
Ed Litzenberger, RW.......................1961-62
Bill Lochead, RW................1974-75 to 78-79
Mark Lofthouse, RW.........1981-82 to 82-83
Claude Loiselle, C............1981-82 to 85-86
Barry Long, D...................................1979-80
Clem Loughlin, D................1926-27 to 27-28
Ron Low, G.......................................1977-78
Larry Lozinski, G.............................1980-81
Dave Lucas, D.................................1962-63
Don Luce, C......................................1970-71
Harry Lumley, G.................1943-44 to 49-50
Len Lunde, C-RW..............1958-59 to 61-62
Tord Lundstrom, LW........................1973-74
Pat Lundy, C.....................1945-46 to 48-49
Chris Luongo, D...............................1990-91
George Lyle, LW...............1979-80 to 81-82
Jack Lynch, D...................1973-74 to 74-75
Vic Lynn, D.......................................1943-44

M

Lowell MacDonald, RW...1961-62 to 64-65
Parker MacDonald, LW.......1960-61 to 66-67
Bruce MacGregor, RW........1960-61 to 70-71
Calum MacKay, LW............1946-47; 48-49
Howard Mackie, RW...........1936-37 to 37-38
Paul MacLean, RW...........................1988-89
Rick MacLeish, LW..........................1983-84
Brian MacLellan, LW........................1991-92
John MacMillan, LW...........1963-64 to 64-65
Frank Mahovlich, LW.........1967-68 to 70-71
Pete Mahovlich, C.............1965-66 to 68-69;
                                      79-80 to 80-81
Steve Maltais, LW............................1993-94
Dan Maloney, LW...............1975-76 to 77-78
Randy Manery, D................1970-71 to 71-72
Ken Mann, RW..................................1975-76
Bob Manno, LW-D.............1983-84 to 84-85
Lou Marcon, D.....1958-59 to 59-60; 62-63
Gus Marker, RW.................1932-33 to 33-34
Brad Marsh, D...................1990-91 to 91-92
Gary Marsh, LW...............................1967-68
Bert Marshall, D...............1965-66 to 67-68
Clare Martin, D...................1949-50 to 50-51
Pit Martin, C..........1961-62; 63-64 to 65-66
Don Martineau, RW............1975-76 to 76-77
Steve Martinson, D..........................1987-88
Charlie Mason, RW..........................1938-39
Roland Matte, D...............................1929-30
Gary McAdam, RW...........................1980-81

Jud McAtee, LW.................1943-44 to 44-45
Stan McCabe, LW...............1929-30 to 30-31
Doug McCaig, D.....1941-42; 45-46 to 47-48
Rick McCann, C....1967-68 to 71-72; 74-75
Tom McCarthy, LW.............1956-57 to 58-59
Darren McCarty, LW..............1993-94 to 95
Kevin McClelland, RW........1989-90 to 90-91
Bob McCord, D...................1965-66 to 67-68
Dale McCourt, C.................1977-78 to 81-82
Bill McCreary, LW.............................1957-58
Brad McCrimmon, D..........1990-91 to 92-93
Brian McCutcheon, LW......1974-75 to 76-77
Ab McDonald, LW....1965-66 to 66-67; 71-72
Bucko McDonald, D............1934-35 to 38-39
Byron McDonald, LW..........1939-40; 44-45
Al McDonough, RW...........................1977-78
Bill McDougall, C..............................1990-91
Pete McDuffe, G..............................1975-76
Mike McEwen, D...............................1985-86
Jim McFadden, C...............1946-47 to 50-51
Bob McGill, D....................................1991-92
Tom McGratton, G............................1947-48
Bert McInenly, LW..............1930-31 to 31-32
Doug McKay, LW...............................1949-50
Randy McKay, RW..............1988-89 to 90-91
Jack McIntyre, LW..............1957-58 to 59-60
Walt McKechnie, C............1974-75 to 76-77;
                                      81-82 to 82-83
Tony McKegney, RW..........................1989-90
Don McKenney, LW...........................1965-66
Bill McKenzie, G.................1973-74 to 74-75
John McKenzie, RW...........1959-60 to 60-61
Andrew McKim, C..................................1995
Rollie McLenahan, D.......................1945-46
Al McLeod, D.....................................1973-74
Don McLeod, G.................................1970-71
Mike McMahon, D.............................1969-70
Max McNab, C....................1947-48 to 50-51
Billy McNeill, RW...............1956-57 to 59-60;
                                      62-63 to 63-64
Stu McNeill, C....................1957-58 to 59-60
Basil McRae, LW................1985-86 to 86-87
Chris McRae, LW..............................1989-90
Pat McReavy, LW.............................1941-42
Harry Meeking, LW...........................1926-27
Tom Mellor, D....................1973-74 to 74-75
Gerry Melnyk, C....1955-56; 59-60 to 60-61
Barry Melrose, D................1983-84; 85-86
Howie Menard, C.............................1963-64
Glenn Merkosky, LW..........1985-86; 89-90
Corrado Micalef, G............1981-82 to 85-86
Nick Mickoski, LW..............1957-58 to 58-59
Hugh Millar, D...................................1946-47
Greg Millen, G..................................1991-92
Kevin Miller, RW.................1990-91 to 91-92
Perry Miller, D....................1977-78 to 80-81
Tom Miller, C.....................................1970-71
Eddie Mio, G......................1983-84 to 85-86
John Miszuk, D.................................1963-64
Bill Mitchell, D..................................1963-64
John Mokosak, D...............1988-89 to 89-90
Ron Moffatt, LW.................1932-33 to 34-35
Gary Monahan, LW...........................1969-70
Hank Montieth, LW.............1968-69 to 70-71
Alfie Moore, G..................................1939-40
Don Morrison, C.................1947-48 to 48-49
Jim Morrison, D.................................1959-60
Rod Morrison, RW............................1947-48
Dean Morton, D................................1989-90
Gus Mortson, D.................................1958-59
Alex Motter, D....................1937-38 to 42-43

John Mowers, G ......1940-41 to 42-43; 46-47
Wayne Muloin, D 1963-64
Don Murdoch, RW 1981-82
Brian Murphy, C..............................1974-75
Joe Murphy, C-RW ....1986-87 to 89-90
Ron Murphy, LW ....1964-65 to 65-66
Ken Murray, D..................................1972-73
Terry Murray, D................................1976-77

N

Jim Nahrgang, D ....1974-75 to 76-77
Vaclav Nedomansky, C-RW .1977-78 to 81-82
Rick Newell, D ....1972-73 to 73-74
John Newman, C...............................1930-31
Eddie Nicholson, D 1947-48
Jim Niekamp, D ....1970-71 to 71-72
Jim Nill, RW ....1987-88 to 89-90
Reg Noble, D ....1927-28 to 32-33
Ted Nolan, LW.....................1981-82; 83-84
Lee Norwood, D ....1986-87 to 90-91
Hank Nowak, LW...............................1974-75

O

Adam Oates, C...................1985-86 to 88-89
Russ Oatman, LW 1926-27
Mike O'Connell, D ....1985-86 to 89-90
Gerry Odrowski, D.............1960-61 to 62-63
John Ogrodnick, LW..........1979-80 to 86-87;
                                               92-93
Murray Oliver, C ....1957-58; 59-60 to 60-61
Dennis Olson, LW.............................1957-58
Jimmy Orlando, D.............1936-37 to 37-38;
                                               39-40 to 42-43
Mark Osborne, LW.............1981-82 to 82-83
Chris Osgood, G ....1993-94 to 95

P

Pete Palangio, LW 1927-28
Brad Park, D......................1983-84 to 84-85
Joe Paterson, LW ....1980-81 to 83-84
George Patterson, RW 1934-35
Butch Paul, C...................................1964-65
Marty Pavelich, LW ....1947-48 to 56-57
Jim Pavese, D ....1987-88 to 88-89
Mark Pederson, LW 1993-94
Bert Peer, RW..................................1939-40
Bob Perreault, G...............................1958-59
Jim Peters, Jr., C ....1964-65 to 67-68
Jim Peters, Sr., RW ...1949-50 to 50-51; 53-54
Brent Peterson, C..............1978-79 to 81-82
Gord Pettinger, C ....1933-34 to 37-38
Robert Picard, D...............................1989-90
Alex Pirus, RW 1979-80
Rob Plumb, LW ....1977-78 to 78-79
Nellie Podolsky, LW 1948-49
Bud Poile, RW 1948-49
Don Poile, C-RW 1954-55; 57-58
Dennis Polonich, RW ....1974-75 to 80-81;
                                               82-83
Poul Popiel, D ....1968-69 to 69-70
Marc Potvin, LW.................1990-91 to 91-92
Dean Prentice, LW ....1965-66 to 68-69
Noel Price, D....................................1961-62
Keith Primeau, C/LW ....1990-91 to 95
Bob Probert, LW-RW ....1985-86 to 93-94
Andre Pronovost, LW ....1962-63 to 64-65
Marcel Pronovost, D ....1949-50 to 64-65
Metro Prystai, RW-C ....1950-51 to 57-58
Cliff Purpur, RW...............................1944-45
Chris Pusey, G..................................1985-86
Nelson Pyatt, C..................1973-74 to 74-75

Q

Bill Quackenbush, D..........1942-43 to 48-49

R

Yves Racine, D...................1989-90 to 92-93
Clare Raglan, D.................................1950-51
Mike Ramsey, D................................1995
Matt Ravlich, D..................................1969-70
Marc Reaume, D................1959-60 to 60-61
Billy Reay, C ....1943-44 to 44-45
Mickey Redmond, RW.........1970-71 to 75-76
Dutch Reibel, C..................1953-54 to 57-58
Gerry Reid, C.....................................1948-49
Leo Reise, D ....1946-47 to 51-52
Dave Richardson, LW 1967-68
Terry Richardson, G ....1973-74 to 76-77
Steve Richmond, D 1985-86
Vincent Riendeau, G ....1991-92 to 93-94
Dennis Riggin, G 1959-60; 62-63
Jim Riley, RW....................................1926-27
Bob Ritchie, LW ....1976-77 to 77-78
Wayne Rivers, RW.............................1961-62
John Ross Roach, G ....1932-33 to 34-35
Phil Roberto, RW................1974-75 to 75-76
Doug Roberts, RW.............1965-66 to 67-68;
                                               73-74 to 74-75
Earl Robertson, G.............................1936-37
Fred Robertson, D.............................1933-34
Torrie Robertson, LW ....1988-89 to 89-90
Mike Robitaille, D 1970-71
Desse Roche, RW 1934-35
Earl Roche, LW.................................1934-35
Dave Rochefort, C 1966-67
Leon Rochefort, RW ....1971-72 to 72-73
Harvey Rockburn, D ....1929-30 to 30-31
Dale Rolfe, D ....1969-70 to 70-71
Rollie Rossignol, LW 1943-44; 45-46
Rolly Roulston, D..............................1936-37
Bob Rouse, D 1995
Tom Rowe, RW..................................1982-83
Bernie Ruelle, LW.............................1943-44
Pat Rupp, G......................................1963-64
Jimmy Rutherford, G..........1970-71;
                                               73-74 to 80-81; 82-83

S

Andre St. Laurent, C...........1977-78 to 78-79;
                                               83-84
Sam St. Laurent, G ....1986-87 to 89-90
Borje Salming, D 1989-90
Barry Salovaara, D ....1974-75 to 75-76
Ed Sanford, C...................................1955-56
Bob Sauve, G 1981-82
Terry Sawchuk, G ....1949-50 to 54-55;
                                               57-58 to 63-64; 68-69
Kevin Schamehorn, RW........1976-77; 79-80
Jim Schoenfeld, D ....1981-82 to 82-83
Dwight Schofield, D...........................1976-77
Enio Sclisizzl, LW ...1946-47 to 49-50; 51-52
Earl Seibert, D...................1944-45 to 45-46
Ric Seiling, RW.................................1986-87
Daniel Shank, RW..............1989-90 to 90-91
Jeff Sharples, D..................1986-87 to 88-89
Doug Shedden, RW ....1985-86 to 86-87
Bobby Sheehan, C.............................1976-77
Tim Sheehy, RW................................1977-78
Frank Sheppard, C.............................1927-28
John Sheppard, LW ....1926-27 to 27-28
Ray Sheppard, RW.............1991-92 to 95
Gord Sherritt, D.................................1943-44
John Sherf, LW ....1935-36 to 38-39; 43-44
Jim Shires, LW 1970-71

Steve Short, D..................................1978-79
Gary Shuchuk, RW.........................1990-91
Dave Silk, RW 1984-85
Mike Sillinger, C ....1990-91 to 95
Cully Simon, D ....1942-43 to 44-45
Thain Simon, D 1946-47
Cliff Simpson, C.................1946-47 to 47-48
Reg Sinclair, RW.............................1952-53
Darryl Sittler, C-LW 1984-85
Bjorne Skaare, D.............................1978-79
Glen Skov, C.....................1949-50 to 54-55
Al Smith, G 1971-72
Alex Smith, D 1931-32
Brad Smith, RW.................1980-81 to 84-85
Brian Smith, LW....................1957-58; 60-61
Carl Smith, LW 1943-44
Derek Smith, C ....1981-82 to 82-83
Floyd Smith, RW................1962-63 to 67-68
Greg Smith, D ....1981-82 to 85-86
Nakina Dalton Smith, LW 1943-44
Normie Smith, G...........................1934-35;
                38-39; 43-44 to 44-45
Rick Smith, D...................................1980-81
Ted Snell, RW 1974-75
Harold Snepsts, D ....1985-86 to 87-88
Sandy Snow, RW.............................1968-69
Dennis Sobchuk, C..........................1979-80
Ken Solheim, LW 1982-83
Bob Solinger, LW 1959-60
John Sorrell, LW ....1930-31 to 37-38
Fred Speck, C....................1968-69 to 69-70
Ted Speers, RW 1985-86
Irv Spencer, D-LW.............1963-64 to 65-66;
                          67-68
Ron Stackhouse, D ....1971-72 to 73-74
Ed Stankiewicz, LW.............1953-54; 55-56
Wilf Starr, C ....1933-34 to 35-36
Vic Stasiuk, RW-LW...........1950-51 to 54-55;
                   60-61 to 62-63
Ray Staszak, RW 1985-86
Frank Steele, LW 1930-31
Greg Stefan, G ....1981-82 to 89-90
Pete Stemkowski, C ....1967-68 to 70-71
Blair Stewart, LW ....1973-74 to 74-75
Gaye Stewart, LW............................1950-51
Jack Stewart, D ....1938-39 to 42-43;
                   45-46 to 49-50
Gord Strate, D ....1956-57 to 58-59
Art Stratton, C..................................1963-64
Herb Stuart, G 1926-27
Barry Sullivan, RW...........................1947-48
Bill Sutherland, LW..........................1971-72

T

John Taft, D......................................1978-79
Jean-Guy Talbot, D..........................1967-68
Chris Tancill, C ....1991-92 to 92-93
Billy Taylor, D 1946-47
Ted Taylor, LW.................................1966-67
Tim Taylor, LW ....1993-94 to 95
Harvey Teno, G................................1938-39
Larry Thibeault, LW 1944-45
Billy Thomson, RW...............1938-39; 43-44
Cecil Thompson, G ....1938-39 to 39-40
Errol Thompson, LW ....1977-78 to 80-81
Jerry Toppazzini, RW 1955-56
Larry Trader, D 1982-83; 84-85
Percy Traub, D ....1927-28 to 28-29
Dave Trottier, LW 1938-39
Joe Turner, G 1941-42

U

Norm Ullman, C ....1955-56 to 67-78
Garry Unger, C ....1967-68 to 70-71

V

Rogie Vachon, G.................1978-79 to 79-80
Eric Vail, LW 1981-82
Rick Vasko, D ....1979-80 to 80-81
Darren Veitch, D ....1985-86 to 87-88
Mike Vernon, G 1995
Dennis Vial, D ....1990-91 to 92-93
Doug Volmer, RW ....1969-70 to 71-72
Carl Voss, C.....................................1932-33

W

Jack Walker, LW ....1926-27 to 27-28
Bob Wall, D............1964-64 to 66-67; 71-72
Aaron Ward, D ....1993-94 to 95
Eddie Wares, RW................1937-38 to 42-43
Bryan Watson, D ....1965-66 to 66-67;
                     73-74 to 76-77
Harry Watson, LW 1942-43; 45-46
Jim Watson, D ....1963-64 to 65-66;
                   67-68 to 69-70
Brian Watts, LW 1975-76
Tom Webster, RW .....1970-71 to 71-72; 79-80
Cooney Weiland, C.............1933-34 to 34-35
Stan Weir, C.....................................1982-83
Carl Wetzel, G 1964-65
Bob Whitelaw, D.................1940-41 to 41-42
Archie Wilder, LW 1940-41
Bob Wilkie, D 1990-91
Burr Williams, D 1933-34; 36-37
Carl Williams, D 1931-32
Dave "Tiger" Williams, LW................1984-85
Fred Williams, C...............................1976-77
John Wilson, LW ....1949-50 to 54-55;
                 57-58 to 58-59
Larry Wilson, C....1949-50; 51-52 to 52-53
Lefty Wilson, G.................................1953-54
Rick Wilson, D 1976-77
Murray Wing, D 1973-74
Eddie Wiseman, RW..........1932-33 to 35-36
Steve Wochy, C-RW...............1944-45; 46-47
Benny Woit, D....................1950-51 to 54-55
Mike Wong, C...................................1975-76
Paul Woods, LW ....1977-78 to 83-84
Larry Wright, RW-C...........................1977-78

Y

Jason York, D ....1992-93 to 95
Doug Young, D ....1931-32 to 38-39
Howie Young, D ....1960-61 to 62-63;
                 66-67 to 67-68
Warren Young, LW...........................1985-86
Paul Ysebaert, LW.............1990-91 to 92-93
Steve Yzerman, C ....1983-84 to 95

Z

Larry Zeidel, D...................1951-52 to 52-53
Ed Zeniuk, D.....................................1954-55
Rick Zombo, D ....1984-85 to 91-92
Rudy Zunich, D.................................1943-44

(780 players through 1995)

No. 1

Harry Holmes	1926-27 to 27-28
Dolly Dolson	1928-29 to 30-31
Bill Beveridge	1929-30
Alex Connell	1931-32
John Ross Roach	1932-33 to 34-35
Abbie Cox	1933-34
Wilf Cude	1933-34
Norm Smith	1934-35 to 38-39, 43-44 to 44-45
Earl Robertson	1936-37
Jim Franks	1936-37 to 37-38, 43-44
Harvey Teno	1938-39
Cecil Thompson	1938-39 to 39-40
Alf Moore	1939-40
Claude Bourque	1939-40
John Mowers	1940-41 to 42-43
Joe Turner	1941-42
Connie Dior	1943-44 to 44-45
Harry Lumley	1943-44 to 49-50
Ralph Adams	1946-47
Terry Sawchuk	1949-50 to 54-55, 57-58 to 63-64 (Retired Mar. 6, 1994)
Dave Gatherum	1953-54
Lefty Wilson	1953-54
Glenn Hall	1954-55 to 56-57
Bob Perrault	1958-59
Dennis Riggin	1959-60, 62-63
Gilles Boisvert	1959-60
Hank Bassen	1960-61 to 62-63
Roger Crozier	1964-65 to 69-70
Roy Edwards	1967-68, 72-73 to 73-74
Jim Rutherford	1970-71, 74-75 to 80-81
Don McLeod	1970-71
Joe Daley	1971-72
Terry Richardson	1973-74, 75-76
Bill McKenzie	1973-74
Gilles Gilbert	1980-81 to 82-83
Corrado Micalef	1983-84 to 85-86
Glen Hanlon	1986-87 to 90-91

No. 2

Clem Loughlin	1926-27 to 27-28
Percy Traub	1928-29
Harvey Rockburn	1929-30 to 30-31
Alex Smith	1931-32
Doug Young	1932-33 to 38-39
Burr Williams	1936-37
Rolly Roulston	1936-37
John Gallagher	1936-37
Jack Stewart	1939-40 to 42-43, 45-46 to 49-50
Buck Jones	1941-42
Clarence Behling	1942-43
Cully Simon	1943-44 to 44-45
Gerry Couture	1944-45
Bob Goldham	1950-51 to 55-56
Larry Hillman	1956-57
Al Arbour	1956-57 to 57-58

Pete Goegon	1958-59 to 61-62, 65-66
Jim Morrison	1959-60
Noel Price	1961-62
Jack Hendrickson	1961-62
Howie Young	1962-63
Ron Ingram	1963-64
Al Langlois	1963-64 to 64-65
Jim Watson	1963-64
Bob McCord	1965-66
Dwight Carruthers	1965-66
Warren Godfrey	1965-66
Gary Bergman	1966-67 to 74-75
Mike Korney	1973-74
Al McLeod	1973-74
Terry Harper	1975-76 to 78-79
Barry Long	1979-80
Rick Smith	1980-81
John Barrett	1980-81
Jim Schoenfield	1981-82 to 82-83
Larry Trader	1984-85
Barry Melrose	1985-86
Mike O'Connell	1985-86 to 89-90
Brad McCrimmon	1990-91 to 92-93
Terry Carkner	1993-94 to 95

No. 3

Slim Halderson	1926-27
Pete Bellefeuille	1926-27
Reg Noble	1927-28 to 32-33
Emil Hanson	1932-33
Carl Voss	1932-33
John Gallagher	1932-33
Stu Evans	1933-34
Ted Graham	1933-34 to 34-35
Bucko McDonald	1934-35 to 38-39
Jack Stewart	1938-39
Scotty Bowman	1938-39 to 39-40
Don Deacon	1939-40
Alex Motter	1939-40 to 42-43
Buck Jones	1941-42
Gordie Sherritt	1943-44
Vic Lynn	1943-44
Murray Armstrong	1943-44 to 45-46
Bill Quackenbush	1946-47 to 48-49
Clare Martin	1949-50 to 50-51
Ben Woit	1951-52
Marcel Pronovost	1952-53 to 64-65
Bill Mitchell	1963-64
Gary Bergman	1965-66
Bert Marshall	1965-66 to 66-67
Bob McCord	1967-68
Jean Guy Talbot	1967-68
Warren Godfrey	1967-68
Bob Falkenberg	1967-68 to 68-69, 71-72
Paul Popeil	1968-69 to 69-70
Jim Watson	1969-70
Gerry Hart	1969-70
Dale Rolfe	1970-71
Jim Niekamp	1971-72
Larry Johnston	1971-72 to 73-74
Murray Wing	1973-74
Jack Lynch	1974-75

Jim Nahrgang 1974-75,76-77
Larry Giroux ....1975-76 to 76-77
Perry Miller ....1977-78 to 80-81
Rick Vasko...1979-80
John Barrett.........................1981-82 to 85-86
Steve Chiasson.................1986-87 to 93-94
Bob Rouse 1995

No. 4

Harry Meeking 1926-27
Archie Briden..1926-27
George Hay ....1927-28 to 30-31
Herb Lewis.............................1931-32 to 38-39
John Sorrell...1937-38
Gus Giesebrecht 1939-40
Sid Abel..1939-40
Jim Orlando..........................1940-41 to 42-43
Harold Jackson ....1943-44 to 46-47
Jim McFadden..1946-47
Doug McCaig ....1947-48 to 48-49
Al Dewsbury..1947-48
Len "Red" Kelly.....................1948-49 to 59-60
Marc Reaume ....1959-60 to 60-61
Howie Young..1960-61
Bill Gadsby ....1961-62 to 65-66
Ron Harris...1963-64
Bob Wall...1964-65
Leo Boivin 1966-67
Howie Young..1967-68
Bob Baun..............................1968-69 to 70-71
Larry Brown..1970-71
Arnie Brown ....1970-71 to 71-72
Thommie Bergman ....1972-73 to 74-75,
                                                          77-78 to 79-80
Bart Crashley 1974-75
Rick Lapointe ....1975-76 to 76-77
Terry Murray...1976-77
Larry Giroux 1977-78
John Hilworth...1977-78
Rick Vasko.............................1977-78, 80-81
Tom Bladon 1980-81
Rejean Cloutier 1981-82
Colin Campbell...................1982-83 to 84-85
Tim Friday...1985-86
Jim Leavins 1985-86
Jeff Sharples 1986-87
Rick Zombo ....1986-87 to 91-92
Bob McGill 1991-92
Mark Howe ....1992-93 to 1995

No. 5

Frank Frederickson 1926-27
Duke Keats ....19-26-27 to 27-28
Gord Fraser ....1927-28 to 28-29
Bill Brydge...1928-29
Bob Connors 1929-30
Ebbie Goodfellow ....1930-31 to 42-43
Pete Bessone 1937-38
John Doran 1937-38
Jim Orlando..1937-38
Buck Jones 1938-39, 41-42
Eddie Bush 1941-42
Doug McCaig...1941-42
Clarence Behling.....................................1942-43
Hal Jackson..1942-43

Pat Egan..1943-44
Bill "Flash" Hollett.............1943-44 to 45-46
Hugh Millar...1946-47
Al Dewsbury...1946-47
Leo Reise ....1946-47 to 51-52
Ben Woit...............................1952-53 to 54-55
Warren Godfrey ....1955-56 to 61-62
Al Arbour 1955-56
Rich Healey 1960-61
Doug Barkley ....1962-63 to 65-66
John Misuk...1963-64
Bob Wall...1966-67
Doug Harvey 1966-67
Bob Falkenberg..1966-67
Bert Marshall 1967-68
Kent Douglas ....1967-68 to 68-69
Carl Brewer...1969-70
Serje Lajeunesse 1970-71
Marcel Dionne....................1971-72 to 73-74
Jean Hamel ....1974-75 to 80-81
Greg Smith ....1981-82 to 85-86
Darren Veitch ....1985-86 to 87-88
John Mokosak 1988-89
Dean Morton 1989-90
Peter Dineen..1989-90
Chris McRae 1989-90
Rick Green 1990-91
Nicklas Lidstrom ....1991-92 to 95

No. 6

Jack Walker.........................1926-27 to 27-28
Larry Aurie ....1928-29 to 38-39
Cumming Burton ....1957-58 to 58-59

No. 7

Russ Oatman 1926-27
Stan Brown 1927-28
Pete Palangio 1927-28
Jim Herberts 1928-29
Herb Lewis ....1929-30 to 30-31
Hec Kilrea 1931-32
Art Gagne 1931-32
Leroy Goldsworthy..................................1932-33
George Hay...1932-33
Carl Voss 1933-34
Cooney Weiland ....1933-34 to 34-35
Marty Barry ....1935-36 to 38-39
Alex Motter 1939-40
Don Deacon 1939-40
Sid Abel..1939-40
Ken Kilrea 1940-41
Carl Liscombe ....1940-41 to 45-46
Ted Lindsay.........................1946-47 to 56-57
                                                 (Retired Nov. 10, 1991)
Billy Dea...1957-58
Hec Lalande 1957-58
Murray Oliver 1957-58
Brian Kilrea 1957-58
Norm Ullman ....1958-59 to 67-68
Garry Unger ....1968-69 to 70-71
Red Berenson ....1970-71 to 74-75
Dave Kryskow 1974-75
Dan Maloney ....1975-76 to 77-78
Willie Huber ....1978-79 to 82-83

Joe Paterson	1983-84
Milan Chalupa	1984-85
Mike McEwen	1985-86
Steve Richmond	1985-86
Eddie Johnstone	1986-87
Doug Halward	1986-87 to 88-89
Brent Fedyk	1988-89
Tony McKegney	1989-90
Robert Picard	1989-90
Tom Bissett	1990-91

No. 8

Art Duncan	1926-27
Carson Cooper	1927-28 to 29-30
Stu Evans	1930-31
Danny Cox	1931-32
Eddie Wiseman	1932-33 to 34-35
Yip Foster	1934-35
Syd Howe	1934-35 to 45-46
Don Deacon	1936-37
Billy Rea	1944-45
Cliff Purpur	1944-45
Pat Lundy	1945-46 to 48-49
George Gee	1948-49 to 50-51
Tony Leswick	1951-52 to 54-55
Dutch Reibel	1955-56 to 57-58
John Wilson	1957-58 to 58-59
Barry Cullen	1959-60
Murray Oliver	1960-61
Leo Labine	1960-61 to 61-62
Forbes Kennedy	1961-62
Lowell MacDonald	1961-62 to 63-64
Floyd Smith	1962-63
Art Stratton	1963-64
Claude Laforge	1963-64
Pat Martin	1963-64 to 64-65
Val Fonteyne	1966-67
Gary Jarrett	1966-67 to 67-68
Bart Crashley	1968-69
Rick McCann	1968-69 to 69-70
Rene Leclerc	1968-69
Fred Speck	1969-70
Tom Webster	1970-71
Bill Sutherland	1971-72
Dan Johnson	1971-72
Guy Charron	1972-73 to 74-75
Ted Snell	1974-75
Brian McCutcheon	1974-75
Dennis Polonich	1075-76 to 80-81, 82-83
Claude Loiselle	1981-82
Joe Paterson	1982-83
Tom Rowe	1982-83
Ted Nolan	1983-84
Dave Silk	1984-85
Ray Staszak	1985-86
Mark Lamb	1986-87
Jim Nill	1987-88 to 89-90
Bobby Dollas	1990-91 to 91-92
Gord Kruppke	1992-93
Steve Konroyd	1993-94
Aaron Ward	1995

No. 9

John Sheppard	1926-27 to 27-28
Herb Lewis	1928-29
Harold Hicks	1929-30

Roalnd Matte	1929-30
Bert McInenly	1930-31 to 31-32
Frank Carson	1931-32 to 33-34
Tom Anderson	1934-35
Ed Wiseman	1934-35
Wally Kilrea	1935-36 to 36-37
Pete Kelly	1937-38
Mud Bruneteau	1937-38 to 45-46
John Sorrell	1937-38
Joe Lamb	1937-38
John Sherf	1938-39
Connie Brown	1938-39
Ken Kilrea	1938-39
Ed Bruneteau	1943-44
Billy Thompson	1943-44
Sid Abel	1945-46
Roy Conacher	1946-47
Gordie Howe	1947-48 to 70-71
	(Retired Mar. 12, 1972)

No. 10

Frank Foyston	1926-27 to 27-28
Frank Sheppard	1927-28
Bob Connors	1928-29
Ebbie Goodfellow	1929-30
Carson Cooper	1930-31 to 31-32
John Sorrell	1932-33 to 37-38
Clarence Droulliard	1937-38
Carl Liscombe	1937-38 to 39-40
Don Grosso	1939-40 to 44-45
Bill Jennings	1943-44
Billy Reay	1943-44 to 44-45
Cliff Purpur	1944-45
Steve Wochy	1944-45
Fern Gauthier	1945-46 to 47-48
Gerry Brown	1945-46
Gerry Couture	1946-47 to 47-48
Max McNab	1948-49
Ed Bruneteau	1948-49
Jim Peters	1949-50 to 50-51
Metro Prystai	1951-52 to 54-55
Alex Delvecchio	1954-55 to 73-74
	(Retired Nov. 10, 1991)
Dale McCourt	1977-78 to 81-82
Mark Lofthouse	1981-82
Claude Loiselle	1982-83
Ron Duguay	1983-84 to 85-86
Joe Murphy	1986-87 to 89-90
Jimmy Carson	1989-90 to 91-92

No. 11

Hobie Kitchen	1926-27
Jim Riley	1926-27
Bernie Brophy	1928-29 to 29-30
Jim Herberts	1929-30
Tom Filmore	1930-31 to 31-32
Frank Steele	1930-31
Art Gagne	1931-32
Carl Williams	1931-32
Hap Emms	1931-32 to 33-34
Gord Pettinger	1934-35 to 37-38
Earl Roche	1934-35
Scotty Bowman	1934-35
Wally Kilrea	1934-35
Red Beattie	1937-38

Ken Doraty 1937-38
Eddie Wares ....1937-38 to 42-43
Billy Thompson..............................1938-39
Sid Abel 1939-40
Adam Brown ....1943-44, 45-46 to 46-47
Jud McAtee 1944-45
Byron McDonald.............................1944-45
Pete Horeck ....1946-47 to 48-49
Barry Sullivan.................................1947-48
Max McNab......................................1949-50
Gaye Stewart..................................1950-51
Marty Pavelich ....1951-52 to 56-57
John Wilson 1957-58
Nick Mickowski ....1957-58 to 58-59
Gary Aldcorn ....1959-60 to 60-61
Vic Stasiuk ....1960-61 to 62-63
Warren Godfrey 1963-64
Irv Spencer.........................1963-64 to 64-65
Lowell MacDonald 1964-65
John MacMillan 1964-65
Bob Dillabough...............................1964-65
Jim Watson.....................................1964-65
Val Fonteyne ....1964-65 to 65-66
Pete Mahovlich...................1966-67, 68-69
Jim Peters Jr. ....1966-67 to 67-68
Gerry Abel......................................1966-67
Gary Monahan.................................1969-70
Gary Croteau 1969-70
Hank Monteith...................1969-70 to 70-71
Don Luce...1970-71
Leon Rochefort ....1971-72 to 72-73
Brian Lavender 1972-73
Len Fontaine 1973-74
Chris Evans.....................................1973-74
Hank Nowak....................................1974-75
Walt McKechnie..................1974-75 to 76-77,
                                        81-82 to 82-83
Rick Bowness..................................1977-78
John Taft...1978-79
Lorry Gloeckner 1978-79
Pete Mahovlich ....1979-80 to 80-81
Murray Craven................................1983-84
Blake Dunlop..................................1983-84
Brad Smith......................................1984-85
Rick Zombo 1984-85
Ted Speers 1985-86
Shawn Burr ....1984-85 to 95

No. 12

Fred Gordon 1926-27
Larry Aurie.....................................1927-28
Pete Bellefeuille.............................1928-29
Red Green.......................................1928-29
Jim Herberts...................................1929-30
Stan McCabe 1929-30
John Sorrell ....1930-31 to 31-32
Walt Buswell ....1932-33 to 34-35
Hec Kilrea ....1935-36 to 39-40
Byron McDonald..............................1939-40
Sid Abel.....1940-41 to 42-43, 46-47 to 51-52
                              (Retired Apr. 29, 1995)
Joe Carveth.......................1943-44 to 45-46
Glen Skov..........................1952-53 to 54-55
Ed Sanford 1955-56

Metro Prystai ....1955-56 to 57-58
Bill Dineen......................................1957-58
Tony Leswick 1957-58
Dunc Fisher.....................................1958-59
Gene Achtymichuk 1958-59
Stu McNeill 1958-59
Chuck Holmes..................................1958-59
Val Fonteyne ....1959-60 to 61-62
Alex Faulkner ....1962-63 to 63-64
Pit Martin 1963-64
John MacMillan 1963-64
Bob Dillabough...............................1963-64
Ron Murphy........................1964-65 to 65-66
Bruce MacGregor ....1965-66 to 70-71
Tom Miller 1970-71
Ab McDonald...................................1971-72
Henry Boucha 1971-72
Randy Manery 1971-72
Bob Cook...1972-73
Garnet Bailey ....1972-73 to 73-74
Dan Gruen 1973-74
Marcel Dionne 1974-75
Bryan Hextall 1975-76
J.P. Leblanc.........................1975-76 to 77-78
Fern Leblanc 1977-78
Errol Thompson ....1977-78 to 80-81
Brent Peterson ....1980-81 to 81-82
Tom Rowe..1982-83
Ivan Boldirev......................1982-83 to 84-85
Adam Oates 1985-86
Billy Carroll ....1985-86 to 86-87
Adam Graves......................1987-88 to 89-90
Sheldon Kennedy...............1989-90 to 90-91
Jimmy Carson ....1991-92 to 92-93
Mile Sillinger.....................1993-94 to 95
Bob Errey..1995

No. 13

Harold Hart 1926-27
Vyacheslav Kozlov ....1991-92 to 95

No. 14

Herb Stuart 1926-27
Percy Traub.....................................1927-28
Frank Daley 1928-29
Rusty Hughes...................................1929-30
Stan McCabe....................................1930-31
Doug Young 1931-32
Stu Evans 1932-33
Fred Robertson 1933-34
Lloyd Gross 1933-34
Gus Marker......................................1933-34
Desse Roche 1934-35
Lorne Duguid 1934-35
Wilf Starr 1935-36
Mud Bruneteau...................1935-36 to 37-38
Hal Mackie ....1936-37 to 37-38
Alex Motter ....1937-38 to 38-39
Sid Abel..1938-39
Gus Giesebrecht ....1939-40 to 41-42
Ken Kilrea 1939-40
Joe Fisher 1939-40
Gerry Brown....................................1941-42
Joe Carveth 1942-43
Bernie Ruelle...................................1943-44

Bill Jennings 1943-44
Ted Lindsay.....................1944-45 to 46-47
Bep Guidolin ....1947-48 to 48-49
Bud Poile 1948-49
Pete Babando.....................................1949-50
Metro Prystai 1950-51
Glen Skov ....1950-51 to 51-52
Reg Sinclair 1952-53
Dutch Reibel.....................1953-54 to 54-55
Real Chevrifils 1955-56
Lorne Ferguson ....1955-56 to 57-58
Jack McIntyre ....1957-58 to 58-59
Claude Laforge 1958-59
Gerry Melnyk....................1959-60 to 60-61
Ed Litzenberger 1961-62
Len Lunde 1961-62
Bill McNeill 1962-63
Larry Jeffrey ....1962-63 to 64-65
Butch Paul 1964-65
Billy Harris 1965-66
Parker MacDonald ....1965-66 to 66-67
Murray Hall.......................................1966-67
Doug Roberts ....1966-67 to 67-68
Real Lemieux 1966-67
Craig Cameron 1966-67
Gary Marsh.......................................1967-68
Nick Libett ....1967-68 to 78-79
Dennis Sobchuk 1979-80
Alex Pirus 1979-80
Mike Blaisdell 1980-81
Mal Davis 1980-81
Don Murdoch 1981-82
Stan Weir..1982-83
Lane Lambert....................1983-84 to 85-86
Doug Shedden...................1985-86 to 86-87
Brent Ashton ....1986-87 to 87-88
Miroslav Frycer..................................1988-89
Randy McKay 1988-89
Torrie Robertson ....1988-89 to 89-90
Brent Fedyk ....1990-91 to 91-92
Jim Hiller 1992-93
Andrew McKim 1995

No. 15

Jack Arbour 1926-27
Frank Sheppard 1927-28
Pete Bellefeuille.................................1929-30
Roland Matte......................................1929-30
Jim Creighton ....1930-31 to 31-32
John Newman.....................................1930-31
Hec Kilrea 1931-32
Gus Marken...1932-33
Ron Moffatt 1932-33
Gord Pettinger 1933-34
Gene Carrigan 1933-34
George Patterson 1934-35
Lloyd Gross 1934-35
Wilf Starr 1934-35
Pete Kelly ....1935-36 to 36-37
John Sherf ....1937-38 to 38-39
Clarence Droulliard 1937-38
Carl Liscombe.....................................1937-38
Ron Hudson.......................................1937-38
Don Deacon 1938-39
Dave Trottier......................................1938-39

Phil Besler 1938-39
Eddie Bush 1938-39
Buck Jones...1938-39
Jack Keating.......................................1939-40
Connie Brown 1939-40, 41-42
Archie Wilder 1940-41
Ed Bruneteau...........1940-41, 44-45 to 47-48
Ken Kilrea 1941-42, 42-43
Bill Quackenbush 1942-43
Cully Simon 1942-43
Frank Bennett.....................................1943-44
Dalton Smith.......................................1943-44
Billy Reay 1943-44
Lude Check 1943-44
Larry Thibeault 1944-45
Enio Sclisizzi......................................1947-48
Fern Gauthier 1948-49
Nelson Podolsky.................................1948-49
Marty Pavelich ....1949-50 to 50-51
Larry Wilson......................................1951-52
Alex Delvecchio ....1951-52 to 54-55
Lorne Davis 1954-55
Larry Hillman.....................1954-55 to 55-56
Billy Dea ....1956-57 to 57-58
Metro Prystai......................................1957-58
Dennis Olson 1957-58
Don Poile 1957-58
Billy McNeill......................1958-59 to 59-60
Jack McIntyre 1959-60
Howie Glover ....1960-61 to 61-62
Charlie Holmes 1961-62
Wayne Rivers......................................1961-62
Pit Martin..1961-62
Allan Johnson....................................1962-63
Andre Pronovost ....1962-63 to 63-64
Ted Lindsay 1964-65
Irv Spencer 1965-66
Gary Jarrett 1966-67
Ray Cullen...1966-67
Bart Crashley 1967-68
Galen Head 1967-68
Ron Anderson 1968-69
Fred Speck...1968-69
Sandy Snow 1968-69
Hank Monteith ....1968-69 to 69-70
Al Karlander ....1969-70 to 72-73
Rene Leclerc 1970-71
Robbie Ftorek.....................................1973-74
Bill Hogaboam...................1973-74 to 75-76
Brian Watts 1975-76
Fred Williams 1976-77
Paul Woods ....1977-78 to 83-84
Claude Loiselle 1984-85
Chris Cichocki...................1985-86 to 86-87
Mel Bridgman....................1986-87 to 87-88
Paul MacLean.....................................1988-89
Brent Fedyk 1989-90
Johan Garpenlov ....1990-91 to 91-92
Sheldon Kennedy ....1992-93 to 93-94
Mike Ramsey.......................................1995

No. 16

Harold Hicks 1930-31
Leroy Goldsworthy..............................1930-31

Emil Hanson	1932-33	Don Deacon	1936-37
Carl Voss	1932-33	Hal Mackie	1936-37
Gus Marker	1933-34	John Gallagher	1936-37
Harry Foster	1933-34	Jim Orlando	1936-37 to 37-38
Wilf Starr	1933-34	Carl Liscombe	1937-38
Ron Moffatt	1933-34	Ron Hudson	1937-38
Yank Boyd	1934-35	Pete Bessone	1937-38
Scotty Bowman	1935-36 to 38-39	Ken Doraty	1937-38
John Gallagher	1936-37	John Doran	1937-38
Rollie Roulston	1936-37 to 37-38	John Sorrell	1937-38
Buck Jones	1938-39	Mud Bruneteau	1937-38
Jack Stewart	1938-39	Charlie Conacher	1938-39
Jim Orlando	1939-40	Cecil Dillion	1939-40
Les Douglas	1940-41	Bert Peer	1939-40
Clarence Behling	1940-41	Joe Carveth	1940-41 to 41-42
Bill Jennings	1940-41 to 42-43	Joe Fisher	1940-41
Joe Fisher	1941-42 to 42-43	Bob Whitelaw	1941-42
Adam Brown	1941-42 to 42-43	Harry Watson	1942-43
Connie Brown	1942-43	John Sherf	1943-44
Bill Quackenbush	1943-44 to 45-46	Frank Kane	1943-44
Rollie Rossignol	1943-44	Jud McAtee	1943-44
Steve Wochy	1946-47	Ken Kilrea	1943-44
Gerry Couture	1946-47	Hy Buller	1943-44
Lloyd Doran	1946-47	Tony Bukovich	1943-44
Calum MacKay	1946-47	Billy Thompson	1943-44
Jim McFadden	1947-48 to 50-51	Steve Wochy	1944-45
John Wilson	1951-52 to 54-55	Earl Siebert	1944-45 to 45-46
Fred Glover	1951-52	Doug McCaig	1945-46
Enio Sclisizzi	1951-52	Gordie Howe	1946-47 to 47-48
Norm Ullman	1955-56 to 57-58	Don Morrison	1947-48 to 48-49
Jack Hendrickson	1958-59	Pat Lundy	1948-49
Jake McIntyre	1958-59 to 59-60	Fred Glover	1949-50, 51-52
Brian Smith	1959-60 to 60-61	Joe Carveth	1949-50 to 50-51
Claude Laforge	1960-61	Metro Prystai	1950-51
Ed Diachuk	1960-61	Alex Delvecchio	1950-51
Bruce MacGregor	1960-61 to 65-66	John Wilson	1951-52
Bob Wall	1965-66	Red Almas	1952-53
Ted Hampson	1966-67 to 67-68	Larry Wilson	1952-53
Garry Unger	1967-68	Marcel Bonin	1952-53 to 53-54
Ron Harris	1968-69 to 71-72	Bill Dineen	1953-54 to 56-57
Henry Boucha	1972-73 to 73-74	Forbes Kennedy	1957-58 to 59-60
Earl Anderson	1974-75	Murray Oliver	1959-60
Michel Bergeron	1974-75 to 77-78	Allan Johnson	1960-61
Andre St. Laurent	1977-78 to 78-79	Claude Laforge	1961-62
Tom Webster	1979-80	Bo Elik	1962-63
Rejean Cloutier	1979-80	Roger Lafreniere	1962-63
Jody Gage	1980-81	Floyd Smith	1962-63 to 67-68
Mark Kirton	1981-82 to 82-83	Ted Hampson	1964-65
Bobby Francis	1982-83	Wayne Connelly	1968-69 to 70-71
Kelly Kisio	1982-83 to 85-86	Tim Ecclestone	1970-71 to 73-74
Ric Seiling	1986-87	Pierre Jarry	1973-74 to 74-75
John Chabot	1987-88 to 90-91	Brian Murphy	1974-75
Vladimir Konstantinov	1991-92 to 95	Ken Mann	1975-76
		Bobby Sheehan	1976-77

No. 17

Frank Frederickson	1930-31	Steve Coates	1976-77
Leroy Goldsworthy	1932-33	Al McDonough	1977-78
Ron Moffatt	1933-34 to 34-35	Dave Hanson	1978-79
Burr Williams	1933-34	Rob Plumb	1978-79
Gene Carrigan	1933-34	Mike Foligno	1979-80 to 81-82
Ed Wiseman	1935-36	Jody Gage	1981-82
Wally Kilrea	1935-36, 37-38	Mark Lofthouse	1982-83
Art Giroux	1935-36	Bob Crawford	1982-83
John Sherf	1935-36	Brad Smith	1982-83
		Ed Johnstone	1983-84

Gerald Gallant....................1984-85 to 92-93
Doug Brown...1995

No. 18

Bob Davis...1932-33
Ron Moffatt..1933-34
Rollie Roulston 1935-36
John Sherf..1936-37
Charlie Mason 1938-39
Jack Stewart...1938-39
Connie Brown 1938-39, 40-41
Pete Kelly...1938-39
Don Grosso..1939-40
Hec Kilrea..1939-40
Dutch Hiller..1941-42
Pat McReavy...1941-42
Doug McCaig..1941-42
Cully Simon..1942-43
John Holota.........................1942-43, 45-46
Les Douglas 1942-43
Jud McAtee..1942-43
Bernie Ruelle...1943-44
Ed Bruneteau....................1943-44 to 44-45
Hy Buller..1943-44
Gerry Brown 1945-46
Rollie Rossignol.....................................1945-46
Jim Conacher....................1945-46 to 48-49
Doug Baldwin..1946-47
Gerry Couture ....1948-49 to 50-51
Marcel Pronovost 1951-52
Larry Ziedel 1952-53
Bill Folk...1952-53
Jim Hay 1952-53, 54-55
Al Arbour 1953-54
Ed Zeniuk 1954-55
Keith Allen 1954-55
Bucky Hollingworth ....1955-56 to 56-57
Dale Anderson 1956-57
Gord Strate 1957-58
Pete Goegon ....1957-58, 62-63 to 64-65
Gus Mortson 1958-59
Jim Morrison 1959-60
Lloyd Haddon 1959-60
Gerry Odrowski..................1960-61 to 61-62
Ron Harris 1962-63
Dave Lucas 1962-63
Ian Cushenan..1963-64
John Miszuk 1963-64
Gary Bergman 1964-65
Bryan Watson...................1965-66 to 66-67
Ted Taylor..1966-67
Warren Godfrey 1966-67
Jim Watson 1967-68
Dan Lawson 1968-69
Ed Hatoum 1968-69
Matt Ravlich 1969-70
Dale Rolfe 1969-70
Gerry Hart...........................1970-71 to 71-72
Bill Sutherland 1971-72
Rick McCann..1971-72
Len Fontaine 1972-73
Blair Stewart..1973-74
Brian Lavender.......................................1973-74
Bryan Watson ....1973-74 to 76-77

Kevin Schamehorn..............................1976-77
Rob Plumb...1977-78
Fern Leblanc 1978-79
J.P. Leblanc 1978-79
Mal Davis 1978-79
George Lyle......................1979-80 to 81-82
Danny Gare ....1981-82 to 85-86
Basil McRae 1986-87
Mark Kumpel ....1986-87 to 87-88
Kris King 1988-89
Kevin McClelland...............1989-90 to 90-91
Alan Kerr...1991-92
John Ogrodnick 1992-93
Chris Tancill 1992-93
Mark Pederson 1993-94
Mike Krushelnyski.................................1995

No. 19

Jack Stewart...1938-39
Sid Abel 1938-39
Gus Giesebrecht 1938-39
Ron Hudson 1939-40
Art Herchenratter 1940-41
Hal Jackson 1940-41
Harry Watson 1945-46
Cliff Simpson 1946-47
Les Douglas 1946-47
Tony Licari 1946-47
Hugh Millar 1946-47
Max McNab 1947-48
Marty Pavelich ....1947-48 to 48-49
Steve Black ....1949-50 to 50-51
Vic Stasiuk ....1950-51, 52-53 to 54-55
Larry Ziedel ....1951-52 to 52-53
Bill Folk 1951-52
Larry Jankowski.....................................1952-53
Steve Hrymnak 1952-53
Keith Allen 1953-54
Don Poile 1954-55
Jerry Toppazini 1955-56
Murray Costello.................1955-56 to 56-57
Billy McNeill 1956-57, 63-64
Tom McCarthy ....1957-58 to 58-59
Brian Smith 1957-58
Dave Amadio 1957-58
Bucky Hollingworth 1957-58
Gerry Ehman...1958-59
Gord Strate 1958-59
Lou Marcon ....1958-59 to 59-60
Pete Goegon 1959-60
Parker MacDonald 1960-61
Marc Roileau 1961-62
Bob Dillabough 1961-62
Val Fonteyne..1962-63
Wayne Muloin 1963-64
John MacMillan 1963-64
Paul Henderson.................1963-64 to 67-68
Pete Stemkowski ....1968-69 to 70-71
Hank Monteith..1970-71
Doug Volmar 1970-71
Jim Krulicki...1970-71
Bob Wall 1971-72
Gary Doak..1972-73
Rick Foley 1973-74

Ted Harris	1973-74
Jean Hamel	1973-74
Mike Korney	1974-75 to 75-76
Barry Salovaara	1974-75
Mike Wong	1975-76
Rick Wilson	1976-77
John Hilworth	1977-78
Dennis Hull	1977-78
Roland Cloutier	1978-79
Dan Bolduc	1978-79 to 79-80
Mal Davis	1980-81
Gary MacAdam	1980-81
Eric Vail	1981-82
Ivan Boldirev	1982-83
Randy Ladouceur	1982-83
Steve Yzerman	1983-84 to 95

No. 20

Sid Abel	1938-39
Jack Keating	1938-39
Bob Whitelaw	1940-41
Rudy Zunich	1943-44
Tony Bukovich	1944-45
Gerry Couture	1945-46
John Mowers	1946-47
Red Kelly	1947-48 to 48-49
Enio Sclisizzi	1948-49 to 49-50
Larry Wilson	1949-50
Glen Skov	1949-50
Gord Haidy	1949-50
Leo Gravelle	1950-51
Max McNab	1950-51
Jim Hay	1953-54
Jim Peeters	1953-54
Marcel Bonin	1954-55
John Bucyk	1955-56 to 56-57
Don Poile	1957-58
Bob Bailey	1957-58
Len Lunde	1958-59 to 61-62
Bob Solinger	1959-60
Howie Young	1961-62
Parker MacDonald	1961-62 to 64-65
Don McKenney	1965-66
Murray Hall	1965-66
Dean Prentice	1965-66 to 68-69
Ed Hatoum	1969-70
Jim Niekamp	1970-71
Mickey Redmond	1970-71 to 75-76
Dwight Schofield	1976-77
Don Martineau	1976-77
Vaclav Nedomansky	1977-78 to 81-82
Dwight Foster	1982-83 to 85-86
Tim Higgins	1986-87 to 88-89
Greg C. Adams	1989-90
Marc Potvin	1990-91
Brad Marsh	1990-91 to 91-92
Martin Lapointe	1992-93 to 95

No. 21

Pete Kelly	1938-39
Ken Kilrea	1938-39, 40-41
Carl Smith	1943-44
Doug McCaig	1945-46
Rollie McLenahan	1945-46

Thain Simon	1946-47
Al Dewsberry	1946-47
Enio Sclisizzi	1947-48
Rod Morrison	1947-48
Lee Fogolin	1948-49
Marcel Pronovost	1950-51
Guyle Fielder	1952-53
Bill Dineen	1953-54
Earl Johnson	1953-54
Gilles Dube	1953-54
Norm Corcoran	1955-56
Ed Stankiewicz	1955-56
Cummy Burton	1955-56
Gerry Melnyk	1955-56
Gord Strate	1956-57
Tom McCarthy	1956-57
Bob Bailey	1956-57
Bucky Hollingworth	1957-58
Jack Hendrickson	1957-58
Billy McNeill	1957-58
Charlie Burns	1958-59
John McKenzie	1959-60 to 60-61
Lou Marcon	1960-61, 62-63
Larry Jeffrey	1961-62 to 62-63
Eddie Royal	1962-63 to 64-65
Ted Hampson	1963-64
Val Fonteyne	1964-65
Andre Pronovost	1964-65
Claude Laforge	1964-65
Jim Peters Jr.	1964-65
Andy Bathgate	1965-66 to 66-67
Warren Godfrey	1967-68
John Brennamen	1967-68
Irv Spencer	1967-68
Pete Mahovlich	1967-68
Jim Watson	1968-69
Gerry Hart	1968-69
Mike McMahon	1969-70
Billy Dea	1969-70 to 70-71
Mike Robitaille	1970-71
Serge Lajeunesse	1971-72
Ron Stackhouse	1971-72 to 73-74
Jack Lynch	1973-74
Danny Grant	1974-75 to 77-78
Roland Cloutier	1977-78
J.P. Leblanc	1977-78
Dan Labraaten	1978-79 to 80-81
Earl Ingarfield	1980-81
Mike Blaisdell	1981-82 to 82-83
Claude Loiselle	1983-84, 85-86
Brad Smith	1983-84
Jody Gage	1983-84
Frank Cernik	1984-85
Adam Oates	1986-87 to 88-89
Borje Salming	1989-90
Paul Ysebaert	1990-91 to 92-93
Bob Halkidis	1993-94 to 1995
Mark Ferner	1995
Bob Errey	1995

No. 22

Don Deacon	1938-39
Hy Buller	1944-45
Les Douglas	1945-46

Doug McCaig 1946-47	Tord Lundstrom 1973-74
Ed Bruneteau...................................1947-48	Nelson Pyatt....................................1973-74
Fred Glover......................................1948-49	Nelson DeBenedet...........................1973-74
Al Dewsbury 1949-50	Bill Lochead.........................1974-75 to 78-79
Marcel Pronovost..............................1949-50	Roland Cloutier................................1978-79
Clare Raglan 1950-51	Glen Hicks.......................................1979-80
Ben Woit 1950-51	Mark Kirton......................................1980-81
Vic Stasiuk......................................1951-52	Mark Osborne ....1981-82 to 82-83
Glenn Hall 1952-53	Bob Manno.........................1983-84 to 84-85
Len Haley ....1959-60 to 60-61	Rick MacLeish.................................1983-84
Stu McNeill......................................1959-60	Basil McRae.....................................1985-86
Paul Henderson................................1962-63	Rick Zombo......................................1985-86
Gerry Odrowski 1962-63	Lee Norwood......................1986-87 to 90-91
Bob Dillabough................................1962-63	Kevin Miller........................1990-91 to 91-92
Roger Crozier 1963-64	Mike Sillinger 1992-93
Harrison Gray...................................1963-64	Greg Johnson.........................1993-94 to 95
Pat Rupp 1963-64	
Bob Champoux 1963-64	**No. 24**
Carl Wetzel 1964-65	Calum MacKay..................................1948-49
Butch Paul 1964-65	Gerry Reid 1948-49
Pete Goegan 1964-65	Al Dewsbury 1949-50
Ab McDonald ....1965-66 to 66-67	Fred Glover......................................1950-51
Howie Young 1966-67	Bob Dillabough.................................1964-65
Dan Lawson.....................................1967-68	Bart Crashley ....1965-66 to 66-67
Nick Libett.......................................1967-68	Gary Doak..1965-66
Ron Anderson...................................1967-68	Pete Mahovlich................................1965-66
Bob Falkenberg................................1970-71	Jim Watson......................................1965-66
Rick McCann 1970-71	Leo Boivin..1965-66
Bill Collins..........................1970-71 to 73-74	Bob McCord 1966-67
Blair Stewart....................................1973-74	Randy Manery 1970-71
Nelson Pyatt.....................................1974-75	Brian Conacher 1971-72
Dennis Polonich 1974-75	Ken Murray.......................................1972-73
Larry Giroux 1974-75	Brent Hughes 1973-74
Mike Wong 1975-76	Rick McCann.....................................1974-75
Dennis Hextall.....................1975-76 to 78-79	Tom Mellor..1974-75
Bill Hogaboam....................1978-79 to 79-80	Rene Drolet......................................1974-75
Glen Hicks.......................................1980-81	Frank Bathe........................1974-75 to 75-76
Greg Joly ....1981-82 to 82-83	Jim Nahrgang 1975-76
Murray Craven...................................1982-83	Greg Joly ....1976-77 to 80-81
Brad Park ....1983-84 to 84-85	Derek Smith.......................1981-82 to 82-83
Doug Houda 1985-86	Brian Johnson 1983-84
Glenn Merkosky 1985-86	Murray Craven...................................1983-84
Dave Barr...........................1986-87 to 90-91	Larry Trader......................................1984-85
Martin Lapointe.................................1991-92	Pierre Aubry 1984-85
Dino Ciccarelli ....1992-93 to 95	Bob Probert........................1985-86 to 93-94
No. 23	**No. 25**
Enio Schlisizzi 1946-47	Don Grosso 1938-39
Ed Nicholson 1947-48	Fern Gauthier 1946-47
John Wilson........................1949-50 to 50-51	Cliff Simpson 1946-47
Marcel Pronovost..............................1950-51	Tom Gratton.....................................1947-48
Warren Godfrey 1964-65	Leo Fogolin......................................1947-48
Bob Wall 1964-65	Ed Stankiewicz 1953-54
Gary Bergman...................................1965-66	Hank Bassen.....................................1963-64
Pete Goegan 1966-67	Murray Hall ....1964-65 to 65-66
Dave Rochefort.................................1966-67	Warren Godfrey 1965-66
Pete Stemkowski 1967-68	Jim Peters..1965-66
Doug Volmar.....................................1969-70	Doug Roberts 1965-66
Jim Shires 1970-71	Bob McCord 1965-66
Guy Charron 1970-71	George Gardner 1965-66
Robbie Ftorek 1972-73	Serje Lajeunesse..............................1972-73
Rick Newell 1972-73	Tom Mellor..1973-74
Bill Hogaboam 1972-73	Rick Newell 1973-74
Dan Gruen 1972-73	Blair Stewart....................................1974-75

Mike Bloom ....1974-75 to 76-77
Dave Kelly 1976-77
Larry Wright 1977-78
Bjorn Skaare 1978-79
Greg Carroll.......................................1979-80
Kevin Schamehorn 1979-80
Dave Lewis ....1986-87 to 87-88
Jim Pavese ....1987-88 to 88-89
Randy McKay......................................1988-89
Mark Habscheid ....1989-90 to 90-91
Troy Crowder 1991-92
Darrin McCarty........................1993-94 to 95

No. 26
Nelson Pyatt......................................1973-74
Doug Roberts ....1973-74 to 74-75
Al Cameron ....1975-76 to 78-79
Steve Short 1978-79
Jim Korn ....1979-80 to 81-82
Larry Trader..1982-83
Ken Solheim 1982-83
Barry Melrose 1983-84
Joe Kocur ....1984-85 to 90-91
Ray Sheppard.........................1991-92 to 95

No. 27
Max McNab 1947-48
Doug McKay.......................................1949-50
Frank Mahovlich.................1967-68 to 70-71
Doug Volmar.......................................1971-72
Denis Dejordy.....................................1973-74
Jim Rutherford 1973-74
Brian McCutcheon 1974-75
Phil Roberto ....1974-75 to 75-76
Buster Harvey ....1975-76 to 76-77
Bob Ritchie ....1976-77 to 77-78
Brent Peterson ....1978-79 to 80-81
Brad Smith ....1980-81 to 81-82, 83-84
Reg Leach 1982-83
Pierre Aubry 1983-84
Darryl Sittler......................................1984-85
Harold Snepsts..................1985-86 to 87-88
Doug Houda........................1988-89 to 90-91
Brian MacLellan..................................1991-92
Jim Cummins 1992-93
Micah Aivazoff....................................1993-94
Jason York 1995
Mark Ferner 1995

No. 28
Barry Salovaara 1975-76
Reed Larson ....1976-77 to 85-86
Dale Krentz 1986-87; 1988-89
Brent Fedyk 1987-88
Bob Wilkie 1990-91
Sheldon Kennedy 1991-92
Dallas Drake ....1992-93 to 93-94

No. 29
Terry Sawchuk....................................1968-69
Don Martineau 1975-76
Brian McCutcheon ....1975-76 to 76-77
Fred Berry 1976-77
Tim Sheehy 1977-78
John Hilworth.....................1978-79 to 79-80

Joe Paterson ....1980-81 to 81-82
Greg Stefan 1981-82
Ted Nolan 1981-82
Jim Rutherford ....1983-84 to 86-87
Randy Ladouceur ....1983-84 to 86-87
Gilbert Delorme..................1986-87 to 88-89
Chris Kotsopoulos 1989-90
Randy McKay......................1989-90 to 90-91
Doug Crossman...................................1991-92
Dennis Vial 1992-93
Aaron Ward 1993-94
Sergei Bautin......................................1993-94
Mike Vernon..1995

No. 30
Hank Bassen ....1965-66 to 66-67
George Gardner ....1966-67 to 67-68
Roger Crozier 1967-68
Roy Edwards.......................1968-69 to 70-71
Jim Rutherford 1970-71
Gerry Gray 1970-71
Don McLeod..1970-71
Al Smith 1971-72
Denis DeJordy 1972-73
Doug Grant 1973-74
Bill McKenzie......................................1974-75
Terry Richardson 1974-75, 76-77
Pete McDuffe 1975-76
Ron Low 1977-78
Rogie Vachon ....1978-79 to 79-80
Gilles Gilbert.......................................1980-81
Corrado Micalef..................................1981-82
Greg Stefan........................1982-83 to 89-90
Chris Osgood ....1993-94 to 95

No. 31
Andy Brown ....1971-72 to 72-73
Doug Grant.........................1974-75 to 75-76
Ed Giacomin ....1975-76 to 77-78
Larry Lozinski 1980-81
Claude Legris ....1980-81 to 81-82
Al Jensen..1980-81
Bob Sauve...1981-82
Corrado Micalef 1982-83
Chris Pusey...1985-86
Mark Laforest ....1985-86 to 86-87
Darren Eliot..1987-88
Tim Cheveldae 1988-89
Alain Chevrier.....................................1990-91
Scott King 1991-92
Peter Ing..1993-94

No. 32
Bruce Eakin..1985-86
Jeff Sharples.......................................1986-87
Sam St. Laurent...................................1987-88
Tim Cheveldae ....1989-90 to 93-94
Stu Grimson 1995

No. 33
Bob Manno.........................1983-84 to 84-85
Brent Ashton 1986-87
Doug Houda..1987-88
John Blum 1988-89
Yves Racine ....1989-90 to 92-93
Kris Draper ....1993-94 to 95

No. 34

Andre St. Laurent	1983-84
Ed Johnstone	1985-86
Sam St. Laurent	1986-87
Jeff Sharples	1987-88 to 88-89
Daniel Shank	1989-90 to 90-91
Greg Millen	1991-92
Steve Maltais	1993-94

No. 35

Ken Holland	1983-84
Warren Young	1985-86
Gilbert Delorme	1986-87
Miroslav Ihnacak	1988-89
Sam St. Laurent	1988-89 to 89-90
Dave Gagnon	1990-91
Allan Bester	1990-91to 91-92
Bob Essensa	1993-94

No. 36

Steve Martinson	1987-88
Per Djoos	1990-91
Dennis Vial	1990-91 to 91-92

No. 37

Kris King	1987-88
John Mokosak	1989-90
Chris Luongo	1990-91
Vincent Riendeau	1991-92 to 93-94
Tim Taylor	1995

No. 38

Murray Eaves	1987-88
Jeff Brubaker	1988-89
Scott King	1990-91
Jason York	1992-93
Bobby Dollas	1992-93
Jason York	1993-94
Tim Taylor	1993-94

No. 39

Dale Krentz	1987-88
Brent Fedyk	1988-89
Doug Crossman	1990-91

No. 40

Rogie Vachon	1978-79
Gord Kruppke	1990-91
Jason York	1995

No. 41

Ed Mio	1983-84 to 85-86

No. 42

Bernie Federko	1989-90

No. 43

Murray Eaves	1989-90
Bill McDougall	1990-91

No. 44

Glenn Merkosky	1989-90
Gord Kruppke	1993-94
Viacheslav Fetisov	1995

No. 46

Marc Potvin	1990-91 to 91-92

No. 47

Jim Cummins	1991-92

No. 48

Gary Shuchuk	1990-91
Chris Tancill	1991-92

No. 52

Dave Lewis	1986-87

No. 55

Dave "Tiger" Williams	1984-85
Keith Primeau	1990-91 to 95

No. 72

Brad Smith	1984-85

No. 77

Paul Coffey	1992-93 to 95

No. 85

Petr Klima	1985-86 to 89-90

No. 91

Sergei Fedorov	1990-91 to 95

1994-95 AHL STANDINGS

NORTHERN DIVISION

	GP	W	L	T	GF	GA	PTS
Albany	80	46	17	17	293	219	109
Portland	80	46	22	12	333	233	104
Providence	80	39	30	11	300	268	89
ADIRONDACK	**80**	**32**	**38**	**10**	**271**	**294**	**74**
Springfield	80	31	37	12	269	289	74
Worcester	80	24	45	11	234	300	59

SOUTHERN DIVISION

	GP	W	L	T	GF	GA	PTS
Binghamton	80	43	30	7	302	261	93
Cornwall	80	38	33	9	236	248	85
Hershey	80	34	36	10	275	300	78
Rochester	80	35	38	7	300	304	77
Syracuse	80	29	42	9	288	325	67

ATLANTIC DIVISION

	GP	W	L	T	GF	GA	PTS
Prince Edward Island	80	41	31	8	305	271	90
St. John's	80	33	37	10	263	263	76
Fredericton	80	35	40	5	274	288	75
St. John	80	27	40	13	250	286	67
Cape Breton	80	27	44	9	298	342	63

CALDER CUP WINNER: Albany

ADIRONDACK RED WINGS
American Hockey League

Glens Falls Civic Center – 1 Civic Center Plaza – Glens Falls, NY 12801
Capacity: 4,405   Phone: (518) 798-0366   Press Box: (518) 798-3544   FAX: (518) 798-0816

Owner/President .... Mike Ilitch
Owner/Secretary–Treasurer .... Marian Ilitch
Vice–Presidents .... Atanas Ilitch, Chris Ilitch
Governor/General Manager .... Ken Holland
Director of Operations .... Ed Krayer
Head Coach .... Newell Brown
Assistant Coach .... Murray Eaves
Director of Public Relations/Broadcaster .... Greg Hollaman
Head Trainer .... Piet VanZant
Assistant Trainer .... Rob Gagne

NEWELL BROWN
Head Coach

1994-95 ADIRONDACK RED WINGS' STATISTICS

	Regular Season					Playoffs				
	GP	G	A	PTS	PIM	GP	G	A	PTS	PIM
Andrew McKim	77	39	55	94	22	4	3	3	6	0
Jason Miller	77	32	33	65	39	4	1	0	1	0
Mike Casselman	60	17	43	60	42	4	0	0	0	2
Martin Lapointe	39	29	16	45	80	–	–	–	–	–
Kurt Miller	78	22	18	40	45	4	1	1	2	2
Jason MacDonald	68	14	21	35	238	4	0	0	0	2
Aaron Ward	76	11	24	35	87	4	0	1	1	0
Sylvain Cloutier	71	7	26	33	144	–	–	–	–	–
Chris Govedaris	24	19	11	30	34	4	2	1	3	10
Scott Hollis	48	12	15	27	118	–	–	–	–	–
Jeff Bloemberg	44	5	19	24	10	4	0	0	0	0
Troy Neumeier	60	4	17	21	26	4	0	0	0	2
Curtis Bowen	64	6	11	17	71	4	0	2	2	4
Tod Hartje	31	6	10	16	33	4	0	0	0	4
Jason Gladney	44	3	13	16	65	–	–	–	–	–
Lev Berdichevsky	38	4	9	13	28	–	–	–	–	–
Jamie Pushor	58	2	10	12	129	4	0	1	1	0
Gord Kruppke	48	2	9	11	157	–	–	–	–	–
Sergei Bautin	32	0	10	10	57	1	0	0	0	4
Yan Golubovsky	57	4	2	6	39	–	–	–	–	–
Dimitri Motkov	31	1	5	6	49	–	–	–	–	–
Darren Banks	20	3	2	5	65	–	–	–	–	–
Jason York	5	1	3	4	4	–	–	–	–	–
Brandon Smith	14	1	2	3	7	3	0	0	0	2
Mark Green	4	0	3	3	2	–	–	–	–	–
Norm Maracle	39	0	2	2	4	–	–	–	–	–
Lorne Knauft	2	0	1	1	6	–	–	–	–	–
Murray Eaves	4	0	1	1	0	–	–	–	–	–
Darren Perkins	4	0	1	1	0	–	–	–	–	–
Cam Brown	10	0	1	1	30	4	0	0	0	24
Kevin Hodson	51	0	1	1	4	4	0	0	0	0
Todd Walker	1	0	0	0	0	–	–	–	–	–
Mike Latendresse	2	0	0	0	0	–	–	–	–	–
Tim Spitzig	2	0	0	0	0	–	–	–	–	–
Chris Osgood	2	0	0	0	2	–	–	–	–	–
Mark Ferner	3	0	0	0	2	1	0	0	0	0
Stacy Roest	3	0	0	0	0	–	–	–	–	–
Derek Grant	3	0	0	0	15	–	–	–	–	–
Clark Poglase	3	0	0	0	7	–	–	–	–	–
BENCH	–	–	–	–	20	–	–	–	–	0
TOTALS	**80**	**271**	**422**	**693**	**1805**	**4**	**7**	**9**	**16**	**66**

GOALTENDERS

Regular Season

	GP	MIN	GAA	W	L	T	EN	SO	GA	SA	SPCT
Chris Osgood	2	120	3.00	1	1	0	0	0	6	63	.905
Kevin Hodson	51	2734	3.53	19	22	8	3	1	161	1564	.897
Norm Maracle	39	1998	3.57	12	15	2	5	0	119	1144	.896
TOTALS	**80**	**4852**	**3.54**	**32**	**38**	**10**	**8**	**1**	**286**	**2771**	**.897**

Playoffs

	GP	MIN	GAA	W	L	EN	SO	GA	SA	SPCT
Kevin Hodson	4	237	3.75	0	4	1	0	14	130	.892
TOTALS	**4**	**237**	**3.75**	**0**	**4**	**1**	**0**	**14**	**130**	**.892**

PRESS, RADIO, TV INFORMATION

The Red Wings are happy to serve you and appreciate your cooperation. Please phone Public Relations office at (313) 396-7537 with questions, comments or suggestions. Thank you.

SEASON PASS: Valid for preseason, regular-season games; available only to authorized media covering majority of games.

GAME PASS: Valid for one specific game; available to authorized media covering limited number of games.

HOW TO APPLY: Applications for season or single-game passes must be submitted on company letterhead to Red Wings' Public Relations Office, Joe Louis Arena, Detroit, MI 48226, or by FAX, (313) 567-0296. Single-game passes must be requested 24 hours in advance. Credential requests subject to review by Detroit chapter of Professional Hockey Writers' Association or Detroit Sports Broadcasters' Association. Please enter arena through West Gate press entrance, located on Third Avenue.

PRESS BOX & RADIO-TV BOOTHS: Located at top of arena seats on west side of building and reached by East Gate or West Gate elevator to third floor. Equipped with Charge-a-Call phones, VDT outlets. Coffee, soda, popcorn available. Smoking prohibited in arena. City law prohibits taking beverage cans from press box into arena seating area.

MEDIA LOUNGE: Located in hallway near Red Wings' dressing room on side of arena facing Detroit River. Credentials must be displayed to gain entrance. Opens two hours before game, remains open 45 minutes after game. Hot meals and pizza served before games. Coffee, soda available. Due to limited space, guests are not permitted.

PRACTICE SESSIONS: Dressing room closed to media before and during practice and opens 10 minutes after head coach leaves ice following practice. Access limited to 30 minutes, although exceptions could be made. In event of team meeting immediately after practice, the room opens at conclusion of meeting.

GAME DAY/NIGHT: Dressing room open to until 5:30 p.m. on game nights, with players available until 5:45; until 11 a.m. for matinees, with players available until 11:15. Room open to media no later than 10 minutes after game and access limited to a 45 minutes, although exceptions could be made.

PREGAME TV-RADIO INTERVIEWS: Television and radio stations seeking live or taped pregame interviews must request coach or player and state specific time of interview to P.R. staff before or during game-day morning skate. Interviews are to be done apart from players' locker area, no later than 5:45 before night game, 11:15 for matinee.

BETWEEN-PERIOD TV INTERVIEWS: Requests are to be made before or during game-day morning skate.

OFF-LIMITS: Not open to media are medical room, weight room, shower and sink area, and players' lounge.

PHOTOGRAPHERS: Those requiring specific vantage points are to phone P.R. office no later than 2 p.m. for night game, 10 a.m. for matinee at (313) 396-7537. Please state how long photographer will stay at game.

PARKING: Reporters/photographers for daily newspapers/wire services or reporters/camerapersons from TV/radio stations who cover majority of games may park at no charge in media section of Joe Louis Arena Garage. City-owned parking garage has limited space and charges P.R. department for each media car parked; therefore, Red Wings regretfully are unable to accomodate everyone for free. Receipts available.

RED WINGS' ATTENDANCE RECORDS

ALL-STAR GAME
*21,002 — Feb. 5, 1980 (Wales Conference 6, Campbell Conference 3)

REGULAR-SEASON GAME
21,019 — Nov. 25, 1983 (DETROIT 7, Pittsburgh 4)

PLAYOFF GAME
20,090 — Apr. 7, 1984 (St. Louis 4, DETROIT 3, 2 OTs)

TOP SEASON TOTALS
*812,640 — 1993-94 Season — 19,820 average for 41 games
808,282 — 1992-93 Season — 19,714 average for 41 games
788,920 — 1991-92 Season — 19,723 average for 40 games
788,102 — 1988-89 Season — 19,703 average for 40 games
786,548 — 1990-91 Season — 19,664 average for 40 games
785,532 — 1987-88 Season — 19,638 average for 40 games
781,679 — 1989-90 Season — 19,542 average for 40 games

HOME OPENERS
19,955 — Oct. 10, 1985 (DETROIT 6, Minnesota 6)
19,875 (5)$ — Jan. 20, 1995 (DETROIT 4, Chicago 1)

OPPOSING TEAMS (Regular Season)
Anaheim (3)$ — 19,875 — Apr. 21, 1995 (DETROIT 6, Anaheim 5)
Boston — 19,880 — Nov. 10, 1984 (Boston 4, DETROIT 2)
Buffalo — 19,875 (4)$ — Mar. 6, 1994 (Buffalo 3, DETROIT 2)
@Calgary — 19,875 (7)$ — Apr. 2, 1994 (Calgary 3, DETROIT 3 OT)
Chicago — 19,875 (17)$ — Apr. 30, 1995 (Chicago 4, DETROIT 0)
+Dallas — 19,955 — Oct. 10, 1985 (DETROIT 6, Minnesota 6)
Edmonton — 20,794 — Feb. 9, 1985 (Edmonton 6, DETROIT 5)
Florida — 19,875 — Feb. 16, 1994 (DETROIT 7, Florida 3)
Hartford — 19,905 — Jan. 12, 1980 (Hartford 6, DETROIT 4)
Los Angeles — 19,875 (11)$ — Mar. 14, 1995 (DETROIT 5, Los Angeles 2)
Montreal — 19,875 (4)$ — Apr. 13, 1994 (DETROIT 9, Montreal 0)
#New Jersey — 19,875 (5)$ — Feb. 23, 1994 (New Jersey 7, DETROIT 2)
NY Islanders — 19,817 — Feb. 8, 1991 (DETROIT 8, NY Islanders 4)
NY Rangers — 19,875 (7)$ — Dec. 17, 1993 (DETROIT 6, NY Rangers 4)
Ottawa — 19,875 (2)$ — Dec. 3, 1993 (DETROIT 8, Ottawa 1)
Philadelphia — 20,339 — Feb. 14, 1981 (Philadelphia 3, DETROIT 1)
Pittsburgh — 21,019 — Nov. 25, 1983 (DETROIT 7, Pittsburgh 4)
Quebec — 19,875 (2)$ — Mar. 31, 1994 (Quebec 4, DETROIT 2)
San Jose — 19,875 (3)$ — Apr. 13, 1995 (DETROIT 3, San Jose 0)
St. Louis — 19,875 (9)$ — Apr. 2, 1995 (St. Louis 3, DETROIT 3 OT)
Tampa Bay — 19,713 — Feb. 17, 1993 (DETROIT 3, Tampa Bay 1)
Toronto — 20,328 — Nov. 23, 1984 (DETROIT 6, Toronto 5)
Vancouver — 19,875 (5)$ — Mar. 17, 1995 (DETROIT 3, Vancouver 1)
Washington — 19,875 — Mar. 25, 1994 (Washington 2, DETROIT 2 OT)
Winnipeg — 19,875 (4)$ — Apr. 19, 1995 (Winnipeg 5, DETROIT 5 OT)

MATINEE GAMES
19,875 (21)$ — Apr. 30, 1995 (Chicago 4, DETROIT 0)

FIRST GAME AT JOE LOUIS ARENA
Dec. 27, 1979 — St. Louis 3, DETROIT 2 — 19,742

LAST GAME AT OLYMPIA STADIUM
Dec. 15, 1979 — DETROIT 4, Quebec 4 — 15,609

*- NHL Record
@-Formerly Atlanta
+-Formerly Minnesota
#-Formerly Kansas City, Colorado
$-Most recent game

GAME	DATE	OPPOSITION	SCORE	RESULT	RECORD	DECIDING GOAL
1	10- 6-95	@ Colorado				
2	10- 8-95	@ Edmonton				
3	10- 9-95	@ Vancouver				
4	10-13-95	Edmonton				
5	10-15-95	@ Winnipeg				
6	10-17-95	Calgary				
7	10-19-95	@ New Jersey				
8	10-21-95	Boston*				
9	10-24-95	Ottawa				
10	10-27-95	@ Calgary				
11	10-30-95	@ Winnipeg				
12	11- 1-95	@ Buffalo				
13	11- 2-95	@ Boston				
14	11- 4-95	Dallas*				
15	11- 7-95	Edmonton				
16	11-11-95	@ San Jose				
17	11-14-95	@ Los Angeles				
18	11-17-95	@ Edmonton				
19	11-22-95	San Jose				
20	11-24-95	@ Philadelphia*				
21	11-25-95	NY Rangers				
22	11-28-95	Montreal				
23	12- 1-95	Anaheim*				
24	12- 2-95	@ Montreal				
25	12- 5-95	Philadelphia				
26	12- 7-95	Dallas				
27	12- 8-95	@ NY Rangers				
28	12-12-95	@ St. Louis				
29	12-13-95	Chicago				
30	12-15-95	New Jersey				
31	12-20-95	@ Anaheim				
32	12-22-95	@ Calgary				
33	12-23-95	@ Vancouver				
34	12-26-95	St. Louis				
35	12-29-95	@ Dallas				
36	12-31-95	Hartford				
37	1- 3-96	Dallas				
38	1- 5-96	@ Pittsburgh				
39	1- 6-96	Chicago				
40	1- 8-96	Winnipeg				
41	1-10-96	@ Dallas				

*-Matinee Game

1995-96 SCHEDULE

GAME	DATE	OPPOSITION	SCORE	RESULT	RECORD	DECIDING GOAL
42	1-12-96	Los Angeles				
43	1-13-96	@ Washington				
44	1-17-96	Colorado				
45	1-24-96	San Jose				
46	1-25-96	@ Ottawa				
47	1-27-96	@ Chicago*				
48	1-30-96	Toronto				
49	2- 3-96	Pittsburgh*				
50	2- 6-96	Florida				
51	2- 8-96	@ Florida				
52	2-10-96	@ Tampa Bay*				
53	2-13-96	Los Angeles				
54	2-15-96	Washington				
55	2-16-96	@ St. Louis				
56	2-18-96	@ Toronto*				
57	2-19-96	Vancouver				
58	2-22-96	Toronto				
59	2-24-96	Tampa Bay				
60	2-27-96	@ NY Islanders				
61	2-29-96	NY Islanders				
62	3- 2-96	Vancouver*				
63	3- 3-96	@ Chicago				
64	3- 6-96	@ Hartford				
65	3- 8-96	@ Colorado				
66	3-10-96	@ Winnipeg				
67	3-12-96	Winnipeg				
68	3-17-95	Calgary*				
69	3-19-96	Toronto				
70	3-20-96	@ Toronto				
71	3-22-96	Colorado				
72	3-24-96	@ St. Louis				
73	3-25-96	Anaheim				
74	3-27-96	Buffalo				
75	3-31-96	St. Louis*				
76	4- 2-96	@ San Jose				
77	4- 3-96	@ Los Angeles				
78	4- 5-96	@ Anaheim				
79	4- 7-96	@ Chicago*				
80	4-10-96	Winnipeg				
81	4-12-96	Chicago				
82	4-14-96	@ Dallas*				

*-Matinee Game

ANAHEIM MIGHTY DUCKS
Pond of Anaheim
2695 Katella Avenue
P.O. Box 61077
Anaheim, CA 92803
(714) 704-2700
General Manager: Jack Ferreira
Coach: Ron Wilson
PR Director: Bill Robertson

BOSTON BRUINS
FleetCenter
Boston, MA 02114
(617) 624-1050
General Manager: Harry Sinden
Coach: Steve Kasper
PR Director: Heidi Holland

BUFFALO SABRES
Memorial Auditorium
140 Main Street
Buffalo, NY 14202
(716) 856-7300
General Manager: John Muckler
Coach: Ted Nolan
PR Director: Jeff Holbrook

CALGARY FLAMES
Olympic Saddledome
P.O. Box 1540, Station M
Calgary, AB T2P 3B9
(403) 777-2177
General Manager:
 Doug Risebrough
Coach: Pierre Page
PR Director: Rick Skaggs

CHICAGO BLACKHAWKS
United Center
1901 West Madison Street
Chicago, IL 60612
(312) 455-7000
General Manager: Bob Pulford
Coach: Craig Hartsburg
PR Director: Jim DeMaria

COLORADO AVALANCHE
McNichols Arena
1635 Clay Street
Denver, CO 80204
(303) 893-6700
General Manager: Pierre Lacroix
Coach: Marc Crawford
PR Director: Jean Martineau

DALLAS STARS
StarCenter
211 Cowboys Parkway
Irving, TX 75063
(214) 868-2890
General Manager/Coach:
 Bob Gainey
PR Director: Larry Kelly

EDMONTON OILERS
Edmonton Coliseum
7424 – 118 Avenue
Edmonton, AB T5B 4M9
(403) 474-8561
General Manager: Glen Sather
Coach: Ron Low
PR Director: Bill Tuele

FLORIDA PANTHERS
100 N.E. Third Avenue
Fort Lauderdale, FL 33301
(305) 768-1900
General Manager: Bryan Murray
Coach: Doug MacLean
PR Director: Greg Bouris

HARTFORD WHALERS
242 Trumbull St., 8th Floor
Hartford, CT 06103
(203) 728-3366
General Manager: Jim Rutherford
Coach: Paul Holmgren
PR Director: Chris Brown

LOS ANGELES KINGS
The Great Western Forum
3900 W. Manchester Blvd.
Inglewood, CA 90306
(213) 419-3160
General Manager: Sam McMaster
Coach: Larry Robinson
PR Director: Rick Minch

MONTREAL CANADIENS
Montreal Forum
2313 Ste-Catherine West
Montreal, PQ H3H 1N2
(514) 932-2582
General Manager: Serge Savard
Coach: Jacques Demers
PR Director: Donald Beauchamp

NEW JERSEY DEVILS
Byrne Meadowlands Arena
P.O. Box 504
East Rutherford, NJ 07073
(201) 935-6050
General Manager: Lou Lamoriello
Coach: Jacques Lemaire
PR Director: Mike Levine

NEW YORK ISLANDERS
Nassau Coliseum
Uniondale, NY 11553
(516) 794-4100
General Manager: Don Maloney
Coach: Mike Milbury
PR Director: Ginger Killian

NEW YORK RANGERS
Madison Square Garden, 14th Floor
2 Penn Plaza
New York, NY 10121
(212) 465-6486
General Manager: Neil Smith
Coach: Colin Campbell
PR Director: Brooks Thomas

OTTAWA SENATORS
301 Moodie Drive, Suite 200
Nepean, ON K2H 9C4
(613) 721-4327
General Manager: Randy Sexton
Coach: Rick Bowness
PR Director: Laurent Benoit

PHILADELPHIA FLYERS
CoreStates Spectrum
Philadelphia, PA 19148
(215) 465-4500
General Manager: Bob Clarke
Coach: Terry Murray
PR Director: Mark Piazza

PITTSBURGH PENGUINS
Civic Arena, Gate 9
Pittsburgh, PA 15219
(412) 642-1300
General Manager: Craig Patrick
Coach: Ed Johnston
PR Director: Harry Sanders

ST. LOUIS BLUES
Kiel Center
1401 Clark Avenue
St. Louis, MO 63103
(314) 622-2500
General Manager/Coach:
 Mike Keenan
PR Director: Adam Fell

SAN JOSE SHARKS
San Jose Arena
525 W. Santa Clara Street
San Jose, CA 95113
(408) 287-7070
General Manager: Dean Lombardi
Coach: Kevin Constantine
PR Director: Ken Arnold

TAMPA BAY LIGHTNING
501 East Kennedy Blvd.
Suite 175
Tampa, FL 33602
(813) 229-2658
General Manager: Phil Esposito
Coach: Terry Crisp
PR Director: Gerry Helper

TORONTO MAPLE LEAFS
Maple Leaf Gardens
60 Carlton Street
Toronto, ON M5B 1L1
(416) 977-1641
General Manager: Cliff Fletcher
Coach: Pat Burns
PR Director: Bob Stellick

VANCOUVER CANUCKS
Pacific Coliseum
100 North Renfrew Street
Vancouver, BC V5K 3N7
(604) 254-5141
General Manager: Pat Quinn
Coach: Rick Ley
PR Director: Steve Tambellini

WASHINGTON CAPITALS
USAir Arena
Landover, MD 20785
(301) 386-7084
General Manager: David Poile
Coach: Jim Schoenfeld
PR Director: Nancy Yasharoff

WINNIPEG JETS
1661 Portage Avenue
10th Floor
Winnipeg, MB R3J 3T7
(204) 982-5387
General Manager: John Paddock
Coach: Terry Simpson
PR Director: Richard Nairn

——NHL DIVISIONAL ALIGNMENT & SCHEDULING——

WESTERN CONFERENCE

CENTRAL DIVISION
Detroit Red Wings
Chicago Blackhawks
Dallas Stars
St. Louis Blues
Toronto Maple Leafs
Winnipeg Jets

PACIFIC DIVISION
Anaheim Mighty Ducks
Calgary Flames
Colorado Avalanche
Edmonton Oilers
Los Angeles Kings
San Jose Sharks
Vancouver Canucks

EASTERN CONFERENCE

ATLANTIC DIVISION
New Jersey Devils
New York Islanders
New York Rangers
Philadelphia Flyers
Florida Panthers
Tampa Bay Lightning
Washington Capitals

NORTHEAST DIVISION
Boston Bruins
Buffalo Sabres
Hartford Whalers
Montreal Canadiens
Ottawa Senators
Pittsburgh Penguins

SCHEDULE

Each team plays 82-game schedule.

Teams in Detroit's Central Division of Western Conference play six games each against three divisional opponents (18 games), five contests each against remaining two divisional opponents (10 games), four games each against seven teams in Pacific Division (28 games) and two contests each against 13 teams in Northeast and Atlantic divisions of Eastern Conference (26 games).

TIE-BREAKER FORMULA

To break tie in final regular-season standings, following methods are used:

1. Most overall victories; 2. Best record in games between tied teams; 3. Best differential between goals for and goals against during 82-game regular season; 4. Meeting or conference call between league general managers.

STANLEY CUP PLAYOFFS

Conference-based system matches No. 1 team vs. No. 8, No. 2 vs. No. 7, No. 3 vs. No. 6, No. 4 vs. No. 5. Four division winners receive first two seeds in each conference; No. 2 seed could be division winner with fewer points than lower seeds, retaining that seed through conference championship.

All series best-of-seven, with home-ice rotating on 2-2-1-1-1 basis. In series between Central and Pacific division clubs, team with most points could choose to start series at home or on road and opt for 2-3-2 format.

Western, Eastern conference champions meet in Stanley Cup final.

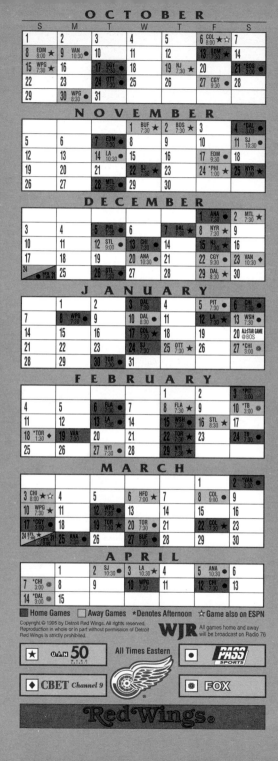

O C T O B E R

S	M	T	W	T	F	S
1	2	3	4	5	6 COL 8:00 ★☆	7
8 EDM 8:00 ★	9 VAN 10:30 ●	10	11	12	13 EDM 7:30 ★	14
15 WPG 7:30 ★	16	17 CGY 7:30 ●	18	19 NJ 7:30 ★	20	21 BOS 3:00 ●
22	23	24 OTT 7:30 ●	25	26	27 CGY 9:30 ●	28
29	30 WPG 8:30 ●	31				

N O V E M B E R

			1 BUF 7:30 ★	2 BOS 7:30 ★	3	4 *DAL 3:00 ●
5	6	7 EDM 7:30 ●	8	9	10	11 SJ 10:30 ●
12	13	14 LA 10:30 ●	15	16	17 EDM 9:30 ●	18
19	20	21	22 SJ 7:30 ★	23	24 *PHI 1:00 ★	25 NYR 7:30 ★
26	27	28 MTL 7:30 ●	29	30		

D E C E M B E R

					1 ANA 7:30 ●	2 MTL 7:30 ★
3	4	5 PHI 7:30 ●	6	7 DAL 7:30 ●	8 NYR 7:30 ★	9
10	11	12 STL 9:00 ●	13 CHI 7:30 ●	14	15 NJ 7:30 ●	16
17	18	19	20 ANA 10:30 ●	21	22 CGY 9:30 ●	23 VAN 10:30 ◆
24 WPG 7:30 ● 31	25	26 STL 7:30 ●	27	28	29 DAL 8:30 ●	30

J A N U A R Y

	1	2	3 DAL 7:30 ●	4	5 PIT 7:30 ●	6 CHI 7:30 ●
7	8 WPG 7:30 ●	9	10 DAL 8:30 ●	11	12 LA 7:30 ★	13 WSH 7:30 ●
14	15	16	17 COL 7:30 ★	18	19	20 ALL-STAR GAME @BOS
21	22	23	24 SJ 7:30 ●	25 OTT 7:30 ★	26	27 *CHI 3:00 ●
28	29	30 TOR 7:30 ●	31			

F E B R U A R Y

				1	2	3 *PIT 7:30 ●
4	5	6 FLA 7:30 ●	7	8 FLA 7:30 ★	9	10 *TB 3:00 ●
11	12	13 LA 7:30 ●	14	15 WSH 7:30 ●	16 STL 8:30 ★	17
18 *TOR 1:30 ◆	19 VAN 7:30	20	21	22 TOR 7:30 ★	23	24 TB 7:30 ●
25	26	27 NYI 7:30 ●	28	29 NYI 7:30 ★		

M A R C H

					1	2 *VAN 3:00 ●
3 CHI 8:00 ★☆	4	5	6 HFD 7:00 ★	7	8 COL 9:00 ●	9
10 WPG 7:30 ★	11	12 WPG 7:30 ●	13	14	15	16
17 *CGY 3:00 ●	18	19 WPG 7:30 ●	20 TOR 7:30 ●	21	22 COL 7:30 ★	23
24 STL 7:30 ★ 31	25 ANA 7:30 ●	26	27 BUF 7:30 ●	28	29	30

A P R I L

	1	2 SJ 10:30 ●	3 LA 10:30 ★	4	5 ANA 10:30 ●	6
7 *CHI 3:00 ●	8	9	10 WPG 7:30 ●	11	12 CHI 7:30 ●	13
14 *DAL 3:00 ●	15					

■ **Home Games** □ **Away Games** ★Denotes Afternoon ☆ Game also on ESPN

WJR All games home and away will be broadcast on Radio 76

★ ⊕AN 50 | **All Times Eastern** | ● **PASS** SPORTS

◆ **CBET** Channel 9 | | ◉ **FOX**

RedWings®